Approaches to Teaching
World Literature

Joseph Gibaldi, series editor

For a complete listing of titles,
see the last pages of this book.

Approaches to Teaching Duras's *Ourika*

Edited by

Mary Ellen Birkett

and

Christopher Rivers

The Modern Language Association of America
New York   2009

MLA and the MODERN LANGUAGE ASSOCIATION are trademarks
owned by the Modern Language Association of America. For
information about obtaining permission to reprint material from
MLA book publications, send your request by mail (see address below),
e-mail (permissions@mla.org), or fax (646 458-0030).

Library of Congress Cataloging-in-Publication Data

Approaches to teaching Duras's Ourika /
edited by Mary Ellen Birkett and Christopher Rivers.
p. cm. — (Approaches to teaching world literature ; 107)
Includes bibliographical references and index.
ISBN 978-1-60329-018-0 (hardcover : alk. paper)
ISBN 978-1-60329-019-7 (pbk. : alk. paper)
1. Duras, Claire de Durfort, duchesse de, 1777–1828. Ourika.
2. Duras, Claire de Durfort, duchesse de, 1777–1828—Study and
teaching. I. Birkett, Mary Ellen. II. Rivers, Christopher.
PQ2235.D65O832 2009
843'.7—dc22   2008054596

Approaches to Teaching World Literature 107
ISSN 1059-1133

Cover illustration of the paperback edition: *Tête de jeune fille*,
by Jean-Antoine Houdon, c. 1781. Photo Musée de Soissons / Michel Minetto

Printed on recycled paper

Published by The Modern Language Association of America
26 Broadway, New York, New York 10004-1789
www.mla.org

CONTENTS

PREFACE TO THE SERIES

In *The Art of Teaching* Gilbert Highet wrote, "Bad teaching wastes a great deal of effort, and spoils many lives which might have been full of energy and happiness." All too many teachers have failed in their work, Highet argued, simply "because they have not thought about it." We hope that the Approaches to Teaching World Literature series, sponsored by the Modern Language Association's Publications Committee, will not only improve the craft—as well as the art—of teaching but also encourage serious and continuing discussion of the aims and methods of teaching literature.

The principal objective of the series is to collect within each volume different points of view on teaching a specific literary work, a literary tradition, or a writer widely taught at the undergraduate level. The preparation of each volume begins with a wide-ranging survey of instructors, thus enabling us to include in the volume the philosophies and approaches, thoughts and methods of scores of experienced teachers. The result is a sourcebook of material, information, and ideas on teaching the subject of the volume to undergraduates.

The series is intended to serve nonspecialists as well as specialists, inexperienced as well as experienced teachers, graduate students who wish to learn effective ways of teaching as well as senior professors who wish to compare their own approaches with the approaches of colleagues in other schools. Of course, no volume in the series can ever substitute for erudition, intelligence, creativity, and sensitivity in teaching. We hope merely that each book will point readers in useful directions; at most each will offer only a first step in the long journey to successful teaching.

Joseph Gibaldi
Series Editor

PREFACE TO THE VOLUME

Ourika, a slim novel written by the French noblewoman Claire-Louisa Lechat de Coëtnempren de Kersaint, duchesse de Duras, was first published, anonymously, in 1823. Almost immediately, the novel became a best seller and sparked interest and debate in France and throughout Europe. Between twenty-five and forty copies of the 1823 edition of *Ourika* were in circulation the year the text was published (Scheler 12; Little, "Bibliographie"); a year later, in 1824, seven thousand copies were sold (Little, "Peau" viii), and four plays, adapted from the novel, opened in Paris theaters (Chalaye, *Les Ourika* xiii). The reasons for the success of this particular book, at that particular place and time, are complex and ambiguous and are treated by many of the essays in this volume.

What is unambiguous, however, is the fact that the narrator-protagonist of the novel, the eponymous Ourika, a young Senegalese girl rescued by a French nobleman from slavery and raised by his sister in Paris as her adopted daughter, is the first black woman narrator in French literature. Indeed, as John Fowles has said, the novel represents "the first serious attempt by a white novelist to enter a black mind" (Foreword xxx). Set against the backdrop of the French Revolution, the Terror, and the restoration, as well as colonialism and slavery, it raises profound and complex questions about historical matters and problems of personal identity. It is most compelling in its expert intertwining of the two registers: Ourika can be seen at once as a victim of history and a timeless tragic heroine; her *mal du siècle* is both specific to her circumstance and an age-old problem.

Despite its brevity, the novel is almost impossibly rich. It is easy to understand why teachers of a range of courses and in a range of institutions have found it an irresistible addition to their syllabi. It has been widely taught since 1979, when Claudine Herrmann's edition was published by Des Femmes, and much more extensively since 1994, when the excellent and accessible MLA Texts and Translations volumes, both French text and English translation, appeared (De-Jean; Fowles).

Responses to our questionnaire reveal that *Ourika* figures on the syllabus of an array of courses from an array of disciplines. Students read *Ourika* in first-year seminars and in French language courses. Duras's text is commonly studied in courses featuring the principal authors of the French tradition, where *Ourika* is frequently taught in conjunction with François-René de Chateaubriand's *René*. Most often, *Ourika* is taught in advanced literature courses: either broad-based surveys on nineteenth-century French literature or courses that span the late eighteenth and early nineteenth centuries. Here too *Ourika* is often read alongside *René*, though other revealing combinations pair it with Françoise de Graffigny's *Lettres d'une Péruvienne*, Germaine de Staël's *Mirza*, or George Sand's *Lavinia*. *Ourika* also has a place in thematically designed nineteenth-century courses that treat visual as well as textual representations of *Ourika*.

In courses devoted to the relationships between France and its colonies or former colonies *Ourika* works remarkably well, whether reading *Ourika* together with Charles Baudelaire's "La Belle Dorothée," comparing the idealized representation of an African male in Victor Hugo's *Bug-Jargal* with the representation of an African woman in *Ourika*, or pairing *Ourika* with Victor Séjour's *Le Mulâtre*.

Outside the French department, *Ourika* can be found on the syllabus of an interdisciplinary nineteenth-century studies course where *Ourika* links *René* to Honoré de Balzac's *Eugénie Grandet*, of gender studies courses where *Ourika* is twinned with *René* or with Oscar Wilde's *The Picture of Dorian Gray*, and of English courses where *Ourika* is read and discussed with Mary Wollstonecraft Shelley's *Frankenstein*.

Teachers who answered our survey were universally enthusiastic about the response the novel receives from students in all these diverse pedagogical settings. Many people spoke of how easily undergraduates in particular identify with the heroine of the novel (several spoke of an "intense" identification) and how effective this identification is in fostering lively and engaged classroom discussion. They observed that the themes of race, gender, and otherness in the novel have topical relevance for students. Respondents mentioned that the brevity and accessibility of the novel make it especially desirable ("the text is short but substantial"). Others described it as an effective means of melding literature and history, of blurring the lines between text and context.

Among the comments we received concerning *Ourika*'s usefulness in the classroom are these:

> [A]s it exhibits characteristics both of classicism and Romanticism, this novella constitutes an excellent example of a transition work between the two literary movements in French literature.
> (Chantal Bertrand-Jennings, University of Toronto, Scarborough)

> My students' reactions to reading *Ourika* illustrated beautifully the way that literature does connect to real life.
> (Carolyn Fay, Penn State University, Altoona)

> [Students] are generally most intrigued by the question of whether Ourika's sufferings are of her own or of society's making.
> (Kathryn M. Grossman, Penn State University, University Park)

> I often teach it to demonstrate the difficulty of political and cultural transitions in France from the ancien régime to the revolution to the Napoleonic régime.   (Deborah Jenson, University of Wisconsin, Madison)

> The value of *Ourika* lies in its remarkable representation of the social construction of identity—gender, race, and class.
> (Dorothy Kelly, Boston University)

I teach the novella . . . primarily because it is an early example of a nascent historical consciousness in French narrative. [I]t is very useful in dramatizing issues pertaining to individual identity emerging from the French Revolution (pertaining to the status of the citizen with respect to women and blacks).   (Marshall C. Olds, University of Nebraska, Lincoln)

[I]t enables me to historically situate the issue of subjectivation and to talk about different historical forms of European "creolization" at a time when issues of identity were debated and reconfigured.
                    (Mireille Rosello, Northwestern University)

It's one of the few texts that bring the race question to the fore in a direct and emotionally immediate way. [T]he fact that it is first-person ventriloquism by a wealthy white woman author complicates the question of identity and identification nicely.   (Margaret Waller, Pomona College)

It's short and "manageable" . . . but its scope is large. Therefore, I can ask [students] to make ambitious arguments about it while keeping them honest about the textual evidence and not having them get lost in a larger, more detailed text.   (Jen Hill, University of Nevada, Reno)

This praise notwithstanding, from the perspective of a teacher *Ourika* can represent something of a paradox. For all its richness, it is the perfect example of a text that might seem to teach itself. Written in easily understandable prose, using a narrow range of vocabulary, the novel is short, its narrative structure uncomplicated, and its plot straightforward. The main character, Ourika, is sympathetic because she tells a tale that movingly reveals the social prejudices of her time. "Simple" readings of *Ourika* are thus quite possible.

But because this work raises complex aesthetic and historical questions and because the text and its context are of equal and interconnected importance, it proves particularly challenging to teachers who seek to transcend simple readings. Those who wish to present *Ourika* in a way that genuinely reflects its complexity, profundity, and unique historical and literary-historical status will find few resources for teaching the novel. In recent years, scholars have begun to articulate sensitive, historically accurate, and critically sophisticated interpretations of this text; however, pedagogical approaches to *Ourika* are notably absent from the growing list of studies of this work. There are many perspectives from which the novel's themes and questions of identity, inequality, exclusion, power, and racial difference can be viewed. The goal of our volume is thus to provide teachers—many of whom will no doubt be people like us, with expertise in related fields and considerable experience as pedagogues but not specialists per se—with concrete information, perspectives, and strategies that will allow them to move beyond the level of simple readings.

The intention of this volume is threefold: to present a forum for analysis of the cultural, social, literary, and historical contexts of *Ourika*; to suggest specific strategies for reading the novel; and to offer examples of successful pedagogical approaches.

In part 1, we offer a brief overview of French editions and English translations of *Ourika* and of the secondary sources instructors are likely to find most useful, including introductions to and critical studies of the novel; biographical and historical works; and sources treating questions of race, gender, and class. We also present a timeline situating Claire de Duras's life within its historical framework, specifically in relation to matters of slavery and abolition.

Part 2 contains the approaches themselves, essays written by scholars who have researched and written on *Ourika* and by teachers who have taught the novel (most of our contributors are both). The essays span a breadth of subject matter and perspective: some are explicitly and concretely pedagogical, while others are more concerned with contextualizing *Ourika*, either historically, biographically, conceptually, or in other ways. To help the reader navigate the essays, we have grouped them into (admittedly somewhat arbitrary) categories: the first section offers historical approaches; the second focuses on race, class, and gender; and the third proposes intertextual readings—ways of pairing *Ourika* with other texts that provide illuminating and sometimes unexpected views of the novel. The fourth and final section presents different types of courses or pedagogical situations and the ways in which the novel may best be taught in a particular context.

Throughout this volume, unless otherwise specified, the edition of *Ourika* referred to is the MLA Texts and Translations edition of 1994 cited above, edited by Joan DeJean and splendidly introduced by DeJean and Margaret Waller. The English translation used is its companion volume, the John Fowles translation. Where the author of an essay cites a French text other than *Ourika*, the accompanying English translation may be assumed to be his or her own unless another translation is specified.

Our sincere thanks go to all those who responded to our survey about *Ourika*, as well as to our marvelous roster of contributors. Felicia Leveille helped with our initial mailing. Liane Hartman provided assistance with the technical task of putting this volume together. Aprile Gallant and Margaret Oppenheim gave excellent recommendations in matters of visual culture. Joseph Gibaldi was enthusiastic and supportive, as well as clear, courteous, and genuinely helpful, from the very start. We are particularly indebted to Christopher Miller, who was generous with his library, his counsel, and his vast knowledge of *Ourika* and related topics, and to Peter Searl, who offered a healthy dose of perspective throughout all phases of this project.

Finally, we would be remiss if we failed to mention Bart's, of Amherst, Massachusetts, the legendary ice cream parlor cum coffee shop where an inordinate, almost embarrassing, amount of the work on this volume took place.

MEB and CR

Part One

MATERIALS

Editions and Translations

French Editions

Ourika was first published in 1823, and numerous reprintings quickly followed. The first modern edition, which enjoyed relatively wide circulation, was Claudine Herrmann's, published in 1979 by Des Femmes. This edition effected a renaissance of Duras's novel. Roger Little produced an excellent edition, complete with a substantial scholarly apparatus, in 1993 (reprinted in 1998). Many of the respondents to our survey praised Little's edition and its prefatory material and numerous appendixes. In addition, the novel was included in *Romans de femmes du XVIII* siècle, a volume published in 1996 by Robert Laffont and edited by Raymond Trousson. The most recent editions of the novel are Christiane Chaulet Achour's, published in 2006; Marie-Bénédicte Diethelm's Folio Classique edition, *Madame de Duras:* Ourika, Edouard, *and* Olivier, published in 2007; and the Bibliothèque Nationale de France's electronic version of the text, available through the Bibliothèque Numérique Gallica at http://gallica.bnf.fr.

The Modern Language Association's 1994 edition of Duras's novel (DeJean), which is affordable, well designed, and readily available, is almost universally used, according to the responses to our survey. The complementary introductions by Joan DeJean and Margaret Waller also receive high marks from respondents. One respondent notes that the typographical distinction made in the MLA edition between Ourika's narrative and the doctor's tale (the frame narrative) alerts students to the distinction between the two levels of narration.

English Translations

The first English translation of *Ourika* was published in London in 1824. An anonymous translation that appeared in 1829 (*Ourika: A Tale from the French*) may be the same text as the 1824 version. The standard modern translation of *Ourika* is the one by the well-known British novelist John Fowles, first published in a limited edition of some five hundred copies by W. Taylor Thomas in 1977. Fowles later revised his text slightly, and the MLA published the new version in 1994, with the same introductions by DeJean and Waller.

In 1993, Françoise Massardier-Kenney and Claire Salardenne published a translation of *Ourika* in *Translating Slavery: Gender and Race in French Women's Writing, 1783–1823*, edited by Doris Y. Kadish and Massardier-Kenney. This volume also contains an essay by Massardier-Kenney on race and class in *Ourika* and a fascinating and extremely pertinent comparative study by Kadish of the 1829 (anonymous), 1977 (Fowles), and 1993 (Massardier-Kenney and Salardenne) translations ("*Ourika's* Three Versions"). Kadish examines not only the linguistic variations among the three texts but, more to the point, the range of ideological stances those variations represent. In short, her reading is that the 1829 translation is characterized by an "abolitionist tone" (218), which Fowles downplays in his version. Kadish argues that Fowles often reduces the importance of race and "diminish[es] the resistant thrust of Duras's treatment of that issue" (222). The Massardier-Kenney and Salardenne translation attempts to bring that issue back into focus. Kadish's study is highly recommended reading for anyone teaching *Ourika* in translation.

Background Readings

History

Books devoted to the historical context of the period are too numerous for us even to attempt a complete list here. Among many others, the following merit attention: William Doyle's *French Revolution: A Very Short Introduction*, Lynn Hunt's *The Family Romance of the French Revolution*, Philip Mansel's *Paris between Empires, 1814–1852*, and Simon Schama's *Citizens: A Chronicle of the French Revolution*.

Works about the real-life models for the Ourika story include the chevalier de Boufflers's letters to Madame de Sabran (published in "livre de poche" format in 1998), Nicole Vaget-Grangeat's *Le chevalier de Boufflers et son temps: Étude d'un échec*, and Paul Bouteiller's *Le chevalier de Boufflers et le Sénégal de son temps (1785–1788)*. See also Little's "Le nom et les origines d'Ourika" and Amy Ransom's "Mademoiselle Aïssé: Inspiration for Claire de Duras's *Ourika*?"

Biography

Biographical materials concerning Claire de Duras are few and far between. To date, there have been only two book-length biographical studies, both of them written circa 1900: Agénor Bardoux's *Études sociales et politiques: La duchesse de Duras* and the abbé Gabriel Pailhès's *La duchesse de Duras et Chateaubriand d'après des documents inédits*. From the same era is Catherine Mary Charlton Bearne's *Four Fascinating French Women*, which includes a section on Duras. Christopher L. Miller's *The French Atlantic Triangle: Literature and Culture of the Slave Trade* revisits the facts and myths of Duras's life and the sources thereof, particularly with respect to the questions of race, slavery, and abolition.

Teachers interested in a biographical perspective might find the following articles of interest: Charles-Augustin Sainte-Beuve's essay on Duras (one of his *Portraits de femmes*, most readily available in the 1951 Gallimard-Pléiade edition of his complete works); an essay by R. Tezenas du Montcel, "Madame de Duras, cette inconnue"; and Alain Paraillous's "Chateaubriand et la duchesse de Duras." The memoirs of two of Claire de Duras's contemporaries, the maréchale princesse de Beauvau and the comtesse de Genlis (*Mémoires*), also contain useful biographical information.

Race and Slavery

Materials in this category are numerous. The Code Noir (the document that sets forth French law regarding the treatment of slaves in French colonies), an indispensable primary source, can be found in Louis Sala-Molins, *Le Code noir, ou, Le calvaire de Canaan*. Another foundational text is Frantz Fanon's classic *Peau noire, masques blancs*.

Among book-length studies pertinent for examining race and slavery in relation to *Ourika* are William Cohen's *The French Encounter with Africans: White Response to Blacks, 1530–1880*, David Brion Davis's *The Problem of Slavery in the Age of Revolution, 1770–1823*, Léon-François Hoffmann's classic *Le nègre romantique*, Christopher L. Miller's *Blank Darkness: Africanist Discourse in French*, Sue Peabody's *"There Are No Slaves in France": The Political Culture of Race and Slavery in the Ancien Régime*, and T. Denean Sharpley Whiting's *Black Venus: Sexualized Savages, Primal Fears, and Primitive Narratives in French*. The volume by Kadish and Massardier-Kenney mentioned above is also invaluable.

Articles teachers might find useful include Peggy McIntosh's "White Privilege: Unpacking the Invisible Knapsack," David O'Connell's "*Ourika*: Black Face, White Mask," and Richard Switzer's "Mme de Staël, Mme de Duras, and the Question of Race."

Literary History

Among the many books placing *Ourika* in its literary historical context, noteworthy ones include Natalie Datlof, Jean Fuchs, and David Powell's *World of George Sand* and Margaret Waller's *The Male Malady: Fictions of Impotence in the French Romantic Novel*; articles include David O'Connell's "The Black Hero in French Romantic Fiction," Nancy Rogers's "The Wasting Away of Romantic Heroines," and Kari Weil's "Romantic Exile and the Melancholia of Identification."

Gender in History and Literature

A basic reference book on gender in France is Maïté Albistur and Daniel Armogathe's *Histoire du féminisme français du Moyen-age à nos jours*. Essential books include Alison Finch's *Women's Writing in Nineteenth-Century France*, Lynn Hunt's *The French Revolution and Human Rights: A Brief Documentary History*, Joan Wallach Scott's *Gender and the Politics of History*, and Tzvetan

Todorov's *Nous et les autres: La réflexion française sur la diversité humaine*. Among the relevant articles are Elinor Ann Acampo's "Integrating Women and Gender into the Teaching of French History, 1789 to the Present" and Chantal Bertrand-Jennings's "Condition féminine et impuissance sociale: Les romans de la duchesse de Duras" and "Problématique d'un sujet féminin en régime patriarcal." Nathaniel Wing's chapter "Admissions of Difference: Gender and Ethnicity in *Ourika*," in his *Between Genders: Narrating Difference in Early French Modernism*, encompasses questions of both race and gender.

Studies of *Ourika*

Introductions

As previously mentioned, the 1994 MLA Texts and Translations editions of *Ourika* contain brief but excellent introductions by Joan DeJean and Margaret Waller. Claudine Herrmann gives a good introduction to her 1979 Des Femmes edition as well. Roger Little's presentation and studies of the novel, in both his 1993 and 1998 edition of the novel, are invaluable ("Peau," "Cahier," "Madame de Duras"). In *Romans de femmes au XVIIIᵉ siècle*, Raymond Trousson provides a lengthy introduction to *Ourika*.

Books

Literary scholars have paid quite a bit of attention to *Ourika* in the past three decades. Book-length studies include Grant Crichfield's *Three Novels of Madame de Duras: Ourika, Edouard, Olivier*; Chantal Bertrand-Jennings's *D'un siècle à l'autre: Romans de Claire de Duras*; and Sylvie Chalaye's *Les Ourika du boulevard*. Marylee S. Crofts's 1992 PhD dissertation, "Duras's *Ourika*: Race and Gender in Text and Context," is also an important resource, as is Thérèse De Raedt's comprehensive dissertation, "Ourika en noir et blanc: Une femme africaine en France."

Articles

Among the key essays devoted to *Ourika* are Barbara T. Cooper's "Staging *Ourika* and the Spectacle of Difference"; Martine Delvaux's "Le tiers espace de la folie dans *Ourika, Juletane* et *L'amant*"; Thérèse De Raedt's "*Ourika* in Black and White: Textual and Visual Interplay" and "Ourika: L'inspiration de Mme de Duras"; Earl G. Ingersoll's "The Appropriation of Black Experience in the *Ourika* of Claire de Duras"; Doris Y. Kadish's "Rewriting Women's Stories: *Ourika* and *The French Lieutenant's Woman*"; Valérie Magdelaine-Andrianjafitrimo's "La

Galatée noire ou la force d'un mot: *Ourika de Claire de Duras, 1823*"; Daniel-Henri Pageux's "Ourika ou la religieuse sénégalaise"; Anjali Prabhu's "Deux nègres à Paris: La voix de l'autre"; Carol L. Sherman's "Race, Melancholy, and Therapeutic Narrative in *Ourika*"; Marie-Ange Somdah's "Ourika ou l'univers antithétique d'une héroïne"; Eileen Warburton's "Ashes, Ashes, We All Fall Down: *Ourika, Cinderella*, and *The French Lieutenant's Woman*"; and, finally, Stendhal's "*Ourika, ou la négresse*, par Mme la duchesse de ———— " in *Chroniques pour l'Angleterre.*

Media Resources

Film and Web resources are countless, so the following is by no means an exhaustive list but rather a sampling. Films concerning the French slave trade include Michael Apted's *Amazing Grace*, a chronicle of the famous late-eighteenth- and early-nineteenth-century British abolitionist William Wilberforce and his success at bringing about the end of the British slave trade; Jean-Claude Barny's *Tropiques amers*, a French television miniseries on slavery in Martinique at the time of the French Revolution, with a screenplay cowritten by the historian Myriam Cottias; John Berry's *Tamango*, an adaptation of the Prosper Mérimée novella of the same title; Guy Deslauriers's *Passage du milieu*, whose script was written by Patrick Chamoiseau; Bernard Giraudeau's *Les caprices d'un fleuve*, a story set in 1786 based on the adventures of the chevalier de Boufflers; and Roger Gnoan M'Bala's *Adanggaman*, a historical depiction of the slave trade inside Africa.

Documentaries concerning the French Revolution include *La Révolution française*, a pedagogical film with good basic information about the revolution, and Doug Shultz's *The French Revolution*, a feature-length film using reenactments, period images, accounts from contemporary journals, and commentary by historians.

Feature films representing the revolutionary period that provide background and atmosphere for the events of *Ourika* include Patrice Leconte's *Ridicule* (see David R. Ellison's essay in this volume); Eric Rohmer's *L'Anglaise et le duc* (released in the United States under the title *The Lady and the Duke*); Ettore Scola's *La nuit de Varennes*; and Andrzej Wajda's *Danton*.

Instructors seeking material on the Haitian Revolution might consider Robin Lloyd and Doreen Kraft's *Black Dawn*, a short, animated children's film using Haitian art to portray the Middle Passage and the revolution.

There are vast resources available on the Web that can inform and enrich the teaching of *Ourika*. Web sites related to the slave trade include *Comité pour la mémoire de l'esclavage* (www.comite-memoire-esclavage.fr), the site of the committee convened by Jacques Chirac, chaired by Maryse Condé, and charged with the administration of France's public memory of the slave trade; UNESCO's

Slave Trade Archives Project (www.portal.unesco.org; path: Site map; Archives; Projects; Slave Trade Archives Project), with links, multimedia, and extensive information about the history of slavery and the slave trade; Jerome S. Handler and Michael L. Tuite, Jr.'s *The Atlantic Slave Trade and Slave Life in the Americas* (http://hitchcock.itc.virginia.edu/Slavery/index.php), a collection of images of the slave trade; and *Francophone Slavery* (www.uga.edu/slavery), a site maintained by Doris Y. Kadish that contains information about slavery in general and its resonances in the francophone world.

Web sites about the French and Haitian Revolutions include *Liberty, Equality, Fraternity* (http://chnm/gmu.edu/revolution/), an extensive collection of primary documents including texts, images, and maps; *EuroDocs* (http://eudocs.lib.byu .edu/index.php/; path: France; France: 1789–1871); Bob Corbett's *Bibliography on the Haitian Revolution* (www.hartford-hwp.com/archives/43a/099.html); and the *Journal of the Louverture Project* (http://journal.thelouvertureproject. org)—"Discovery and Discussion about Haiti . . . and the Haitian Revolution of 1791–1804." *About.com* collects a number of links in one place and summarizes what they have to offer (http://europeanhistory.about.com/od/ thefrenchrevolution/The_French_Revolution.htm).

Instructors developing syllabi or working on teaching strategies might want to consult one or more of Adrianna M. Paliyenko's sites, each devoted to a different French course: Provocative Texts: Engaging the World (www.colby.edu/ personal/a/ampaliye/FR252/index.html), an intermediate course designed to instruct students in the art of critical analysis; Cultural Legacies of Nineteenth-Century France (www.colby.edu/personal/a/ampaliye/FR356/index.html), an advanced course on the cultural legacies of the nineteenth century; and Passionate Discontent: Nineteenth-Century Epidemic (www.colby.edu/personal/a/ ampaliye/FR358/index.html), an advanced topics course.

For works of art accessible on the Web and relevant to the teaching of *Ourika*, see the sites discussed by Thérèse De Raedt in her essay in this volume. Instructors may also find relevant Jean-Antoine Houdon's *Tête de jeune fille* in the Musée de Soissons (www.numerique.culture.fr). Additional visual material may be found in the "Cahier iconographique" of Little's edition of *Ourika*.

Significant Events in Duras's Life, the Slave Trade, and French History

Deborah Jenson and Christopher L. Miller

1604–77   The French establish outposts around the Atlantic, permitting them eventually to conduct the triangular trade in goods, slaves, and colonial products such as sugar and cotton. They acquire Saint-

Domingue (the future Haiti), Saint-Louis and Gorée in Senegal, Martinique, and Guadeloupe.

1685	Slavery in the French islands, unregulated up to this point, is brought under the dictates of the Code Noir, which expels all Jews from the colonies (art. 1), defines slaves as movable property (art. 44) but requires that they be baptized and instructed in Catholicism (art. 2), and prescribes punishments and tortures for various crimes such as running away (art. 38).
1691	François d'Alesso, marquis d'Eragny, great-grandfather of Claire de Duras, is briefly governor of the French islands in the Caribbean; he dies in Martinique, where his family remains.
1716	An edict institutes exceptions to the "freedom principle" forbidding slavery in the *métropole*: now certain slaves can be brought to France without being freed.
1738	Slaves' stays in France becomes limited to three years and only for undertaking an apprenticeship.
1742	Birth of the father of Claire de Duras, Armand-Guy-Simon de Coëtnempren, comte de Kersaint, in Paris.
1761	The comte de Kersaint fights against the British occupation of Martinique during the Seven Years' War.
1762	The French government clamps down again on the growing numbers of slaves in France.
1763	The Treaty of Paris ends the Seven Years' War: France loses Canada but regains Martinique and Guadeloupe.
1771	Louis-Sébastien Mercier's *L'an 2440, rêve s'il en fut jamais* contains abolitionist passages including the idea of a black Spartacus, later plagiarized by the abbé Raynal.
1772	Claire Louise Françoise de Paul d'Alesso d'Eragny and the comte de Kersaint are married.
1778	On 22 March Claire-Louisa-Rose-Bonne Lechat de Coëtnempren de Kersaint, the future Madame de Duras, is born in Brest.
1780	The real Ourika may have been born this year (see Sue Peabody's essay in this volume).
1781	The marquis de Condorcet writes his *Réflexions sur l'esclavage des nègres*.
1782	The comte de Kersaint recaptures the British colonies in what is now British Guyana and serves briefly as governor.
1783	Louis-Sébastien Mercier, in his *Tableau de Paris*, documents the vogue among French aristocratic women of keeping African children as pets. Mercier comments that the enslaved father of such a child "groans under the whip of a pitiless master" on a distant sugar plantation (254).

1783–92	The French slave trade returns with a vengeance: more than 1,100 French ships engage in the trade in this period, taking more than 370,000 captives.
1786	The chevalier de Boufflers, governor of Senegal, reports, in a letter dated 8 February, that he has bought "a little Negress, two or three years old, to send to the Duchesse d'Orléans" (60). This unnamed girl is apparently not Ourika. The same year, the real Ourika is brought to France from Senegal by the chevalier de Boufflers and given to Charles Just de Beauvau and his wife. (See Thérèse De Raedt's essay in this volume.) Germaine Necker, the future Mme de Staël, writes her abolitionist novella *Mirza* (first published 1794), which contains a character named Ourika, the first one in French literature. This Ourika stays in Africa and seems to owe nothing but her name to the real Ourika (whom Mme de Staël may have met).
1788	In February La Société des Amis des Noirs is founded by a small group led by Jacques-Pierre Brissot, including Condorcet, Emmanuel-Joseph Sieyès, Necker, and the comte de Mirabeau. This elite group, heavily indebted to English abolitionism, in particular the work of Thomas Clarkson, is active until 1793 and then briefly revives in 1798. (French abolitionism was never a mass movement as it was in England.) Olympe de Gouges publishes *Zamore et Mirzah* and *Réflexions sur les hommes nègres*.
1789	Claire enters the Panthémont convent in Paris, where she is educated until 1791. On 5 May King Louis XVI convenes the Estates-General; debate on the slave trade is blocked there. On 14 July the French Revolution begins (see Mary Jane Cowles's essay in this volume). The revolution leads to a flourishing of French antislavery publications this year, including Lecointe-Marsillac's *Le More-Lack*, Benjamin Frossard's *Cause des esclaves nègres*, and Antoine Edme Pruneau de Pommegorge's *Description de la Nigritie*, as well as Dominique-Harcourt Lamiral's proslavery and pro-slave-trade *L'Affrique et le peuple affriquain*; Olympe de Gouges's *Esclavage des nègres* is performed in December at the Comédie Française.
1790	The first debate on slavery and the slave trade takes place in the Constituent Assembly. The comte de Mirabeau's eloquence is ineffective: the assembly votes for inaction; the slave trade continues to be subsidized by the state. The abbé Raynal publishes his *Histoire des deux Indes*, a compendium of French thoughts on the colonies, containing ambiguous statements about slavery and the slave trade. Over the course of this year, nineteen thousand Africans arrive at the port of Le Cap Français in Saint-Domingue; Nantes has its best year ever in the slave trade.

1791	The French National Assembly condemns slavery (the first such condemnation in Europe). On 22 August insurrection in Saint-Domingue begins; in November Port-au-Prince burns. Gouges's *Déclaration des droits de la femme* compares (French) women to slaves and suggests empire should be sacrificed rather than perpetuate slavery.
1792	Claire's parents are legally separated. On 20 June Parisian revolutionaries raid the Tuileries Palace, residence of King Louis XVI and his family. In August shortages of sugar cause riots in Paris. On 10 August Parisian sansculottes again attack the Tuileries Palace; the king Louis XVI seeks refuge in the National Assembly, which suspends his powers, effectively ending the monarchy. Gouges publishes *L'esclavage des nègres*.
1793–1815	Wars between France and Britain disrupt the entire Atlantic system, including the slave trade.
1793	On 21 January King Louis XVI is guillotined. On 29 August Léger-Félicité Sonthonax (a Girondist-appointed commissioner) abolishes slavery in Saint-Domingue, setting off a global war focused on the Caribbean; the British attack Martinique and Guadeloupe. Maximilien de Robespierre declares terror the order of the day in September; on 5 December the comte de Kersaint, a Girondist deputy, is guillotined.
1794	On 4 February the National Convention votes the abolition of slavery after a proposal by the abbé Grégoire; the measure legally frees the slaves of Saint-Domingue, many of whom had already freed themselves in revolt. The slaves in Guadeloupe and Guyana are in a state of semifreedom. On 28 July Robespierre is guillotined; the Reign of Terror ends. Claire and her mother travel to Philadelphia to reclaim possession of Claire's mother's holdings in British-held Martinique. Eventually the holdings in Martinique—including land and slaves—are sold, to Claire's profit.
1795	Claire and her mother are in London, where Claire meets Amédée-Bretagne-Malo de Durfort, the future duc de Duras, from one of the most illustrious noble families of France. Mme de Staël publishes her *Recueil de morceaux détachés*, containing *Mirza* and *Histoire de Pauline*, novellas dealing with slavery and the slave trade (both written in 1786).
1797	Claire marries Durfort de Duras. (Henceforth she will be referred to here as Mme de Duras. She becomes the duchesse de Duras in 1800, on the death of her father-in-law.)
1798	Mme de Duras gives birth to a daughter, Félicie.
1799	Mme de Duras gives birth to her second and last child, a daughter named Clara. Napoléon becomes head of state.

1800   Death of the real Ourika at the reported age of sixteen. The
              maréchale de Beauvau's touching account of Ourika's death and the
              grief it provoked is recounted in *Souvenirs de la maréchale Prin-
              cesse de Beauvau* (see Thérèse De Raedt's essay in this volume).

1801–08   Mme de Duras visits France numerous times but maintains her
              residence with her family in London.

1801   First Consul Napoléon Bonaparte establishes the Concordat with
              Pope Pius VII, reinstating Catholicism as the religion of the majority
              of French nationals (see Christine De Vinne's essay in this volume).
              Mme de Duras's maternal aunt, Rose Angélique d'Alesso d'Eragny,
              the marquise de Rouvray, a plantation owner in Saint-Domingue,
              dies; her losses—and dire judgments of the slave insurrection—are
              evoked in published family correspondence. (She and her husband,
              in exile in Philadelphia, encountered her sister—Claire's mother—
              and Claire there in 1794.)

1802   Napoléon is confirmed as first consul for life. He sends the general
              Antoine Richepanse to Guadeloupe, where slavery is reestablished
              after explosive resistance led by the mulatto Louis Delgrès. In June
              the French kidnap the best-known leader of the revolution in Saint-
              Domingue, the former slave Toussaint Louverture, and send him
              to a dungeon in the Fort de Joux in the Jura in France, where he
              dies in April 1803.

1803   The French evacuate Saint-Domingue.

1804   Haitian independence is declared (see Deborah Jenson's essay in
              this volume). Napoléon proclaims himself emperor.

1807   Great Britain and the United States ban their slave trades; France
              is more or less cut off from the New World. Mme de Duras buys
              the Château d'Ussé (still owned by her descendants), in the Loire
              Valley, and takes up residence there.

1814   Restoration of the Bourbon monarchy under Louis XVIII (see
              Marshall C. Olds's essay in this volume) leads to a reactivation of the
              French slave trade, even though it is now banned by international
              treaty. The British restore French island colonies (slave-based) to
              French control. Seventeen years of mixed signals and lax enforce-
              ment allow the slave trade to flourish. With the restoration, the duc
              and duchesse de Duras take their places at the pinnacle of French
              society. Mme de Duras leads a brilliant intellectual salon, frequented
              by Chateaubriand, Charles-Maurice de Talleyrand, Alexander von
              Humboldt, Georges Cuvier, and others. Mme de Staël writes the
              abolitionist pamphlet *Appel aux Souverains réunis à Paris pour en
              obtenir l'abolition de la Traite des Nègres* ("Appeal to the Sover-
              eigns Convened in Paris").

1815	The Congress of Vienna condemns the slave trade.
1816	The French slave trade is fully back in business.
1818	The French government declares the slave trade illegal, but enforcement remains lax.
1819	The number of French slave-trading voyages doubles.
1820	Victor Hugo publishes the first version of *Bug-Jargal ou la révolution haïtienne*, a romantic vision of the Haitian Revolution with a black hero (see Kathryn M. Grossman's essay in this volume). Charles-Augustin Sainte-Beuve reports that Mme de Duras recites the story of Ourika to her salon in this year. She also begins writing *Edouard*.
1821	From January to April Mme de Duras writes *Ourika*. Marceline Desbordes-Valmore publishes the colonial novella *Sarah*, inspired by her 1802 travels in the revolutionary Caribbean (see Doris Y. Kadish's essay in this volume).
1823	*Ourika* is published; the novel is a tremendous success. The Académie Française's poetry contest on the theme "L'abolition de la traite des noirs" receives fifty-four entries. French naval patrols against the slave trade become more effective.
1824	An Ourika vogue runs through Paris. In the spring, four plays called *Ourika* open in the boulevard theaters. Mme de Duras's health begins to decline; she writes the novel *Olivier ou le secret*.
1825	On 17 April France recognizes Haitian independence; this recognition provokes outrage in France although Haiti is required to pay huge indemnities to France.
1825	Sophie Doin publishes anti-slave-trade stories *La famille noire* and *Nouvelles blanches et noires* (see Doris Y. Kadish's essay in this volume). Mme de Duras publishes her novel *Edouard*. This is the last big year for the French slave trade.
1828	Mme de Duras dies.
1830	The July Revolution in France ends the Bourbon Restoration and makes Louis-Philippe d'Orléans king of the French; abolitionists such as the baron de Staël and the duc de Broglie come to power.
1831	The final and real abolition of the French slave trade is effected by the law of 4 March, with new draconian sanctions. But the law is silent about slavery itself. New groups favoring the abolition of slavery organize and begin to work.
1848	In February revolution in France leads to the Second Republic; the abolitionist Victor Schoelcher is immediately active and effective; the final abolition of slavery in the French colonies is declared on 4 March. Some slaves in Martinique free themselves by rebellion before news of the emancipation reaches them.

Part Two

APPROACHES

Introduction

Mary Ellen Birkett and Christopher Rivers

The essays in this volume reflect the interests, needs, and desires of those who responded to our survey. Some respondents, for example, requested information about Claire de Duras's life. Many mentioned wanting to know more about the French slave trade, French colonialism in the eighteenth and early nineteenth centuries, and the historical Ourika, and others wanted help placing the novel in the context of the French and Haitian revolutions. Still others were curious about the pedagogical uses of *Ourika* and the various texts, literary and nonliterary, with which it is juxtaposed on a wide range of syllabi.

Literary, historical, and social contexts are inextricably intertwined in the telling of Ourika's story, which provides a rare means of reading race, gender, and class in late-eighteenth- and early-nineteenth-century France. Likewise, scholarly and pedagogical issues continually overlap in this volume. Keeping in mind that no boundaries are absolute, particularly in a work like *Ourika*, we have nonetheless divided the essays into sections that we hope will prove useful to readers.

The first section, "Historical Dimensions," is intended to help teachers bring their students to an understanding of the novel in its historical context, a pedagogical task that is more difficult than it may appear. *Ourika* is a historical novel, written in 1823 and thus molded by the rigid values of Restoration society, but it is set during the events of the French Revolution (1789–99) and the Haitian Revolution (1791–1804).

Mary Jane Cowles's essay puts *Ourika* in the context of the major events of the French Revolution and examines the representation of the revolution and its principles—especially the concept of natural order. Marshall C. Olds discusses the revolution as seen by the Restoration—as a "failed social experiment" much like Ourika's upbringing—and the way in which Duras's novel expresses those perceptions; in so doing, he places *Ourika* in both historical and literary-historical perspective. Christine De Vinne argues that Duras's choice to have Ourika retreat to an Ursuline convent is not an arbitrary one; in a discussion of the Ursuline order, the convent in general, and the religious culture of revolutionary Paris, De Vinne puts *Ourika* in an often overlooked context that is important to any nuanced understanding of the work. Deborah Jenson examines the relation between the French and Haitian revolutions and how the novel reflects both explicitly and implicitly the "simultaneous twinship and radical difference" of the two.

The next two essays present history on a more personal scale. Christopher L. Miller discusses the ways in which Duras's life story, especially her close family ties to the Atlantic economy and thus to slavery, may be brought to bear on an interpretation of the novel and the ways in which the facts of that life story have been reported, distorted, and mythologized. His reading provokes students to ask whether *Ourika*, despite its seemingly sympathetic posture, ultimately defends, albeit subtly, slavery and by extension Duras's own wealth. Thérèse De Raedt provides information about the presence of black child-servants in prerevolutionary aristocratic French households, a context within which she examines visual and textual representations of the real-life Ourika. (Sue Peabody's essay later in the volume complements these representations by citing archival documents concerning the real Ourika.)

The next section, "Race, Class, and Gender Matters," addresses the issues of race, class, and gender that are at the heart of Duras's novel—the aspects of *Ourika* that tend to be most fully explored in today's classrooms. Doris Y. Kadish demonstrates how the works of three French women who wrote about black characters in the 1820s—Henriette de La Tour du Pin, Marceline Desbordes-Valmore, and Sophie Doin—call into question fundamental assumptions about race and gender in Duras's work. (Kadish's essay might well be read in tandem with Miller's, which questions the same assumptions.) After situating Duras in the long tradition of women writers in France, Chantal Bertrand-Jennings offers teachers a close textual analysis of ways in which narrative and linguistic structure translate the marginalization and powerlessness attributed to the biological difference of gender in *Ourika*. Kari Weil enlists psychoanalytic theory to help students examine why the marginalization that Ourika suffers silences her and then brings her to narrate a life story that only hastens her death, in contrast to the *mal du siècle* of male heroes, such as René, which empowers them to live productively and creatively. (Later in the volume, Carolyn Fay returns to this pairing of *Ourika* with *René*, bringing the heroine of *René*, Amélie, into the comparison). Dorothy Kelly uses the critical lens of literary theory—here, Pierre Bourdieu's *Masculine Domination*—to give students a framework for thinking about social construction in the novel. The conjunction of Bourdieu and Duras can lead students to a more complex appreciation of the role of biological reproduction in Duras's text, as well as to an assessment of what it means to be man or woman, black or white, in society. Mireille Rosello approaches *Ourika* through the character of the doctor. She proposes a reading centered on both the doctor's failure as a professional healer and his effectiveness as a listener to and reteller of Ourika's story. Her reading, aimed at disclosing Ourika's secret, asks students to be attentive to the unspoken as well as to the spoken dimensions of Ourika's *mal*.

The essays in the following section illuminate *Ourika* and highlight its originality by juxtaposing it with other literary texts. Adrianna M. Paliyenko informs readers about the literary frame of Romanticism, particularly the Byronic Romanticism to which Duras points in the epigraph to *Ourika*. Inspired by Ourika's reference to the Ovidian myth of Pygmalion and Galatea—the sculptor and his statue-turned-flesh—Damon DiMauro explores Duras's novel as an inversion of this classical philosophical tale of human creativity (as revived by the Enlightenment) into a Romantic meditation on human frailty and divine creation. Kathryn M. Grossman compares *Ourika* with Victor Hugo's 1821 tragic novel of slavery, friendship, and revolution, *Bug-Jargal*. Grossman uses Hugo's revisions to *Bug-Jargal* following Haiti's independence in 1825 to offer a reflection of and on Duras's *Ourika*, bringing home to students the influence that Duras's best seller had on her contemporaries. The perspective of postcolonial black women writers attests to troubling prolongations of Ourika's experience. Dawn Fulton provides a compelling example of the persistence of the themes of urban confinement and negative self-discovery in contemporary francophone Caribbean fiction. By comparing *Ourika* with Gisèle Pineau's *L'exil selon Julia*, she exposes underlying tensions in Julia's and Ourika's assumptions about, and experience of, Paris as a place where a black woman can find safety and refuge. (The motif of salvation that runs through both novels can be linked to the French idea of civilization that Scott M. Powers explores in his essay.)

The final section of this volume, "Across the Curriculum," is the most explicitly pedagogical. Given the variety of courses and disciplines in which *Ourika* is taught, this section offers samples from the range of contexts in which students encounter this novel. The historian Sue Peabody outlines a pedagogy for bringing fiction into history courses, using *Ourika* as an effective example of a novel's function as window, prism, and mirror. Scott M. Powers, too, argues that *Ourika* is not only a reflection and a product of French culture but also an active response to it: he puts Duras's text fruitfully to use in a French civilization course, where it leads to a critique of the notion of civilization itself. Jocelyn Van Tuyl discusses how to teach *Ourika* in two very different pedagogical contexts: an intermediate French language class and a comparative literature course exploring the relation of fiction and history through "doubling strategies." David R. Ellison proposes a pedagogy for using *Ourika* in a "bridge" course—one that takes students from the study of the French language to the study of literature. The first half of a course of this type, he suggests, can begin with straightforward grammar instruction, while the second half can be devoted to the study of the first literary work students read in French, *Ourika*.

Carolyn Fay offers a model for teaching *Ourika* in a gender studies course, and Jen Hill demonstrates the value of teaching *Ourika* in a required humanities course, emphasizing how Duras's text extends the discussion of the political potential and limits of sympathy opened in Aphra Behn's *Oroonoko*. Barbara Woshinsky closes the volume, appropriately, by reflecting not only on how *Ourika* engages students in topics of personal concern to them, such as love, marriage, race relations, and religion, but also on what teachers may learn from student responses to the novel.

The French Revolution in *Ourika*

Mary Jane Cowles

The pages of Claire de Duras's novel *Ourika* depicting the events and effects of the revolution are at the center of the text and merit particular attention (DeJean 18–23; Fowles 18–24). According to Joan DeJean, "Very few previous literary works depicted life during revolutionary times . . . because censorship under all successive regimes had rendered the subject taboo" (Introduction xii). *Ourika* provides, therefore, a rare perspective on the consequences of the revolution. The revolution, however, not only anchors the fictional events in a historical reality, thereby enhancing the value of the narrative as testimony and truth in fiction, but also underwrites the fundamental meaning of the narrative, opening a window of hope for the heroine and embodying the inherent contradictions that seal her fate. There is a paradox in the novel that can be exploited effectively by teachers: in the context of an Enlightenment discourse on reason and natural rights that serves as the foundation for the revolution, Duras portrays the society of the ancien régime as the "natural order"; it is this natural order that lies at the heart of Ourika's tragedy. Moreover, the shared misfortunes occasioned by the revolution are, ironically, the only moments of happiness Ourika knows.

A Brief Summary of the Revolution

Many students will doubtless recognize references to the Bastille or to the Terror, but most will probably be unfamiliar with the historical events alluded to in *Ourika*. It is thus useful to provide them with an overview of the various causes of the revolution: the questioning of authority promoted by the philosophes of the Enlightenment (whose debates Duras evokes in her description of the salon of Mme de B. [18–20; 18–20]); the national economic crisis engendered by years of war; resistance by the nobility to a diminution of their privileges; and, more immediate, a disastrous harvest in 1788, resulting in increased prices and the fear of famine. At the same time, the French colony of Saint-Domingue (now Haiti) represented a significant source of wealth for metropolitan France. With a population of approximately 31,000 whites, 28,000 free people of African or mixed descent, and 465,000 slaves, it was the world's leading producer of sugar and coffee (Dubois 30). Some Enlightenment thinkers, such as the marquis de Condorcet, had already published antislavery essays, and, in 1788, Jacques Pierre Brissot founded the Société des Amis des Noirs, an abolitionist group.

The National Assembly

In the hope of finding a solution to the financial crisis, Louis XVI convened the Estates-General on 5 May 1789. The more numerous deputies of the Third Estate (representing all classes other than the aristocracy and the clergy) demanded that the three orders convene jointly and that votes be counted by head, not by order. By mid-June, they were joined by representatives of the clergy, thereby forming the National Assembly. From its very inception, discussion of civil rights for free persons of color and the problem of slavery figured prominently in the National Assembly's deliberations.

When Louis XVI threatened to dissolve the Estates-General and began massing troops around Paris, the Parisians, anticipating an attack and experiencing dwindling food supplies, formed a bourgeois militia. Accompanied by the crowd, the militia marched on 14 July to the Bastille prison in search of gunpowder and eventually took the fortress. In the provinces, too, the bourgeoisie established armed forces—the National Guard—while the peasants, fearing an aristocratic reaction (*la Grande peur*), besieged local châteaus and burned feudal registers. In response, the National Assembly abolished feudal privileges (4 Aug. 1789) and adopted the Declaration of the Rights of Man and of the Citizen (26 Aug. 1789). The king's failure to approve these decrees and the recurrent fear of food shortages prompted the Parisian populace, led by the women of the market, to march on Versailles and bring the king back with them to Paris.

During this time, plantation owners and the merchants who benefited from colonial trade were attempting to prevent news of the declaration from reaching Saint-Domingue. Despite the demands for equal rights by free men of color, many of whom were French-educated owners of property and slaves, the powerful planters' lobby succeeded in arguing for particular laws to suit the different conditions of the colony; legislation passed in May 1790 was only a compromise measure.

The National Assembly continued its drafting of a constitution for the new nation, giving the king veto power as head of the executive branch of government and instituting an elected legislative body. To address the financial crisis, the assembly nationalized church lands in November 1789 (to the chagrin of the old abbot friend of Mme de B. [22; 23]) and began enacting tax reform. The assembly also limited the power of the king; consequently, Louis XVI and the royal family fled Paris toward the northern border on the night of 20 June 1791 but were arrested in the town of Varennes on 21 June. As a result of this flight, many called for the king's abdication; the assembly, however, moved to preserve the monarchy.

The Constitutional Monarchy

With the constitution in place, the Legislative Assembly was convened in Paris in October 1791, but it faced many challenges. Increasingly, royalist officers were deserting the army to join the king's two brothers in Coblenz, Germany, and fears of an internal conspiracy in support of foreign enemies were rampant. Meanwhile, in August 1791, a rebellion of as many as eighty thousand slaves erupted in Saint-Domingue, hundreds of plantations were destroyed, and some thousand whites were massacred (Bellegarde-Smith 41), an act that makes Ourika ashamed of her race (DeJean 20; Fowles 21). In an effort to quell the revolt by strengthening alliances between whites and free men of color, the assembly now granted civil equality to all free persons of color.

In November 1791, the assembly issued a law declaring the émigrés outlaws (it is this decree that brings Mme de B.'s grandson Charles back to France [21; 22]). Reacting to threats from foreign powers, the assembly declared war against Austria on 20 April 1792. Then, in response to the king's veto of measures to strengthen national defense, protestors invaded the Tuileries Palace on 20 June 1792. In August, Parisians learned of the manifesto of the Duke of Brunswick, commander of the Prussian armies, which warned that Paris would be destroyed if Louis XVI and his family were harmed. The Paris sections organized an insurrection, and an army of sansculottes again invaded the Tuileries Palace on 10 August 1792; the king took refuge with the assembly, which suspended his powers, effectively ending the monarchy. These two "affreuses journées" 'terrible days,' 20 June and 10 August, proved to Ourika that the men of the revolution no longer respected anything (21; 21). In early September 1792, fearing that counterrevolutionary prisoners were waiting to welcome the invading troops, popular courts in Paris summarily executed some twelve hundred prisoners (the September Massacres). Elected to frame a new constitution, the Convention convened on 21 September 1792 and immediately proclaimed the republic.

The Republic

The king was tried by the Convention and then guillotined on 21 January 1793 (Duras describes Mme de B.'s grief on this occasion [21–22; 22]). Given the military crisis, the Jacobins (a republican, centralist, and populist faction within the Convention) proposed a general conscription, which provoked civil war in the west (the Vendée Revolt). The Convention gave executive power to the Committee of Public Safety, led by the Jacobin Maximilien de Robespierre. In September, again in response to demands from the Paris sections, the Convention declared terror the order of the day. Measures included strict price and wage controls (*le maximum*); a policy of de-Christianization; and the Law of Suspects, which sanctioned the arrest of former nobles, priests, and all those who appeared to have federalist or royalist sympathies. It is this law that puts Mme de B. under house arrest (23; 24).

In February 1794, three delegates from Saint-Domingue arrived at the Convention to report that the republican commissioners, to maintain French control of the colony, had granted freedom to the slaves. The Convention promptly voted to abolish slavery throughout the republic (Napoleon would reinstitute it in 1802). The Committee of Public Safety, meanwhile, continued purging the opposition, arresting the leaders of both radical and more moderate factions in March 1794. The number of executions rose dramatically. But support for Robespierre's policies had been declining, and his 26 July speech implicating unnamed deputies of the Convention provoked a reaction. He and his followers were arrested on 27 July 1794 (9 Thermidor) and guillotined the next day. While the work of the republic was hardly over, the following months saw relaxation of the Terror, an increase in personal freedoms, and an end to the threat of imminent invasion.

The Hope of Revolution: "Trouver Ma Place"

Ourika first becomes aware of her racial difference when she overhears Mme de B.'s friend the marquise's warning to Mme de B.:

> [L]a philosophie nous place au-dessus des maux de la fortune, mais elle ne peut rien contre les maux qui viennent d'avoir brisé l'ordre de la nature. Ourika . . . s'est placée dans la société sans sa permission; la société se vengera. (13)

> Reason may help people overcome bad luck. But it's powerless against evils that arise from deliberately upsetting the natural order of things. Ourika . . . has entered society without its permission. It will have its revenge. (14)

It is thus the natural order that causes Ourika's irremediable solitude. (For perspectives on the natural order in *Ourika* see Chilcoat, "Civility" 127 and "Confinement" 15; Crichfield 7; Little, "Madame de Duras" 89–90.)

Students can profitably examine two moments in the narrative at which the ideals of the revolution offer hope for a change in the natural order. The first relates to the abolition of privilege and the concept of equality expressed in the Declaration of the Rights of Man. One can ask students to consider the declaration in the context of *Ourika*, especially the preamble and the first article. For Enlightenment thinkers, the declaration articulates natural rights: men are born equal (Haudrère and Vergès 9). Ourika evokes these ideas in her description of the debates in Mme de B.'s salon (DeJean 18–19; Fowles 18–20).

The reconceptualization of social structures that informed Enlightenment debates—on the church, the system of justice, limits to state authority, recognition of merit independent of social rank, the role of women and marriage—was bound to appeal to Ourika. The "grand désordre" could perhaps pave the way for a new order (18–19; 19), one that would hold a place for a young, well-educated black woman. But students should observe, too, that the fear of excess surfaces even in this most idealized exchange of pure ideas, preparing for later disillusionment with the revolution. (See Bissière's treatment of the hopes offered by the revolution [319–20].)

Ourika envisions her place in society as deriving not from solidarity with others of "tous les rangs confondus" 'all social caste overthrown' (DeJean 19; Fowles 19) but rather from her exceptionality, the unique qualities of her mind and education replacing the isolating singularity of the color of her skin: "si j'avais quelque supériorité d'âme, quelque qualité cachée, on l'apprécierait lorsque ma couleur ne m'isolerait plus au milieu du monde" 'If I truly possessed some superiority of mind, some hidden quality, then it would be appreciated when my color no longer isolated me' (19; 19). Universal social justice would transform her black skin, an opaque covering that hides her imagined qualities, into a transparency that would reveal them.

The second moment of hope occurs as the debates in the salon of Mme de B. turn to the question of slavery. Here, too, Ourika glimpses a change in the social order that could affect her status. Ourika initially believes in the illusion of a fraternity, shared with the slaves of Saint-Domingue. She gives credence to a myth of noble suffering, and, since she also suffers from her misfortunes, she can identify with the slaves. She invests the slaves, however briefly, with idealized qualities of the noble savage, both moral and stoic.

"La Place de la Raison"

Both of these moments of hope, of course, give way to disillusionment. In each case, students should ask themselves what motivates Ourika's judgment of the progress of the revolution. Does Ourika reject or support its underlying principles, and why or why not? It appears that her critique focuses on issues of solidarity with others and on the self-interest of revolutionary leaders. First, her education and generosity of spirit cause her to dissociate herself from the gains of revolutionary social change (19; 19). Second, she realizes that even those gains will not undo centuries of prejudice, since revolutionary leaders were inspired by a false philanthropy (19; 20; see Chilcoat's discussion of the "hypocrisy of Enlightenment egalitarianism" in "Civility" 142). Her renunciation of her own interests contrasts with the ultimately selfish motives that displace the reason of the distinguished men who frequent Mme de B.'s salon (DeJean 19; Fowles 20). But what is meant by "reason"? How is reason portrayed in Duras's novel, and what is its relation to the natural order? What other characters and traits are associated with reason?

Regarding the question of slavery, abolitionists of revolutionary France were clearly appealing to reason in demanding equal rights for all men. But the violence of the 1791 uprisings in Saint-Domingue shocked even abolitionists. The massacres of Saint-Domingue appear the antithesis of reason, in "a world turned upside down" (Dubois 112). In response, Ourika shifts her alliance: instead of identifying with the oppressed slaves, she sympathizes with their oppressors, in the name of order. Is there no place for a middle ground?

The Homeland of Suffering

The slaves in revolt are not the only ones who resort to violence. The evocation of Saint-Domingue is juxtaposed with the violence of the birth of the republic (DeJean 21; Fowles 21). By this point, any ambivalence Ourika may have felt with respect to the revolution has vanished. After she has rejected identification with the revolutionaries, with the slaves of Saint-Domingue, and with the aristocracy that excludes her, what remains for Ourika? Mme de B. responds to the violence of the "affreuses journées," which culminate in the execution of the king, with equally violent grief:

> Ce grand crime avait causé à Mme de B. la plus violente douleur; . . . et son âme était assez forte, pour proportionner l'horreur du forfait à l'immensité du forfait même. Les grandes douleurs, dans la vieillesse, ont quelque chose de frappant: elles ont pour elles l'autorité de la raison.
> (21–22)

> That outrage had caused Mme de B. the most acute grief. She . . . was courageous enough to feel a horror at the crime proportionate to its enormity. There is something striking about great suffering in the old, since it has the authority of reason.   (22)

Here, reason is again linked to suffering and serves not to measure political equality or intellectual judgment but to portion out "l'horreur du forfait à l'immensité du forfait même." There is, however, a problem. If, as Ourika says, "opinion" 'a view of life' is like "une patrie" 'a motherland' (22; 23), it is but a precarious homeland. The return to Mme de B.'s circle of other victims of revolutionary persecution undermines the existence of that homeland as a refuge for Ourika. The more things revert to a natural order, the more isolated Ourika becomes (27; 28).

Students should ask themselves again, What is the natural order of things? Did the revolution really affect that order? Ourika hoped to find a place for herself in a new order, but in the upheaval that results, the persistence of ancien régime values precludes her integration. Does the revolution represent an ideology for Ourika, or is it a structural element in the narrative, offering the hope of order while signifying its absence? Place, order, and reason are practically synonymous in the text, and all contribute to narrow the social field of Ourika's experience until she is ill and confined to a convent. Their function culminates in the law of God, which appears to be the antithesis of revolution: "cette loi," says Ourika, "me montre tous mes devoirs" 'His law . . . shows me what I must do' (44; 46).

The Restoration Looks Back at the Revolution

Marshall C. Olds

Among its seemingly endless applications for teaching, Claire de Duras's novel *Ourika* can contribute to discussion of nineteenth-century views of the French Revolution. I have used the text in teaching courses in nineteenth-century studies on the rise of historical consciousness and the rise of the novel, where study of reactions to the revolution has a prominent role. As my title suggests, the focus here is on a combined historical and literary presentation of the novel. This double optic offers rich perspectives, especially when considered in the context of the period 1775–1823, from the approximate date of the fictive Ourika's arrival in France to the first publication of the novel.[1] Duras was of course inspired by the true story of the historical Ourika (DeJean, Introduction viii). The novelist did not merely transpose that real life to fiction, however. She changed the chronology of the protagonist's life, making the fictional life longer than the real one (Little, "Madame de Duras" 70–91), and aligned the story with the full span of the revolution. These dates define the narrative's specific point of historical reference and also plant the work firmly in the literary practice of the 1820s, an important decade for the development of the French novel, with respect to both form and ideology.

In the work's spare frame, the historical material is abundant and focused. *Ourika* not only offers a chronology for the revolution, from its early days to its effective end with the Concordat signed in 1802, but also evokes important issues of citizenship and civic rights, issues tied to the debates over slavery and the slave trade. In this thematic chronology, we are given a rapid-fire view of an astonishing number of social events that include the uprisings on Saint-Domingue, the execution of the king, the Terror, the aristocratic emigration, and, finally, the reopening of monasteries and convents. On a more intimate scale, there are specific historical indications of the social milieu in which Ourika is raised, the upper reaches of the Parisian aristocracy: Paul-Joseph Barthez, the doctor who first examines Ourika (DeJean 14; Fowles 15), was a physician to Louis XVI and later to Napoléon Bonaparte; the Ursuline convent in the faubourg Saint-Jacques to which she retires was well known for taking daughters from France's most illustrious nobility (Aron 66); and Mme de B. is said to have been a friend of Louis XV's influential minister of foreign affairs, the duc de Choiseul (DeJean 23; Fowles 23).

Discussion of the literary side of this work is no less revealing. Events and comment come to us from a double point of view that reflects (while not representing entirely) the two social classes having the most at stake in the revolution: the aristocracy and the black slaves. An astonishing feature of *Ourika* is that both perspectives come from a single character. Moreover, that character suffers mortally from a secret woe and so is fully a literary creation of the sentimental novel of the empire and restoration. As formulaic as Hollywood movies, works in this genre are structured on the motifs of solitude, impossible love, melancholy, and, inevitably, early death. *Ourika* is an important transitional example of the novel that, on the one hand, is beginning to incorporate specific contemporary social material and that, on the other, is still bound by the rigid formal conventions of the French sentimental novel. This combination offers much that can be explored with students, such as the enactment of *two* revolutions, one public and one private, both ending in failure. Ourika's death signals both the end of her personal development and the end of the social development—ultimately unrealized—she incarnates.

Indeed, from the vantage point of the restored monarchy (1814–30), the revolution of 1789 was often viewed as a failure, whether one sympathized with the specifically revolutionary goal of creating a secular republic or with the spirit of reform that came from the Enlightenment regarding the primacy of the individual. This latter view was held by Duras's father—the comte de Kersaint—and other prominent nobles, such as the marquis de Condorcet and the marquis de Lafayette, among the progressive minds of the period. In 1788, they and others founded the Société des Amis des Noirs and initiated the debate that eventually lead to the 4 February 1794 law abolishing slavery. This law would be reversed on 10 May 1802, when Bonaparte reestablished the civic status of all persons living in the colonies to the condition that obtained before 1789. Kersaint and Condorcet, of course, were both victims of the Terror.

In her combined sense of rejection, self-loathing, and solitude, Ourika has much in common with other heroines and heroes of the period, most bearing signs of what Deborah Jenson has described as the collective trauma caused by the revolution. The novel is significantly at variance with many of its contemporaries, however, and invites us to see a social interpretability that complements that of character and situation. Unlike other eponymous protagonists who live outside of France (Mme de Staël's Corinne) or whose narrative lives antedate the revolution (François-René de Chateaubriand's René), Duras's characters do not leave the *hic et nunc* that give them meaning. Mme de B. and the members of her household who are essential to the tale do not emigrate but remain steadfastly in Paris throughout the revolution. The story told by Ourika is not only that of a uniquely gifted young woman who confronts a social prohibition against interracial love and marriage. Hers is a *récit*, a personal tale, that draws overt parallels between her own story and the specific social dynamism of the times, such that the two must be considered together to take full measure of what is singular about this literary work.

Roger Little points out how the abject solitude of the heroine parallels that of another of her contemporaries, Mary Wollstonecraft Shelley's creature; both characters are uniquely alone in the world and morbidly despondent (Little, "Madame de Duras" 83). There is for us a more significant parallel: Victor Frankenstein's brilliant creation teaches himself French by reading Jean-Jacques Rousseau, a figure whom we associate today with the birth of Romanticism but who, in Duras's and Shelley's day, was considered the progenitor of the French

Revolution. In this light, Shelley's 1818 novel points to the revolution as the broad frame for understanding Frankenstein's failed *social* experiment, but medical success, to create a new man. Like *Frankenstein*, *Ourika* is the story of a social experiment paralleling the revolution's: raising a black orphan of slave parents as a French aristocrat, an undertaking as audaciously revolutionary in its implications as the 1789 revolution, if on a smaller scale.

The novel opens with insistent specificity as to time and place; the references in the all-important first paragraph could not be clearer (3; 3). Our young doctor, whose narrative contains the heroine's, is from Montpellier, a city renowned for both medical education and revolutionary fervor. He is a child of the revolution, raised in the antichurch interval since 1789, who, on crossing the threshold of the newly reopened convent, steps into a France that has restored the institution that was among the most potent reasons for revolution. As expressed here, the official reopening of monasteries and convents—which dates from the concordat in 1802, several years before Bonaparte became emperor in 1804—marks not merely the end of the revolution but the attempted erasure of it as an active social force. The projected repairs of the damage caused during the turmoil signal a return to the *statu quo ante bellum*.

While the plot of the novel has been described as perfectly linear (Crichfield 41), the form is not; it shares the structure typical of the sentimental novel—that of a personal *récit*, embedded in another first-person tale, or witness *récit*—allowing for a return to the initial chronology and hence for a kind of circularity. The social events referred to in Ourika's tale are the revolt of 1789, the debates in the National Assembly over citizenship and rights—specifically those of blacks—the execution of the king, the Terror, recruitment abroad for the prince de Condé's counterrevolutionary army, the slave uprisings on Saint-Domingue, the execution of Maximilien de Robespierre and the end of the Terror, and the return of the émigrés. The doctor's *récit* takes us to the time immediately after the reopening of the convents, the only postconcordat event evoked in his narrative. This *récit* is verification by the witness-narrator, a kind of spot check, of the nature of the events recounted in the personal tale. Both revolutions—the private and the national—end in favor of a third social structure, permitted by the restored church, where racial difference no longer exists and where, as we learn in Ourika's last, unfinished sentence, all objects of pure love can be contemplated—without sin, certainly, but above all without social prohibition (DeJean 45; Fowles 46).

Not all social and political events of the period are evoked: aside from the Terror, we hear nothing of the various revolutionary governments, nothing further of the Napoleonic period, nothing even of the early liberation of the slaves (1794) and Bonaparte's subsequent rescinding of that law (1802). These omissions are justifiable: the intended, proabolitionist readership of 1823 would have been all too familiar with these occurrences. More important, they simply are not necessary to the social and political thrust of the work, which quietly but firmly points to the restoration to generate its full meaning. The jump to the France of the concordat offers a plausible context for the heroine's withdrawal from the society that she feels has shunned her. It provides, too, a major stepping-stone between 1789 and the point of the novel's first readership in 1823, also the presumed date of the doctor's *récit*. To mention first the devastation of the revolution and then the emperor Napoléon in the opening sentences only invites the reader to consider what has happened since: the social tumult put in motion in 1789 has been stopped, the halfway house of the empire is at an end, and if things have not been put absolutely right again, they are beginning to look much like before.

For this novel, then, the restoration, while never named in the text, is the historical vantage point that illuminates the story. More nuanced than the simple question of political direction, the notion of restoration becomes central to how the novel expresses meaning. There are several key markers for this implied restoration found in the frame surrounding Ourika's story. One is afforded by Mme de B.'s friend, the marquise. Her two appearances in the narrative initiate Ourika's double *prise de conscience*—personal and social—and, because the marquise returns from emigration, punctuate the start and the end of the revolution. It is she who tells Mme de B. in no uncertain terms that Ourika's misfortune is sealed because of her benefactress's error of judgment. "Ourika n'a pas rempli sa destinée: elle s'est placée dans la société sans sa permission; la société se vengera" 'Ourika has flouted her natural destiny. She has entered society without its permission. It will have its revenge' (13; 14). Ourika is doomed to solitude, and it is *la société* that will exact this price. Mme de B. pleads the girl's innocence in the matter, but her plea merely underscores her own responsibility. The marquise reveals to Ourika her plight, and she also forces Mme de B. to recognize the profound injustice she has committed by bringing the girl up as a social equal. Mme de B. allows that she could have raised her charge to be of a much lower station, but chose not to. She admits to her friend, "Pour la rendre heureuse, il eût fallu en faire une personne commune" 'To have made her happy, I'd have had to try to turn her into a common servant' (13; 13). In coming to Mme de B. as an infant, Ourika was innocent of knowledge both of the world and of a predestined place in it. Choice, not birth, has determined what her world would be. As mentioned above, there are indeed two revolutions, one public and one private.

Seen in this light, Ourika's plight is not the result of some innate and permanent condition. Although she is black and a woman, the crux of the problem does not lie there. Her condition cannot fully be allied with the melancholy of Chateaubriand's René, with the monstrousness of Shelley's creature, or with the plight of another of Duras's characters, Olivier, who suffers from sexual impotence. The solitude resulting from these flaws is universal because it is everywhere immutable. Ourika's condition is not universally the same: the obstacle to her happiness in France is indeed tied to her race but specifically to the conjunction between her race and her acquired social class (a marriage outside that class is conceivable—if not enviable—but not one within it [13; 13]). Were she to "emigrate" and join others of her race either in slavery or in her native Senegal, she would suffer further isolation because she thinks like a French aristocrat and would not be understood (15; 16). At issue here is not her unchangeable nature but her acquired one. True, it becomes something like an irreversible condition, and critics justifiably put her among the ranks of "nègres blancs" ("Uncle Toms"; Little, "Madame de Duras" 80), although this anachronism evokes a community unavailable to Ourika. She is absolutely alone. Her induced solitude makes the social content of the novel critical to its reach.

That Ourika's social destiny might have been otherwise is made clear by the events subsequent to July 1789. Through the discussions in Mme de B.'s salon, Ourika becomes aware of the new ideas, debated in the National Assembly as early as August, surrounding citizenship and rights. The principal debating body of the Third Estate—those who were neither noble nor of the clergy—was not a monolithic entity but a myriad of distinct groups, such as Protestants, Jews, mulattoes, blacks, and women (Hunt, *French Revolution* 7–12). Ourika was understandably interested in the proposed social changes, particularly with respect to social rank and to color (DeJean 19; Fowles 20). Her hopes were raised by events and then dashed. The failure of the revolution as it collapsed into regicide and slaughter by both races—the massacres on Saint-Domingue and the Terror—was the result not of faulty ideals, however, but of human weakness and error. Speaking of those who would fall short of professed ideals, "je jugeais les petitesses de leurs caractères, je devinais leurs vues secrètes; bientôt leur fausse philanthropie cessa de m'abuser" 'I perceived the smallness of their characters, I guessed their real philosophies. I soon stopped being the dupe of their false notion of fraternity' (19; 20).

Ourika's despondency is personal but also results from her identification with the unattained goals of the revolution. In addition, Ourika is associated with the revolution by the returning émigrés who begin to frequent Mme de B.'s salon. Their expressions of surprise and disdain at finding her there indicate a cruel society that "me rendait responsable du mal qu'elle seule avait fait" 'declared me guilty of a crime it alone had committed' (28; 28–29). While not the cause of the revolution, Ourika nevertheless is seen as having contributed to it. This association provides a key point of overlap between the personal revolution and the social one: they are different in form—ennoblement as opposed to democratization—though they share the belief propounded by the abbé Raynal that blacks differ from whites in skin color only (Hunt, *French Revolution* 51–55). What better way to validate this belief than by raising a child of slaves to the highest level of social and personal accomplishment?

The reaction of the émigrés—their fear turned to scorn—not only formalizes the association of Ourika with revolution, but also signals the beginning of the end of the upheaval and the move toward restoration. That direction will be affirmed by the marriage between Charles and Anaïs de Thémines, whose parents perished during the Terror. Their union and the birth of their child are at once the source of Ourika's final grief and the emblematic bridge over the gulf created by the revolution. We might temper the view that would see Duras's criticism of society as the condemnation of all society by observing that Duras does not show Charles and Anaïs as unworthy of their happiness or the social context of that happiness as unworthy of them. Neither is the case, and therein lies a hesitation regarding the revolution and the restoration that foreshadows Honoré de Balzac's appreciation of the unique complexity of the times.

But Duras is not Balzac. She has quite a different take on what will be for her successor the period's historical dynamism. Along with the story of its protagonist, Duras's short novel powerfully communicates the profound sense in 1823 that history had somehow come to an end, where history is understood precisely as the dynamic of change. The restored social order is seen as the right one, all things considered; but its return does not come without loss. There is the loss of the engaging protagonist and also the loss of the social eventuality by which she could have been fully realized as a human being. The only community to which she can turn, where there are neither blacks nor whites and where all hearts are equal (DeJean 43; Fowles 45)—the ideals of both revolutions—is not of this earth but in the restored church, which admits neither social change nor historical time. This last point, that time has somehow come to an end, is made in the final sentence of the text. Earlier, expressing her longing for death, the heroine exclaimed, "Ourika est un enfant déshérité. . . . O mon Dieu! . . . laissez-la mourir comme la feuille tombe en automne" '[Ourika] was a disinherited child. . . . [L]et her fall as the leaf falls in autumn' (36; 37). In the closing passage, it is the doctor who is speaking as he relates Ourika's death, which occurred in autumn. "Je continuai à lui donner des soins: malheureusement ils furent inutiles; elle mourut à la fin d'octobre; elle tomba avec les dernières feuilles de l'automne" 'I continued to attend her, but my science proved sadly unavailing. She died at the end of October, with the last of the autumn leaves' (45; 47). He has taken her metaphor of time and death and brought it to apply to the real time of the end of the year and the death of nature, to 1802 and by extension 1823. Real time is the time of historical possibility, and, as Ourika dies, so does the last vestige of the possibility that she represents.[2]

NOTES

[1] *Ourika* was printed first at the author's expense in 1823 and then by a commercial editor in 1824. I am considering 1823 as the date of the first readership.

[2] The novel's solemn finality did not prevent it from becoming a call to arms for abolitionist sympathizers and authors such as Victor Hugo (*Misérables*) and Gabrielle de Paban. Read by enlightened minds throughout Europe, its influence was felt beyond French borders. That influence was not always welcome, however; in Spain, where the monarchy was still heavily invested in slavery and the slave trade, *Ourika* was placed on the index of banned books in 1825.

Religion under Revolution in *Ourika*

Christine De Vinne

The frame story for *Ourika* is so short that students are likely to overlook its importance to the novel's historical context. The doctor's opening narrative, however, provides clues essential for understanding a tale that poses the political realities of early empire France as a romantic setting:

> La Révolution avait ruiné une partie de l'édifice; le cloître était à découvert d'un côté par la démolition de l'antique église, dont on ne voyait plus que quelques arceaux. (DeJean 3)

> Part of the building had been destroyed during the Revolution, and the demolition of the ancient church, of which no more than a few vault arches remained, left the cloisters open on one side. (Fowles 3)

Yet the Ursuline convent in the faubourg Saint-Jacques, its ravaged church and ruptured cloister, even the particular black veil that Ourika would have worn there are no mere fictional backdrops, and the image of a life radically affected by forces behind the revolution belongs not just to the dying patient but to every nun in the monastery.

When I teach *Ourika*, in an English course on the European novel in translation, there is little chance that my students will miss these details. On our liberal arts campus, an interdisciplinary core curriculum encourages the study of literature in context. What is more, and I realize I have a distinct home-court advantage, our college is sponsored by a congregation of Ursulines who trace their heritage to Boulogne-sur-Mer and from there to *le grand couvent de Paris*. Admittedly, such insider sensibilities are hard to replicate, but students anywhere can recognize that the overtly religious setting for Ourika's last months is a critical aspect of her story's sociopolitical context. With a basic understanding of the Ursulines of Paris and their experience under the revolution, students can appreciate the subtle but powerful symmetry between Ourika's exile status and that of the outcasts whose ruined monastery becomes her final home.

From the start, Claire de Duras is deliberate in her choice of convent for Ourika. In a district nearly saturated with religious orders—the eighteenth-century faubourg Saint-Jacques was home to Benedictines, Carmelites, Oratorians, Visitandines, Capuchins, and others—Ourika ends her days among Ursulines. Cloistered and professed, dedicated to the instruction of girls, drawn, at least in Paris, from the aristocracy and officer class, the order would have provided her a haven among cultured women brought up, like she had been, in ancien régime privilege, applied now to the educational advantage of the pupils.

Founded by Angela Merici in Brescia, Italy, in 1535, the Ursuline congregation spread to southern France in the 1590s and arrived in Paris by 1607. Confident that the moral and practical education of young women could reform society, the Ursulines needed a high degree of freedom to accomplish their mission. Originally only loosely structured—members lived individually in family homes—they underwent three successive transformations to meet the requirements of their ministry. First, while they were still in Italy, under Charles Borromeo, archbishop of Milan and theologian of the Council of Trent, their independent governance yielded in part to the authority of the local bishop, who lent legitimacy and stability to their work. Then, also under Borromeo, they began living together in community, an adaptation that heightened their sense of mutual support.

As members of a church intent on revitalization in the aftermath of the Protestant Reformation, the Ursulines, who had a new apostolate among the poor and the emerging middle class, represented a major departure from earlier forms of religious life for women. To protect their ministry they underwent a third transformation shortly after reaching Paris. There, by a 1612 papal bull, they accepted solemn vows and enclosure, twin hallmarks of traditional religious life. In doing so, they acknowledged Tridentine reforms that reinforced their religious identity, as well as cultural expectations that precluded women of status from the kind of work on the streets that Angela Merici's early followers had undertaken. Nevertheless, behind walls they were still able to teach, their apostolate now canonically protected by a special vow, "vaquer à l'instruction des petites filles" 'to attend to the instruction of young girls' (*Bulle* 15; my trans.). By adding this ministry to the three monastic vows of poverty, chastity, and obedience, they safeguarded their work among daughters of the wealthy, whom they taught as paid boarders (*pensionnaires*), and of the poor, whom they accepted as free day students (*écolières*).

Once I've given my students a short history of the order, they quickly recognize the aptness of an Ursuline convent for Ourika. In many ways, any monastery could have been her sanctuary, screening her from prying eyes, sublimating through celibacy her longing for marriage, and affording her the solitude of "le seul lieu" 'the one place' where she could think of Charles "sans cesse" 'day and night' (DeJean 45; Fowles 46). Elements of the Ursuline charism, however, prove an exceptional fit for her. She who sat as a child in one of Paris's most distinguished parlors to be schooled in literature, painting, music, and dance joins the first women's congregation dedicated to teaching. When society denies her a chance for motherhood, she adopts the maternal ideals of Angela Merici, whose "Counsels" advised superiors and teachers to treat their charges like "dearly loved daughters" (243). This care extended to members who fell ill, as Ourika would discover; the order's regulations called each infirmarian to tend the sick "avec beaucoup de douceur, de soin, & de diligence, se persuadant qu'elle sert notre Seigneur en ells" 'with much sweetness, care, and diligence, convinced that she serves Our Lord in them' (*Règlemens* 233; my trans.).

The community that Ourika seeks out followed a dual vocation, to the active and the contemplative life, by melding monastic tradition with apostolic vision. They shared all things in common, attended daily Mass, and prayed the liturgical hours, but, to meet the demands of the school week, they more often used the shorter Little Office of the Blessed Virgin than the full Roman breviary. Their rule prescribed private prayer but cautioned against mystical experiences that might interfere with teaching duties and acknowledged the rigors of the classroom as apt substitutes for physical mortification. Their garb, too, was modified to fit an active lifestyle. They wore a one-piece black, ankle-length serge habit, held at the waist by a leather cincture with a metal buckle. A white cloth covered the neck, and a starched white linen bandeau stretched across the forehead. The "grand voile noir" 'large black veil' that "l'enveloppait presque tout entière" '[left Ourika] almost entirely hidden' when the doctor met her would have been made, in Ursuline fashion, of lightweight black fabric doubled over white unstarched linen (DeJean 3; Fowles 3).

A clear hierarchy structured the convent community. Elections identified a mother superior and a council responsible for the congregation's spiritual and temporal welfare, and the bishop, through his clerical visitor, provided external oversight. The common life supported two ranks of members. Most (up to sixty in the eighteenth-century Paris congregation) were choir nuns, obligated to the liturgical hours and responsible for teaching the boarders; addressed as *mère* ("mother"), they were fully cloistered, took solemn vows, and were ultimately admitted to chapter, the convent's decision-making body. A smaller number were accepted as lay sisters (*converses*), who performed domestic chores and taught the day students; addressed as *sœur* ("sister"), these externs lived under simple vows and managed all exchange with the outside world.

Applicants, often drawn from the ranks of boarders, served three to six months as postulants and then two years as novices. Over this probationary period, while they received instruction in teaching and religious life, candidates could be dismissed for reasons ranging from poor health or weak eyesight (a handicap in the classroom) to defects of character or judgment. Once professed, however, they belonged until death, with perpetual vows recognized under canon and civil law. Their dowries, which by the second half of the seventeenth century averaged 10,000 livres for a choir nun, would support the monastery, just as the monastery would support them for the rest of their lives.

Their apostolic work sustained them too. For a fee set in the seventeenth century at 240 livres a year, the convent in the faubourg Saint-Jacques accepted boarding students from ages seven through fifteen, grouped in classes of twenty. In addition to providing moral and catechetical instruction, the curriculum included reading (beginning with Latin and advancing to French), writing, basic spelling, and rudimentary math, mainly the business of making change and keeping accounts. Each school day ended with practical lessons in painting, needlework, or bobbin lace. Day students were taught a simplified curriculum in classes as large as fifty, conducted on convent grounds but outside the cloister.

The Ursuline philosophy of education saw in every student an opportunity to mold a new generation of faith; each girl schooled could in turn educate her entire family. With time, moreover, the Ursulines and other teaching congregations laid a solid foundation for citizenship by training hundreds of thousands of girls in the work ethic and skills needed to support the households of France.

Despite this service to society, the ancien régime remained ambivalent about nuns. If their image in the minds of today's students is shaped by Hollywood—from Whoopi Goldberg's role in *Sister Act* to seemingly chance cameos of sisters in dark blue suits at bustling airports or street corners—the image in the minds of Ourika's contemporaries would have been no more realistic. Even as membership in active congregations surged, the fictional theme of the forced vocation persisted. Best known from Denis Diderot's *La religieuse* of 1796, this vision offered the tragic figure of a beautiful daughter sacrificed to a despotic monastery, where, in happy endings, she was released from her vows and reunited with her true love, or, in unhappy versions, she languished and died, forlorn yet uncomplaining. (A pornographic counterpart to such passive compliance construed the libertine nun whose monastery functioned as the site of her active sexual initiation.) Ourika's variation on the theme provides the apparent free choice of a convent—she begs first Mme de B. and then Charles to let her go—at the same time that society, by declaring her unmarriageable, effectively imposes celibacy on her.

Quite possibly, Ourika has no idea what awaits her. Her postrevolution retreat bears little resemblance to any she could have imagined in her youth, when 350 convents were home to ten thousand French Ursulines, with an estimated fifty thousand girls in their care. Their teaching linked them to newer congregations whose active apostolates provided services in education and nursing vital to the state. Undeniably, however, their solemn vows connected Ursulines to a tradition increasingly associated with the revolution's wider critique of privilege. Inflammatory rhetoric portrayed monasteries as corrupt bastions of aristocracy, their celibate members unnaturally unproductive citizens and their property an unwarranted drain on the national economy. Thus the call for revolution coupled the private space of the cloister with the public space of court and prison; if the Bastille had to fall, so would the convent.

The work of dismantling religious life soon commenced. By late summer 1789, the National Assembly barred monasteries from professing new members and then, after exhaustive inventories of real estate, goods, and outstanding debts, confiscated all church property, exempting, for a time, congregations of teachers and nurses. A failed attempt to empty convents by persuasion—nuns almost universally refused initial offers of laicization with a life pension—served as prelude to the Civil Constitution of the Clergy in July 1790. The required oath of state loyalty led to a schism between those clergy members who, accepting the oath, became government functionaries and those nonjurors who refused and were exiled or driven underground. For nuns, whose obedience to

Rome compelled their loyalty to nonjurors, the results were disastrous. Of the thousand Ursulines imprisoned in the 1790s, for example, most were jailed for aiding and abetting refractory priests in their attempt to bring Mass and sacraments to the faithful.

As the revolution radicalized, so did its treatment of the church. In early autumn 1792, religious orders were suppressed, and their members evicted. Led by their seventy-four-year-old superior, the Ursulines closed their door in the faubourg Saint-Jacques on 1 October, each nun allowed to take with her only the bed and chair from her cell, her personal linens, and her place setting for the table. They sent their old and infirm to a house in Dugny, and the rest found lodging with family, friends, or former students as close as possible to the monastery. What work they could do, continuing to teach students by day, proceeded covertly, its history lost to the gap in congregational chronicles that spanned the Terror.

When subsequent decrees first authorized freedom of worship in 1795, a religious restoration, under strict separation of church and state, began. Churches once converted to meetinghouses, army barracks, horse stables, forges, or fishmongers' stalls were now reclaimed for worship. Nuns began to reappear, resuming their habits in public, attempting to locate members of their congregations or, failing that, assimilate into hybrid clusters. By the close of the century, Ursulines were reestablishing their ministry, and parents were sending students back to them. In Paris, they were able to rent part of their former monastery in the faubourg Saint-Jacques, where they returned to community life, although uncertainty about their future, in both canonical status and temporal welfare, prevented them from accepting new members. Meanwhile, the consulate adopted the wisdom of Napoléon, who valued religion at least for the moral training it could impart to French citizenry. Peace with a disestablished church came under the concordat that he negotiated with the Vatican in 1801.

The convent that Ourika enters, then, has absorbed many of the shocks that France withstood during her lifetime, including the seizure of church property, the nationalization of the clergy, the closing of monasteries, even the execution of counterrevolutionary nuns. The breaches in convent walls that the doctor first observes symbolize much wider fissures whose lingering effects amount to a far-reaching feminization and laicization of religion: a spike in membership for women's congregations, a plummet in male religious practice, a drop in intellectualism and a rise in popular piety, and, inevitably, a decline in overall church membership. Catholicism in France, scholars conclude, has never fully recovered.

Although all this is Ourika's world, students caught up in her tale often miss the panorama that Duras constructs. Surveyed in quasi-reader-response style, my classes confess that they read *Ourika* for its plotline and, left to themselves, ignore its historical context. The italicized introduction that specifies the novel's setting? My students skim it. The revolution that dominates the middle portion of the narrative, when Mme de B.'s friends flee, armed guards surround her home, and Ourika shudders, "Rien ne peut peindre l'état de l'anxiété et de terreur des journées" 'The anxiety and horror of those days are indescribable' (23; 24)? My students miss the import of these material details. Only when they have read through to Ourika's death and we have discussed her history at the level of personal narrative, do I lead them back to the beginning for a second reading. In this rereading, guided by the two internal witnesses who narrate its events, my students come to appreciate how Duras manipulates micro and macro storylines to underscore the text's thematic focus.

Doctor and patient, the two narrators function most obviously as actual characters in *Ourika*, yet they simultaneously represent contrasting perspectives for its religious context. The doctor embodies the empiricism of the Enlightenment and the iconoclasm of the revolution, the entrenched "préjugés" 'anticlerical prejudices' that predispose him to see in Ourika "une nouvelle victime des cloîtres" 'a new victim of the convent system' (3; 3). By contrast, Ourika reads religion through the lens of romantic illusion. For her, the convent signifies not oppression but embrace: "La sœur de la charité, me disai-je, n'est point seule dans la vie, quoiqu'elle ait renoncé à tout; elle s'est créé une famille de choix" 'A nun, I told myself, may have renounced everything, but she is not alone in the world. She has chosen a family' (44; 45). Ourika lives in the hope that her fellow citizens will project divine consolation: "[I]l n'y a pour [Dieu] ni nègres ni blancs: tous les cœurs sont égaux devant ses yeux" 'For [God] there is neither black nor white. All hearts are equal in His eyes' (43; 45). Both narrators, she in her idealism and he in his skepticism, misrepresent a multivalent reality. By casting one as internal audience for the other, Duras highlights the dichotomy between their positions and hints at complex tensions that the revolution fails to resolve.

The narrators' limitations, I suggest to my students, can inspire a more nuanced reading of *Ourika* and an appreciation for Duras's use of a world in turmoil to magnify one character's misery. On the micro level, it is her singularity that pains Ourika; she, alone, is the Senegalese native who has been stolen for Paris and then ostracized by it. Behind the veil that marks her early in life, she suffers exquisitely, with no one to share her pain. On the macro level, however, she is far from alone. The revolution breeds collective anarchy, famine, economic collapse, de-Christianization, and the failure of every organ of social welfare. Emigration, exile, and execution reduce Mme de B.'s elite circle to "débris" 'remnants' (27; 28). Against this backdrop, in the middle ground, Duras sets the Ursulines, who welcome Ourika as one of their own, another black-veiled nun in a desolate monastery. Little wonder that in this barely reclaimed sacred space, she protests too heartily: "Je suis heureuse, me dit elle; jamais je n'ai éprouvé tant de calme et de bonheur" 'But I'm happy now. I've never known such peace and contentment' (4; 4). Abducted, forsaken, disillusioned, Ourika knows a unique, race-specific anguish, yet it heightens the pathos of her story to view her singular pain as Duras reveals it, framed by universal suffering and the history of the worn congregation that shares her last days.

By her illness and death among these nuns, Ourika, in turn, serves metonymically for their wider experience. Nationally, only 105 of the 350 Ursuline convents of the ancien régime survived the revolution, and *le grand couvent de Paris* never returned to glory. Its towering church, spacious buildings, and linden-lined gardens were razed; only its vaulted cellars remained. During World War II, the resistance reportedly used the tunnels as safe passage through the neighborhood. For those wishing to visit today, Voyage Europe travel specialists, who rent "elegant apartments in central Paris" at seasonal rates, claim a townhouse built by an unnamed count in 1790 on the grounds. The Web site for the renovated premises, "[d]ecorated in 18th century antique period complimented with modern furniture and equipped with all the appliances you will need," promises guests, "You'll be received with fresh flowers, bed linens and bath towels" ("Elegant Apartments"). Where parlor, church, and classroom once welcomed royalty—Queen Anne of Austria laid its first stone, Louis XIV learned his catechism there, princesses and duchesses sent their daughters for First Communion—twenty-first-century visitors now find a different kind of hospitality.

This is the historical site that offers Ourika a final home, where hers is the only veil to frame as dark a face in the convent of the faubourg Saint-Jacques. From the doctor's first sight of her to the last, color defines her as terminal, incurable misfit. Her race confounds her class, renders her gender moot, and exiles her to a death among other anomalous women displaced from postrevolutionary culture. To belong then to that Ursuline convent is to belong nowhere except as an evanescent shadow, "les dernières feuilles de l'automne" 'the last of the autumn leaves' (DeJean 45; Fowles 47). A heavily politicized story of race, class, and gender thus concludes in a space defined by religion. An understanding of the ethos of this convent offers students an unexpected window on the meaning of the novel and its author's perspective on the achievements and failures of the revolution.

NOTE

The history of the Ursulines in Paris under the ancien régime is well documented; primary sources range from papal documents and official constitutions to annals, chronicles, obituaries, biographies, and spiritual tracts. The analyses of Marie-Andrée Jégou and Anne Bertout cite extensively from these materials; Jégou follows the convent from its foundation through its fiftieth anniversary in 1662, and Bertout extends its history through the second half of the seventeenth century. Linda Lierheimer discusses the Ursuline educational apostolate, especially its maternal rhetoric. Marie de Chantal Gueudré's detailed three-volume account of the French Ursulines, which incorporates the faubourg Saint-Jacques into wider Ursuline history, is valuable for its inclusion of the revolutionary period, for which few original documents are extant.

Several resources contextualize Ursuline history in the development of female orders. Among them, Laurence Lux-Sterritt compares the mission of the French Ursulines with that of the English Ladies. Elizabeth Rapley's works offer a close look at the evolution and lifestyle of cloistered and noncloistered congregations (*Dévotes* and *Social History*), while Mita Choudhury describes the roles of these congregations in legal, political, and cultural arenas; both make references to Ursulines throughout.

Mirror Insurrections:
Haitian and French Revolutions in *Ourika*

Deborah Jenson

We know that Claire de Duras wrote and published *Ourika* in 1823, but in what year does Ourika tell her story, and what light does that date shed on the history that influences Ourika's life? The following exploration of metaphors of the ruins of history in Ourika's narrative reveals the partially incorporated narrative of anticolonial revolution and the heroine's ambivalent identification with it. I argue here that the Haitian Revolution mirrors the French Revolution in *Ourika* and parallels Ourika's sense of the challenge of her own dark reflection as mirrored back to her by her adoptive French social peers.

The difficult task of establishing a historical date for the narration reminds the reader that history, however objective, is passed down to us in the form of memory. The opening and final scenes, in which the narrator recalls Ourika's account of her life, mark the end point of the fictional events in the novel, but no specific date (other than the month, October, in the final scene) is attached to them. Some oblique hints of chronology nevertheless are scattered through the opening pages. The young doctor from Montpellier tells us that he had been called to the faubourg Saint-Jacques in Paris to see Ourika at a convent belonging to the Ursuline order. The emperor Napoléon, he explains, recently had allowed a few of the convents previously sold as national property during the French Revolution to reopen. Ostensibly, then, to identify the final year of the fictional time period covered, the reader would have only to identify this Ursuline convent in the faubourg Saint-Jacques and pinpoint the historical date of its religious reestablishment—starting sometime after May 1804, when Napoléon Bonaparte was crowned emperor.

But this convent as *lieu de mémoire*, or memory site, to use the expression coined by the French historian Pierre Nora, turns out to be eroded by more than the revolutionary vandalism that had, in Duras's description, left the church's architectural skeleton exposed and some of the tombstones paving its passageways cracked open. It is also destabilized by the subjectivity of the author's own memory, no doubt in conjunction with her attempt to make history into metaphor. The Ursuline convent on the rue du Faubourg Saint-Jacques in Paris, like many French religious establishments, had come under religious persecution during the Terror. This persecution was to some extent reversed when Napoléon, not as emperor (1804–14) but as first consul (1799–1804), initiated a concordat with Pope Pius VII in 1801. The agreement reestablished Catholicism as the religion of the majority of French nationals, but the lands and buildings appropriated by the revolutionary state remained national property. The religious inhabitants of the Ursuline convent in Paris had been renting their former home on a temporary basis since its sale as state property in

1798 (Biver and Biver 290). Under the concordat the Ursulines had to vacate the property, which was then demolished. Some Ursuline religious instructors and nuns in Paris did adapt to this chaos, relocating to carry on their mission in nearby establishments such as the Vache Noire ("Black Cow") and the former *hôtel particulier* of the magistrate Fleury de Brionne (Gueudré 3: 500).

These events do not square with Duras's depiction of the reopening of the convent, where the medical narrator finds his patient languishing in a bower, enveloped in a long black veil. But even once we accept that history merges with fiction in *Ourika*, a coherent fictional date remains elusive. One might plausibly situate the October of Ourika's final year very tentatively in the consulate (1799–1804) after the concordat of 1801, since Duras clearly means to highlight the change in the status of religious orders brought about by Napoléon. Yet this identification, based as it is on the false memory of the reestablishment of the Ursulines, should perhaps yield to the more definitive reference to Emperor Napoléon, which would situate the final date sometime during or after 1804.

This instability of historical memory in *Ourika*, in which different regimes are collapsed into one ruined historical edifice, arguably bears greater significance than a well-defined date either before or after 1804, a critical turning point in French history. Some historians date the French Revolution from 1789 to the end of the consulate in 1804, and certainly by the beginning of the Napoleonic empire the revolution had reached a definitive end. But 1804 was also the conclusion of a long slave insurrection, mirroring the chronology of the revolution, in the French colony of Saint-Domingue. On 1 January 1804, the former slaves of the richest European colony of that era overthrew colonial rule and renamed their independent black republic Hayti (Haiti) after the indigenous name for the island where Columbus had first established a European presence in 1492. Since Napoléon had sent an army to Haiti to reestablish control in 1802, this unprecedented and radical reversal of French colonial mastery was also Napoléon's first major defeat. The obscure pre- or post-1804 chronology of the narrative of a black woman in *Ourika* is symptomatic both of this early postcolonial rupture and of its cultural suppression in France, a suppression that began in the historiography of nineteenth-century France (Bénot 205) and has continued to this day (Miller, "Forget Haiti" 39–41).

Undoubtedly Duras—whose mother was born and raised in Martinique, whose father had engaged in colonial enterprise in Haiti, and whose in-laws were major landholders in Haiti—was aware of the insurrection that we now call the Haitian Revolution. (And so were some of her contemporaries, including François-René de Chateaubriand and Victor Hugo, who also had familial links to colonial commerce in Haiti.) Unlike Hugo's roughly contemporaneous *Bug-Jargal*, which was entirely devoted to the representation of the Haitian Revolution, *Ourika* makes only one direct allusion to this insurrection—to its early phases rather than to the moment of its triumph, in 1804. The phenomenon of simultaneous ideological twinship and mortal conflict between the French and Haitian revolutions is, however, represented indirectly in the novel through the symbolic framework of mirroring and resemblance, which extends beyond Ourika's personal self-consciousness to problems of the subjectivity of historical consciousness.

In effect, *Ourika* presents a nineteenth-century postcolonial mirror, in which colonialism, despite the known horrors of slavery, largely had escaped public criticism as a system or institution. Unlike the postcolonial consciousness of the twentieth century, which rejected colonialism, French consciousness after the independence of Haiti registered the violence of its loss of colonial mastery, without fully processing the ideological similarity of the slaves' conquest of freedom and French citizens' acquisition of revolutionary rights. This consciousness is presented in the novel as a disruption in a mirror stage of identification between blacks and whites.

When Ourika describes her symptoms, the doctor exclaims, "c'est le passé qu'il faut guérir" 'it's the past we must cure' (DeJean 4; Fowles 5). What appears to be a prepsychoanalytic imperative to put pathological affect into words—the talking cure—may also apply less directly in the novel to the need to put the colonial past into words. The aftermath of the independence of Haiti was postcolonial only in the sense that colonial rule had been overturned in France's most profitable colony and that independence had been won by the colonized, inaugurating an era that postdated the colonial. But colonialism had not been renounced by the French in any way, nor had its traumatic legacies been confronted.

In 1938, the Trinidadian social theorist C. L. R. James argued in *The Black Jacobins* that colonial trade and slavery in the Atlantic triangle had given a growing French middle class the economic and political power to challenge the monarchical system of the ancien régime: "The slave trade and slavery were the economic basis of the French Revolution" (47). French revolutionary ideology privileged liberty and equality for all, a rule to which the status of the enslaved presented a glaring exception. But in general terms, the French were more likely to apply the paradigm of slavery to their own oppression as monarchical subjects than to Africans kidnapped from their homelands and forced to labor for life without pay in the interest of European prosperity. The lyrics of "La Marseillaise" represent counterrevolutionary threats with the following couplet: "C'est nous qu'on ose méditer / De rendre à l'antique esclavage!" 'They dare think of returning us / Back to the old slavery!' (my trans.).

This culpable role in the colonial system, masked by identification with its victims, is not without relevance to *Ourika* and the social positioning of Duras herself. But the Haitian Revolution is an important reminder that the French Revolution did have a contagious effect outside the boundaries of the *métropole* and that a transatlantic age of revolution emerged with the Caribbean in dialogue with the French (and American) Revolution. As the title of James's history indicates, Jacobin revolutionaries in France paralleled the "black Jacobins" of the Haitian Revolution. For Yves Bénot, this combination of French blindness to colonial oppression and of colonial dissemination of the revolutionary ideals of liberty poses a fundamental question: "Que peut une idéologie?" 'What can ideology actually do?' (7; my trans.).

Any mirroring of revolutionary ideology in the *métropole* and its colonies inevitably led to antagonism as well as twinship. Shared ideology among black and white Jacobins produced the war of one revolution against the other—the war, in James's terms, of (revolutionary) "property" (6–26) against (revolutionary) "owners" (27–61).

In *Ourika*, the representation (or, conversely, the amnesiac erasure) of this history is achieved not so much through the depiction of events and opinions— few opinions on colonialism are clearly stated in this novel—as through the ambitions and failures of mirroring and identification. In effect, colonial and anticolonial history are presented in Fanonian terms through what Henry Louis Gates calls "the convergence of the problematic of colonialism with that of subject formation" ("Critical Fanonism" 458).

Throughout most of her youth, Ourika occupies a liminal social position in which her racial difference does not evoke overt analogies with that of "property," of slaves [She is welcomed into the intimate spaces of the highly privileged world of an aristocratic Enlightenment salon. But caustic judgments from an unfeeling marquise make her realize that in the face of potential familial and marital alliances, her appearance and origins will always be associated with the social abjection of the slaves she resembles] This emphasis on her color, significant in relation to the social positioning of other people of color in an imperialist world, devastates Ourika's previously secure identification with her benefactor, Mme de B. Before this moment, Mme de B.'s social influence had been so potent that Ourika and her companions believed that their proximity to the noble lady caused them to resemble her: "en la voyant, en l'écoutant, on croyait lui ressembler" '[w]atching her, listening to her, people began to feel they resembled her' (DeJean 8; Fowles 8). This social mimeticism had extended to Ourika's education: she learned by imitating Mme de B. and by striving to please her. Even the malevolent marquise notes to Mme de B. that, as an adult, Ourika "causera comme vous" '[will] be able to converse as well as you' (12; 12).

The disruption of this symbiotic identity results in what Frantz Fanon describes as the "epidermalization" of the racist gaze (*Black Skin* 11). Ourika becomes fearful of her skin and of her image in the mirror; seeing herself is now as alienating as being caught in the racist gaze of the marquise. Her physical resemblance to one group cancels out her potential to be integrated into the group she has been taught to resemble socially and intellectually. In the wake of this epiphany, Ourika repeatedly emphasizes the power of others' perceptions of her as the basis for confirmation of her existence. She represents her rescue from a slave ship and her informal adoption by Mme de B. as a decisive humanization through the benevolent consciousness of the colonizing other. Her luck falls into the category of "ces dons de l'intelligence" '[these gifts of] understanding' (DeJean 7; Fowles 7), as if, outside the edifying gaze of Western European society, her existence would have been like a tree falling in the forest with no one there to hear the sound. This correlates with Fanon's observation that in colonial society, "for the white man The Other is perceived on the level of the body image, absolutely as the not-self—that is, the unidentifiable, the unassimilable" (*Black Skin* 161n25). Ourika internalizes this psychology of un-identifiable otherness.

She considers requesting a repatriation to Senegal but demurs when she realizes that her carefully cultivated likeness to Mme de B. would make her a stranger there, just as her absence of physical likeness to Mme de B. makes her a stranger in the society in which she has been raised (DeJean 15; Fowles 16). The reader can surmise further that Ourika is psychologically uncertain of the existence of a world beyond the European vantage point. Unable to confirm her own existence through her experience rather than through the gaze of others, she has difficulty remaining attached to life (17; 17).

The French Revolution offers a dramatic opportunity to depart from this ontology of the racially hierarchical gaze. Ourika's experience of the revolution diverges sharply from that of her benefactors, even though in theory they share the same Enlightenment preoccupation with the "grands intérêts moraux et politiques que cette Révolution remua jusque dans leur source" 'the vast moral and political questions the Revolution had so profoundly posed' (18; 18–19). The revolution launches a collective interrogation of all values and institutions, and Ourika quickly perceives that it may yield an extraordinary personal opportunity to integrate differently and more fully into society. Revolutionary chaos suspends Ourika's sufferings. She sees the possibility that in "ce grand désordre" 'this great chaos' (18–19; 19), she could find her own place. She feels less foreign in the world once "toutes les fortunes [étaient] renversées, tous les rangs confondus, tous les préjugés évanouis" 'personal destiny was turned upside down, all social caste overthrown, all prejudices had disappeared' (19; 19). It seems plausible to hope that her personal qualities might be appreciated "lorsque ma couleur ne m'isolerait plus au milieu du monde, comme elle avait fait jusqu'alors" 'when my color no longer isolated me, as it had until then, in the heart of society' (19; 19). Ourika has a personal interest, in other words, in a genuine revolution, a revolutionizing of the status of the slave into that of a person. For her benefactors, however, the passage of this interrogation from philosophy to action could only threaten their monopoly on cultural and economic capital and opportunity.

It is in the revolutionary context that Ourika first begins to note the discussion of abolitionist projects and of rights for people of color: "On commençait à parler de la liberté des nègres: il était impossible que cette question ne me touchât pas vivement" 'About this time talk started of emancipating the Negroes. Of course this question passionately interested me' (20; 21). (Much of this social current would have been inspired by the attempts of mulattoes from Haiti to gain representation in the National Assembly, and so it stands as an indirect reference to the rumblings of revolution in Haiti.) For Ourika, the discussion of freedom for blacks suggests that "j'avais des semblables" 'there were others like myself' (20; 21). This identification with blacks elsewhere is short lived, however, to the point that it is characterized as an "illusion" (20; 21). The colonial mirror revolution of the insurrection in France is an occasion not for constructive mirroring but for shame and horror:

> Hélas! je fus promptement détrompée! Les massacres de Saint-Domingue me causèrent une douleur nouvelle et déchirante: jusqu'ici je m'étais affligée d'appartenir à une race proscrite; maintenant j'avais honte d'appartenir à une race de barbares et d'assassins.   (20)

> But alas, I soon learned my lesson. The Santo Domingo massacres gave me cause for fresh and heartrending sadness. Till then I had regretted belonging to a race of outcasts. Now I had the shame of belonging to a race of barbarous murderers.   (21)

Ourika does not contextualize this violent image of the slave insurrection in Haiti as part of a propaganda campaign orchestrated in the interests of French colonial mastery (Bénot 135–56). For Ourika, the mirror is shattered, and she retreats from her revolutionary hopes, unable to desire for long "beaucoup de mal pour un peu de bien personnel" 'so much present evil for my own small future good' (DeJean 19; Fowles 19). In effect, she empathizes with the society of her benefactors, even though the racist scorn of this society has now supplanted her own mirror image: "J'étais poursuivie, plusieurs jours de suite, par le souvenir de cette physionomie dédaigneuse; . . . elle se plaçait devant moi comme ma propre image" 'I was haunted by its sneering face. . . . It stood before me like my own reflection' (28; 29).

The racism of the only society she knows functions in a manner not unlike opinion: "L'opinion est comme une patrie; c'est un bien dont on jouit ensemble; on est frère pour la soutenir et pour la défendre" 'A view of life is like a motherland. It is a possession mutually shared. Those who uphold and defend it are like brothers' (22; 23). History in the "motherland" of colonial bias is indeed a matter of identification, of a mirror in which those who look different are distorted. Duras did not entirely avoid the problem of history through her technique of blurring its colonial and postcolonial boundaries and focusing on her heroine's self-consciousness. Instead, she represented the subjectivity of historical consciousness, a consciousness in which identifications—or the failure to identify beyond a proscribed model of self—have the power to create and maintain categories of the only partly human, of the slave. Revolution represented a great hope in relation to that racial motherland. The small miracle of the mirroring between the French and Haitian revolutions initially promised to install liberty as a transatlantic ideal. But the conflict of interest between those metropolitan and "tropicopolitan" revolutions rendered Ourika's biracial identifications tortuous (Aravamudan 300), making nineteenth-century postcolonial mirroring into a reflection of hostile alterity.

Duras, Biography, and Slavery

Christopher L. Miller

The revival of *Ourika* in recent years and its frequent use in French literature courses in the United States are well justified. *Ourika* is simply one of the most compelling short works of fiction in French and a startlingly modern commentary on race. Here I suggest how *Ourika* can be used to raise pedagogical questions about the relations of an author and of her text to a world-historical problem: slavery and the French Atlantic slave trade. A close reading of one key passage in the novel suggests ways in which *Ourika* sheds an ambiguous light on the slave trade, on the cultured elite to which Claire de Duras belonged, and on plantation slavery itself.

What does an author's life tell us about the words he or she wrote on the page? Biographical criticism has long been disdained as a distraction from the real work of the critic: reading the text itself. But when that text involves itself in a sociohistorical problem like slavery, and when it turns out that the author herself had interests in slavery that were more than intellectual, questions of biography are hard to avoid. Looking at the life of Duras can open students' perspectives in two radically different directions: toward the economic entanglements of the aristocratic French elite during the restoration and toward the lives of slaves they sometimes owned without seeing, across the Atlantic. But a biographical approach to *Ourika* is troubled by a central mystery.

The French slave trade brought roughly one million captive Africans to Martinique, Guadeloupe, and Saint-Domingue (Haiti), which became the world's richest colony and a huge source of revenue for France. The twenty-five-year period from the Treaty of Paris to the French Revolution was the apogee of the triangular, slave-based economy: the slave trade churned, the plantations worked slaves to death in large numbers, which created the need for more slaves brought over from Africa. Opposition to the slave trade and to slavery was late and ineffective in France compared with England, which took the lead in abolitionism. After interruptions caused by the revolution and the Napoleonic Wars, the French slave trade was restored and flourishing, illegally, when Duras was writing *Ourika* (on the French slave trade, see Miller, *French Atlantic Triangle*; Pétré-Grenouilleau; Stein).

Even before her marriage to the wealthy duc de Duras, whose father had been a trustee of the slave-trading Compagnie des Indes and a staunch defender of slavery, the future author of *Ourika*, Claire de Kersaint, had her own family ties to the Atlantic economy. She was, like so many in her social set, very directly linked to the plantation-slave system that dominated the French Atlantic from the late seventeenth century until the final abolition of French slavery, in 1848. Claire's father, Guy-Armand-Simon de Coëtnempren, comte de Kersaint, was a lifelong naval officer. In 1792 he took a moderately abolitionist position, while admitting that he had owned slaves himself in the French islands and that he maintained part of his fortune there (De Raedt, "Ourika en noir" 11). (A Girondist, he was guillotined on 5 December 1793.) The author's mother, née Claire d'Alesso d'Eragny, was a Creole in the French sense (a distinction that must be explained to students): a white French person born in Martinique and an owner of large holdings there. (On the figure of the Creole, students might be interested in Baudelaire's sonnet "À une dame créole"; see Miller, *Blank Darkness* 93–108.) She was not just any *dame créole*. She was descended from one of the most illustrious families of the island: her great-great-grandfather was François d'Alesso, marquis d'Eragny and governor of the French islands of America in 1691; his remains are buried in the cathedral of Fort-de-France, marked by a plaque. He had just distinguished himself by chasing the English off the islands when he died of yellow fever; his son stayed on Martinique, and the family became important landowners ("Alesso"; Banbuck 95). The masters' house of their *habitation*, La Frégate, is, even now, one of the most impressive on the island (for a photograph, see Laguarigue).

The author's parents met when her father was a young naval lieutenant assigned to the defense of Martinique. Their daughter was born at Brest in 1777 and raised in Parisian salon society. In 1794, when the property of émigrés was being confiscated by the revolutionary government, mother and daughter traveled to the New World to rescue their fortune. At the French consulate in Philadelphia (then capital of the United States), they signed various legal documents by which Duras took ownership of her mother's estates in Martinique. At this point the mystery arises.

Did Duras go to Martinique? Much rides on the question. If she did, she would be what Doris Y. Kadish claims her to be, one of very few women writers who "lived in the colonies and responded favorably to African women in their literary works" (Introduction 3). In fact, Duras would be the only such woman author in French literature. Did the remarkable sympathy toward an African woman that we see in *Ourika* grow out of the author's direct contact with slaves in Martinique?

Duras's visit to Martinique, however, is myth rather than history (see Jenson 101); it can neither be proved nor disproved. Charles-Augustin Sainte-Beuve, writing in 1834, gave the version of events that has been repeated by most modern critics:

> Mlle de Kersaint s'embarqua pour l'Amérique avec sa mère. . . . Elle fut à Philadelphie d'abord, puis à la Martinique, où elle géra les possessions de sa mère avec une prudence et une autorité bien au-dessus de son âge. Devenue tout à fait orpheline, et riche héritière malgré les confiscations d'Europe, elle passa en Angleterre, où elle épousa le duc de Duras.
> (1045)

> Mlle de Kersaint embarked for America with her mother. . . . She was in Philadelphia first, *then in Martinique, where she managed her mother's*

estates [*possessions*] with a prudence and an authority that were well in advance of her age. Now truly an orphan and a rich heiress despite confiscations in Europe, she went on to England, where she married the duc de Duras.   (my trans.; emphasis added)

This image of the future author of *Ourika* residing in Martinique for an indeterminate time has become widely accepted. Most of the recent works on Duras claim that the two women traveled from Philadelphia to Martinique. That this story seems to have originated with Sainte-Beuve, the father of biographical literary criticism, is food for thought.

But there are numerous problems with the story. For starters, Martinique was in the hands of the British at the time when the Kersaint women are supposed to have gone there. They are documented in Philadelphia in June 1794; there would have been little time for the daughter to "manage" a plantation in Martinique and then be in Switzerland and England later that same year or in 1795. Neither of the two most significant biographical sources about Duras says that Duras went to Martinique. Agénor Bardoux's narrative strongly suggests that mother and daughter went only to the United States, not to Martinique (49–51). Gabriel Pailhès's work places the two women in Philadelphia, then in Switzerland, then London; he makes no mention of Martinique (34).

Sainte-Beuve's tale placing Duras in Martinique invites both skepticism and reflection. As an eyewitness to (and a proprietor in) the plantation-slave system, she would have a particular status, moral burden, and narrative authority. At sixteen, she would have seen the colonial plantation system firsthand and met and interacted with the slaves whom she was there to claim—or perhaps to sell. Following Sainte-Beuve's description, we imagine Duras issuing orders around the plantation, taking charge; perhaps ordering punishments like whippings, perhaps buying and selling slaves. Fighting adversity and rising out of defeat, she becomes a kind of Scarlett O'Hara figure.

Even leaving aside the hypothesis of Duras's sojourn in Martinique, there are biographical and financial questions that persist: what became of her colonial holdings (or their profits) in later years? Near the end of her life, as she was creating one of the most sympathetic representations of an African in French literature, did Duras still hold title to hundreds of African slaves in Martinique? Even if the plantation and its slaves had been sold at that point, as seems likely, Duras was living on the benefits these assets brought her, some of which may have allowed her to buy her magnificent chateau, Ussé, on the Loire (Bardoux 89; Côme and Clermont-Tonnerre 57). The author of *Ourika* was, in any of these cases, a slave trader: she had owned and had likely sold (or had others sell) human beings as chattel. Before we make Duras into the French Harriet Beecher Stowe, more attention to her involvements might be warranted. At a minimum, then, these biographical dimensions can raise questions in students' minds about the social and economic context in which *Ourika* was created.

What, then, about the text itself? Duras moves her characters around the Atlantic in an original way. Most representations of Africans in French literature before her novel came through real or fictive accounts of Frenchmen traveling in Africa (such as Staël's *Mirza*) or in the slave-island colonies (as in Bernardin de Saint-Pierre's *Paul et Virginie*). Duras chose to tell the converse tale, of a young African girl brought to France. This placement of an African into French society has devastating psychological effects, but as a literary strategy it also allows the author to follow the adage of writing schools: write what you know. The only society represented in *Ourika* is that of the French aristocracy to which the author belonged. Duras does not attempt to represent foreign climes about which she knows little or nothing—with one very important exception in *Ourika*. She does not even mention explicitly her mother's native Martinique. Since Ourika is raised in France from age two, little remains of her African culture, so her difference comes down to one element alone: color.

Ourika, like her real-life counterpart, is rescued from the slave trade, redeemed out of slavery, and brought to France where "there are no slaves" (see Peabody). Because Ourika's enslavement ends nominally, the story is no longer supposed to be about slavery, the slave trade, or the Atlantic; rather it is, and has mostly been read as, an allegory of race, a dramatization of the color bar. In the influential volume *Translating Slavery*, Françoise Massardier-Kenney states that *Ourika* "expose[s] race prejudices" and Duras "take[s] racial equality as a given" (186, 193). My fear is that critics, understandably impressed by Duras's pioneering psychological portrait of racism, have assumed too much about her presentation of slavery and the slave trade. Thus Roger Little asserts that *Ourika* "discretely sensitizes the reader of 1824, by means of art, to the barbaric effects of the slave trade" ("Peau" ix). Ourika is generally, if loosely, associated with abolitionism by many critics. But Little's claim is dubious, and the relation of the tale to abolition needs to be scrutinized.

Slavery and the slave trade are mentioned only four times in the novel: at the beginning, when Ourika is saved from the slave ship (DeJean 7; Fowles 7); during the French Revolution, when the rising Haitian Revolution is discussed with revulsion as a series of "massacres" (20; 21); in one passing allusion to the slave ship from which she was removed (32; 33); and, near the end, when Ourika mentions the "vices of slavery" from which she was saved (44; 46).

Focusing on one particular passage might help students see signs of Duras's personal involvement with and ambivalence about slavery. This passage is an intersection of fiction and biography. Near the end of the tale, Ourika reinvents her life, imagining what it would have been if she had not been rescued from that slave ship. This segment, overlooked by critics, is far more significant than its length suggests:

> Pourquoi ne me laissait-on pas suivre mon sort? Eh bien! je serais la né-
> gresse esclave de quelque riche colon; brûlée par le soleil, je cultiverais

la terre d'un autre: mais j'aurais mon humble cabane pour me retirer le soir; j'aurais un compagnon de ma vie, et des enfants de ma couleur, qui m'appelleraient: Ma mère! Ils appuieraient sans dégoût leur petite bouche sur mon front; ils reposeraient leur tête sur mon cou, et s'endormiraient dans mes bras!   (38)

Why hadn't I been left to follow my own destiny?

What did it matter that I might have been the black slave of some rich planter? Scorched by the sun, I should be laboring on someone else's land. But I would have a poor hut of my own to go to at day's end; a partner in my life, children of my own race who would call me their mother, who would kiss my face without disgust, who would rest their heads against my neck and sleep in my arms.   (39)

Ourika translates her life into the present conditional, moving herself into a different sector of the Atlantic world: the plantations of the New World islands. The first thing to notice here is that the crossing of the Atlantic—the Middle Passage—is instantaneous, invisible, and harmless; Ourika simply appears, years later, in the middle of a life that has already been well established. This is completely inconsistent with the abolitionist effect that Little attributes to *Ourika*: Duras elides the horrors of the Atlantic crossing.

The segment goes on to suggest an emotional-economic calculus: for the small price of cultivating someone else's land during the day, one is offered a perfectly ordered and fulfilling life—replete with family values. The slaves of Martinique might have taken exception to this representation of their lives. Would a female slave's existence have resembled this sentimental fantasy in any way?

Concerning women and slavery in the French islands, the research and insights of recent historians should be juxtaposed to this passage in *Ourika*. The passage can, in fact, be used as a springboard for teaching the realities of French slavery. Helpful sources are the books on women and slavery in the French islands by Arlette Gautier, Bernard Moitt, and Jennifer L. Morgan.

Moitt finds that "the institution of slavery itself was antithetical to the promotion and development of strong family units" and that its burdens, including hard labor, "fell disproportionately upon slave women" (80, 84). Morgan reports that slave owners cherished the idea of slaves' reproduction, even "in the face of sky-high mortality and dismal fertility rates" (68, 150). Despite the wishful thinking of the Code Noir (which made provisions for religious marriage, with the owner's consent), there were, Moitt reports, "few legal marriages among slaves" in the French Antilles (84); Gautier says the same (82, 103). Slaves themselves seem to have resisted the institution of marriage (Moitt 84).

In the light of these circumstances, Duras's choice of the word *compagnon* ("companion" or "partner") instead of *mari* ("husband") is intriguing. Period dictionaries do not suggest that *compagnon* was used at this time to mean "common-law husband," but Duras clearly implies that meaning with the phrase

"compagnon de ma vie." In an otherwise emphatic portrait of close, monoga-
mous, nuclear family bonds, why did the author choose this one slightly off-key
word? I suggest that this may be a rare, perhaps unique, sign of Duras's knowledge of plantation life, information that her mother might have passed on to
her. She may well have known that slaves were more likely to be companions
to each other than spouses. In any case, the solid, lifelong bonds that Duras's
Ourika dreams of in this passage would, in real life, have been embedded in a
context of immense hardship. Furthermore, Duras subtly conveys another comforting and insidious myth about slavery in this passage: an image of fertility.
There were in fact "few children on the plantations" (Gautier 95); slaves on the
French islands "did not reproduce themselves" (Moitt 89–90). As an unspecified number of children press their lips to Ourika's forehead, readers receive a
false and rosy impression about slave life, self-serving propaganda on the part of
the slave-owning class, perhaps. It is hard not to see in this passage by Duras an
implied defense of her mother's Martinique and of the plantations that Duras
herself may still have owned or profited from as she was writing *Ourika*.

This passage of *Ourika*, however, is not a journalistic report on slave life in
the islands; it is a reverie on Ourika's part, built into a novel, and thus doubly
fictional. But ultimately, Ourika's dream is Duras's creation, and nothing in the
tale contradicts its images.

Is *Ourika* abolitionist in any sense? Does Duras actually condemn slavery?
This novel is only abolitionist in an extremely loose sense: by creating a human portrait of the effects of racial exclusion[Duras contributes to the general
project of sympathy for blacks] a precondition of abolition. But she goes no
further than that. The question of color overshadows any consideration of the
institution of slavery in *Ourika*. You can remove a *négresse* from slavery, *Ourika*
tells us, but you can't erase the problem of color[Duras found a way to write
sympathetically about an African while tiptoeing around and soft-pedaling the
problem of slavery.

On the one hand, Duras created an immensely powerful narrative on racial
prejudice, thereby contributing to the pity and sympathy that were the building blocks of abolition. But on the other hand, through Ourika's reverie, she
preserved the image of plantation slavery as a productive and reproductive way
of life, thereby defending her mother's background and perhaps her own invest-
ments, transactions, and fortune. Duras made the experience of racial difference come alive in French literature, but she also gave voice to the comforting
myths about slavery that her mother's (and her own) planter class often circulated in France. The relative weight of these two effects is certainly a matter for
class discussion.

Representations of the Real-Life Ourika

Thérèse De Raedt

Students are always intrigued when they hear that the novel *Ourika* is based on real life. Claire de Duras knew about Ourika's life from firsthand sources because she was linked through family ties to Ourika's benefactors, the prince and princess of Beauvau. In the novel, Duras retains the time frame and events of the real Ourika's story.

When I teach *Ourika*, I try to elucidate the paradoxical situation of the life of the real woman on whom the novel is based: her benefactors loved her as an individual with her own personality but at the same time exhibited her to society as an exotic, decorative object. This apparent contradiction also characterizes the fictional Ourika, who is both integrated into the aristocratic milieu and subjugated to it because of her race. My primary goal is to teach students about the specific political, social, and cultural atmosphere of the end of the eighteenth century and its response to the presence of Africans in Paris. More generally, I aim to give students critical tools for analyzing various types of cultural documents so that they may better understand the novel *Ourika* within its historical context, as it is represented in the visual arts and in nonliterary texts.

Petits Nègres

The chevalier de Boufflers, who becomes "M. le chevalier de B." in Duras's story, was governor of Senegal from 1786 until 1787. At that time the colony was a trading post; in his position as governor, Boufflers supervised the trade of gum arabic, gold, ivory, and, above all, slaves: approximately three thousand were sent to the Americas in 1786 and 1787 (Bessire 11).

Boufflers purchased Ourika in 1786. He gave her to his uncle to thank him for having helped him become governor. (In the novel, it is "Mme de B." who receives Ourika as a gift.) Boufflers wrote to Mme de Sabran, his future wife, on 19 July 1786:

> Il me reste une perruche pour la reine, un cheval pour M. le maréchal de Castries [Ministre de la Marine], une petite captive pour M. de Beauvau [l'oncle de Boufflers], une poule sultane pour le duc de Laon, une autruche pour M. de Nivernois, et un mari pour toi. (169–70)

> I still have a parrot for the queen, a horse for the Marshal of Castries [Minister of the Navy], a little captive for M. de Beauvau [Boufflers's uncle], a sultan hen for the Duke of Laon, an ostrich for M. de Nivernois, and a husband for you. (my trans.)

My students often remark that the chevalier de Boufflers does not distinguish between animals and the "little captive." He offers Ourika as an object, prized in the same way that an exotic animal is prized. As another letter shows, however, he was sensitive to the humanity of a little slave girl in a similar situation to that of Ourika and was appalled that she had been sold like an animal:

> J'achète en ce moment une petite Négresse de deux ou trois ans pour l'envoyer à madame la duchesse d'Orléans. Elle est jolie, non pas comme le jour, mais comme la nuit. Ses yeux sont comme de petites étoiles, et son maintien est si doux, si tranquille, que je me sens touché aux larmes en pensant que cette pauvre enfant a été vendue comme un petit agneau.
> (8 Feb. 1786)

> I am currently purchasing a little two- or three-year-old black girl to send to the Duchess of Orleans. She is beautiful, not like the day, but like the night. Her eyes are like little stars, and her bearing is so sweet, so tranquil, that I am moved to tears when I think that this poor child has been sold like a little lamb.   (my trans.)

This passage allows me to explain the trade of black children as a lesser-known outgrowth of the institution of slavery (Sala-Molins 115). Slave children (in French usually called *petits nègres* or *petits pages*) were very fashionable in high society in the seventeenth and, especially, eighteenth centuries. White European families found them pleasing as servants and entertainers. They represented a status symbol, a sign of wealth and luxury, and an adornment, as three paintings of the period show: *Jeanne Bécu, Comtesse du Barry*, by Jean-Baptiste André Gautier-Dagoty; *Jeune nègre tenant un arc* ("Young Negro Child Holding a Bow"), by Hyacinthe Rigaud; and *Jeune noir tenant une corbeille de fruits et jeune fille caressant un chien* ("Young Black Holding a Fruit Basket and Young Girl Caressing a Dog"), by Antoine Coypel.

The dress of these slave children is revealing: they all wear luxurious clothes and turbanlike headdresses with feathers; but they also wear metal collars around their necks, making visible their status as slave servants as well as likening them to domestic animals. (The collar is particularly visible in Rigaud's painting.) In the portrait of the countess of Barry, her young servant Zamor serves her coffee; he, like coffee, is an exotic import. The young black girl of Coypel's painting is accompanied by two monkeys, one of them grasping her back, the other sitting on the balustrade, trying to steal the fruit basket from her. Whereas the white girl (one presumes she is the mistress) actively caresses the dog, the black girl passively puts up with the monkeys. In this way the artist seems to reinforce the subjugation of the black girl.

The chevalier de Boufflers was known for his generosity in giving African children as presents to his friends and associates in France. He gave an African boy to Mme de Sabran; her children named him Friday. An excerpt from the memoirs of Mme de Sabran's daughter documenting the way Friday's adopted family treated him could be given to students (app. 1). The young boy is not only dehumanized but also represented as a voiceless showpiece, a "product" of Senegal (Maugras and Croze-Lemercier, *Memoirs* 17). He is described as a buffoon (the comparison between Friday and the cat is particularly revealing). Louis-Sébastien Mercier's "Petits Nègres," from *Le tableau de Paris*, is another text that might be assigned to reinforce the notion of little slaves as playthings or pets, kept in a subordinate position and often denigrated.

All these representations indicate that child-slaves, when brought to France, pleased only while they were young. When they had outgrown being playthings for children (and adults), some of them (males) enrolled in the army, while others became runaways. There was no real future for any of them.

Ourika

In many ways, Ourika is treated differently from these *petits nègres* and from other African servants living in high society. For one thing, Ourika's adoptive family does not rename her. Her name indicates that she was most likely of Peul origin, probably from Fouta-Djallon, a hilly region in southeast Senegal, which continues into Guinea (Little, "Le nom").

For another, Mme de Beauvau appears to have been genuinely fond of Ourika and regarded her as a warm, sensitive human being; the benefactress describes Ourika as endowed with originality, a keen mind, and a sense of decency (app. 2). She stresses Ourika's lack of affectation (*le naturel*); this characteristic of her personality, taste, and modesty recalls the innate nobility and purity of mind that Jean-Jacques Rousseau attributed to "noble savages." Nonetheless, Mme de Beauvau also seems to accentuate passive, exterior, and reifying features of Ourika.

Ourika's sincere grief at the death of M. de Beauvau increased Mme de Beauvau's esteem for her: "alors elle m'avoit inspiré la tendresse d'une véritable mère" 'she made me feel the tenderness of a real mother' (147; my trans.). Students are alert to the fact that Mme de Beauvau compares her own feelings for Ourika with those of a mother but that Ourika calls her not "mother" but "amie" and "Madame" (148). The fictional Ourika, too, wishes she could call Mme de B. "mother" (DeJean 17; Fowles 17).

Even though Ourika appears to have been taken care of, genuinely appreciated, and at least partially integrated into the Beauvau household, Mme de Beauvau seems to have loved Ourika less as an individual than as a reminder of her husband. At the end of his life, M. de Beauvau was preoccupied with Ourika's future and may even have left her a dowry. He died a natural death in 1793, the same year that Louis XVI was guillotined. At that time, most of the Beauvaus' friends had fled France. For the lonely Mme de Beauvau, Ourika became an object of interest and affection as well as her sole preoccupation. Mme de Beauvau looked to Ourika for consolation in her old age but was thwarted in this purpose by Ourika's death. As Ourika was dying, however, Mme de Beauvau found solace in the idea that Ourika would soon become her deceased husband's protector and mother.

A painting of the real-life Ourika, *Ourika*, by Sophie de Tott, complements this verbal portrait (see "Ourika: Le mal de la couleur" in Paliyenko). The name Ourika is painted in the upper right-hand corner of the canvas, confirming that this is her portrait. I point out to students that no title or family name is added, an absence that suggests that Ourika is not represented here as a member of the family. She poses with grace, and her twinkling eyes look at the viewer in a delightful manner. The intensity of her gaze engages the viewer and invites a deep level of personal involvement and response. Students imagine that this attractive pose represents the grace that so charmed Mme de Beauvau.

As we analyze the composition of this portrait, students often observe that the white bust of M. de Beauvau, as well as its ornate gilded base, captures and reflects light so that this inanimate object acquires as much importance as, if not more than, Ourika herself. The crown of flowers that Ourika holds above her benefactor's bust—reminiscent of the laurel wreath awarded to heroes in antiquity—also draws attention to the statue. In the context of abolitionism, this gesture becomes one of homage. I suggest that Ourika's role in this painting is to glorify M. de Beauvau, an enlightened person who, as a member of the Société des Amis des Noirs, promoted the abolition of slavery. (Slavery was abolished in the French colonies in 1794; Napoléon reestablished it in 1802.) Ourika pays tribute to her white benefactor as she prepares a crown of glory for him; she signals not only her indebtedness to him but also her admiration for him.

The figure of Ourika wears golden bands on her arms and ankles; I have seen representations of white women wearing arm bands but never ankle bands. Although the ankle bands complement Ourika's earrings and crown, they recall the chains of slavery. Their role appears to be similar to the metal collars in the previously discussed paintings. She is also barefoot (as was Friday), and her feet are big (in contrast to the delicate, thin, and daintily shod feet of young noble women). Ourika wears a drapery of striped fabric that leaves one breast un-veiled—a type of clothing seen in representations of slave markets. Such signs underscore Ourika's difference from the society in which she grew up.

The contradictory iconography of this portrait reflects the tension resulting from the anomaly of Ourika's having been brought to France as a child-slave but subsequently having been educated in a noble household. While cherished by her benefactors for her natural talents, she was also valued as an exotic object, existing mainly to showcase M. de Beauvau's liberality and enlightenment.

Finally, we look at the anonymous portrait *Ourika* (Tourasse 17; Paliyenko). First we compare the way Ourika is represented in this portrait with the way she is depicted in Tott's painting. She seems older, and her innocent gaze no longer engages the viewer: she appears to be elsewhere in her thoughts.

Then we observe the way this Ourika is clothed. She wears a white dress with a tulle shawl going from her upper left shoulder to the middle of her right arm. This outfit seems conventional; it corresponds to the way aristocratic women were portrayed at the time. Students note, however, that Ourika's headdress, fashioned out of the same cloth that covers her shoulder, has a more exotic connotation. (The way the tulle is tied around her head draws attention to its knot and resembles the feather worn by the slave girl in the Coypel painting.)

The text written in roman letters on the frame deserves attention. On the upper frame, we read a text probably composed by Mme de Beauvau: "Son regard triste et doux implore la pitié" 'Her sad and soft look implores pity.' On the lower frame appear the words "Mon père et ma mère m'ont abandonnée, mais le Seigneur a pris pitié de moi" 'My father and my mother abandoned me, but the Lord has taken pity on me.' The first inscription asks that the viewer see Ourika as an object of pity; the second appears to be a quotation from Ourika herself, found by Mme de Beauvau among Ourika's possessions after her death (Beauvau 150; app. 2). This sentence, taken from Psalm 27, verse 10, constitutes, to my knowledge, the only existing text written in Ourika's own hand. It implies that religion saved Ourika, an idea that is further developed in Duras's fictional account when Ourika tells the doctor that she has found happiness in the convent. In dialogue with the text on the upper frame, another interpretation would be that these words serve to glorify both the chevalier de Boufflers and M. and Mme de Beauvau: my father and mother in Africa abandoned me, but the Lord took pity on me; the chevalier de Boufflers purchased me and brought me to the Beauvau family, where I have found happiness.

We might wonder to what extent Ourika represented the goodness of her benefactors. On the one hand, although they fashioned her to become an accomplished young aristocrat, she remained marked with the stigma of having been a slave, deserving of pity because of what was perceived at the time as her innately inferior position. On the other hand, Ourika was appreciated, as were most slave children, for her sweet disposition; more important, she appears to have been the object of genuine interest and care. I finish by reminding students that it is because Ourika had this exceptional destiny that her life story became a widely told anecdote among aristocrats. Duras, known for her storytelling talents, enjoyed narrating it and, following her friends' advice, eventually wrote it down.

In teaching *Ourika*, I emphasize the ambiguity of the eponymous protagonist's situation. We discuss the importance of translating historical and cultural events into fictional ones. At the end of the class, I distribute to students the following quotation from Duras:

> Le fond de l'histoire est vrai. Ourika fut rapportée par le chevalier de Boufflers à Mme la maréchale de Beauvau, mais, hors leurs deux caractères et la triste cause de la fin d'Ourika, tout le reste est d'imagination.
> (Pailhès 279)

The core of the story is true. Ourika was brought [to France] by the chevalier of Boufflers and given to Madame de Beauvau. These two personages
and the sad cause of Ourika's death apart, it is a work of the imagination.
(my trans.)

I ask students to interpret the possible meaning of the quotation. I explain
that the real-life Ourika is said to have died from tuberculosis. I underscore that
Ourika's retreat to the convent is a traditional ending for an eighteenth-century
novel but that in this case it may be somewhat progressive. Duras invents a dig-
nified way for Ourika to leave "the world": knowing that there is no future for
her, Ourika herself makes this decision.

APPENDIX 1
FROM THE *MEMOIRS OF DELPHINE DE SABRAN*

En arrivant [à Paris, après un séjour à la campagne], Mme de Sabran eut
l'agréable surprise de trouver chez elle une lettre du chevalier qui lui annonçait
l'envoi d'un produit de son gouvernement. Quel fut l'étonnement de tous quand
on vit arriver quelques jours après un petit nègre «haut comme une botte» et
«noir comme l'ébène.» Ce petit négrillon qui était, à peu de chose près, tout ce
que produisait le Sénégal, fit le bonheur d'Elzéar et de Delphine, il devint leur
jouet et la joie de la maison. Mme de Sabran écrivait à Boufflers:

«Je te parlerai de ton petit sauvage que mes enfants ont appelé Vendredi;
il fait leur bonheur, et il n'y a pas de joie pareille à celle qu'il a éprouvée le
jour qu'il s'est vu un bel habit sur le corps; il est si emprunté dans ce nouveau
vêtement qu'il fait mourir de rire; il ressemble à ces chats auxquels on met des
papillotes à la queue; il tourne, il se regarde, il n'ose pas remuer, crainte de se
salir, à peine peut-il marcher avec ses souliers, enfin il nous donne la comédie
toute la journée et il nous paraît d'autant plus piquant qu'il est en fait de plaisir
et de distractions notre unique ressource. »

(Maugras and Croze-Lemercier, *Delphine* 27)

When she arrived [in Paris, after a stay in the country], Mme de Sabran was
agreeably surprised to find a letter from the Chevalier de Boufflers saying that
he was sending one of the products of his province. Great was the astonishment
of all when some days later a black child arrived, "as tall as a boot and as black
as ebony." This little black person, practically the only product exported from
Senegal, delighted Elzéar and Delphine, became their plaything and the joy
of the household. Mme de Sabran wrote to Boufflers, "I must tell you of your
little savage, whom my children call Friday. He is a great delight to them, and
no joy can be equal to that which he showed on the day when he was dressed in
livery for the first time. He is so discomfited in his new garments that we nearly
suffocate with laughter; he looks like a cat with curling papers tied to its tail;

he turns around, looks at himself, and is afraid to move for fear of getting dirty; he can hardly walk in his shoes; he amuses us all day long, and is therefore the more valuable to us as he is our only source of pleasure and entertainment."

(Maugras and Croze-Lemercier, *Memoirs* 17; trans. modified by author and Mary Ellen Birkett)

APPENDIX 2
FROM THE *SOUVENIRS DE LA MARÉCHALE DE BEAUVAU*

EXCERPT 1

27 Janvier 1799

La mort d'une enfant de seize ans vient de rouvrir toutes mes plaies. Cette enfant, donnée à Monsieur de Beauvau, sans que ni lui ni moi l'eussions désirée, était devenue promptement pour lui un objet d'intérêt, de goût, de tendresse; j'avois partagé tous ces sentiments, et lorsque je l'ai perdu [M. de Beauvau], l'unique objet du sentiment passionné de toute ma vie; lorsque ses dernières dispositions m'ont fait connaître combien il étoit occupé d'elle et de son avenir; lorsque la douleur profonde et durable qu'elle a montrée de sa perte, avoient augmenté mon vif intérêt pour elle, alors elle m'avoit inspiré la tendresse d'une véritable mère. Jamais fille ne fut plus aimée. Elle justifioit tous mes sentiments; j'ai besoin de les répandre.

Monsieur de Beauvau avoit deviné l'originalité de son caractère; il réunissoit au plus grand naturel une sorte de profondeur qui lui faisoit renfermer jusqu'à sa sensibilité: quand je n'en aurois pas eu la preuve par la durée de ses regrets pour son protecteur, cent fois j'aurois eu cette preuve de sensibilité dans toutes les occasions qui la forçoient en quelque sorte à la laisser paroître; elle m'aimoit avec une préférence qui lui ôtait jusqu'à l'idée qu'elle put vivre sans moi ou loin de moi; la menace seule que je lui en avois faite quelque fois, la jetoit dans une espèce de désespoir.

Hélas! J'avois perdu celui dont depuis tant d'années j'étois le premier objet; je sentois quelque douceur à penser que j'étois encore celui de cette intéressante créature. Jusqu'à son dernier soupir elle m'appeloit avec ce son de voix si touchant, qui étoit un de ses charmes: "Amie, Madame, mon amie, Madame".

Elle étoit née avec beaucoup d'esprit; et la qualité la plus remarquable de son esprit, étoit une justesse et un goût naturel, qui me surprenoient à tout moment dans les lectures que nous faisions ensemble.

Sa pureté ne pouvoit se comparer qu'à celle des Anges. Elle avoit une fierté douce et modeste, une pudeur naturelle, qui l'auroit préservée à jamais des inconvénients que son âge, son état, sa figure, sa couleur auroient pu faire craindre pour elle; sa figure, qui plaisoit à tous ceux qui la voyoient, avoit pour moi un charme particulier.

Je ne l'ai jamais regardée sans plaisir: ses beaux yeux, sa charmante physionomie, sa grâce, sa taille, ce maintien que la nature seule lui avoit donné, sa noblesse, sa bonté, tout me charmoit en elle, et elle m'est enlevée à seize ans; et moi, vieille, affligée, malheureuse, qui la regardois comme ma consolation, comme mon soutien pour le reste de mes tristes jours, je suis condamnée à la pleurer. Je la verrai à tous les moments; je l'appellerai auprès de moi! Sans cesse elle me rappeloit celui qui m'avoit tant aimée, qui la recommandoit si tendrement à sa fille et à moi; et lorsque l'idée d'une mort prochaine me faisoit jeter sur elle de tristes regards, je me consolois en pensant que cette fille chérie qui l'aimoit presque autant que moi, lui tiendroit lieu de protectrice et de mère, et je n'avois plus rien à craindre pour elle.

La mort de ma chère Ourika a été douce comme sa vie; elle n'a pas connu son danger, et les plus affectueux, les plus tendres soins, lui ont été prodigués jusqu'à ses derniers moments, par ceux qui me sont attachés et qui la pleurent avec moi.

J'ai trouvé dans son portefeuille ce passage écrit de sa main: "Mon père et ma mère m'ont abandonnée, mais le Seigneur a pris pitié de moi."

(Beauvau 147–50)

27 January 1799

The death of a sixteen-year-old child has reopened my wounds. This child, given to Monsieur de Beauvau, without either he or I having desired the gift, immediately became for him an object of interest, of appeal, of tenderness; I shared all these feelings, and when I lost him [Monsieur de Beauvau], the unique object of passion in my life; when the provisions of his will made me aware of how concerned he was for her and her future; when the profound and lasting suffering that she had shown at his death deepened my feelings for her, she made me feel the tenderness of a real mother. Never was a girl more loved. She was worthy of all my affection; I need to talk about it.

Monsieur de Beauvau had discovered the originality of her character, whose great naturalness, depth, and sensitivity made her reticent: even if she had not shown long-lasting grief for her protector, I would have known she was sensitive from the hundreds of occasions when she could not help letting it appear; she loved me so exclusively that the idea of living without me or far away from me never occurred to her; the mere suggestion of doing so (which I sometimes made) made her despair.

Alas! I had lost the person for whom I was everything for so many years; I took some comfort from the notion that I was still the center of the world for this interesting creature. With her last breath she called to me, in the touching voice that was one of her charms: "Friend, Madame, my friend, Madame."

She was born with much spirit, and the most remarkable quality of her mind was her sound judgment and her natural good taste, which constantly surprised me when we read together.

Her purity could be compared only to that of Angels. She had a sweet and modest pride, a natural modesty, which would have saved her from the disadvantages that her age, her condition, her appearance, her color made us fear for her; her countenance, which pleased everyone, was for me particularly charming.

I never looked at her without pleasure: her beautiful eyes, her charming physiognomy, her grace, her stature, that bearing that nature alone had given her, her nobility, her goodness, everything about her charmed me, and she was taken away from me at the age of sixteen; and I, old, afflicted, unhappy, who looked upon her as my consolation, as my support in the sad days that remain, I am condemned to mourn her. I will see her always; I will call her to me! She reminded me constantly of him who had loved me so much, who had recommended her so tenderly to his daughter and to me; and when the thought of her approaching death made me look at her with sadness, I found solace in thinking that this cherished young woman who had loved him almost as much as I had would become a kind of protector and mother for him; I no longer had anything to fear for her.

The death of my dear Ourika was as sweet as her life; she did not know the danger of her situation, and the most affectionate and tender care was given to her until the very end by those who are attached to me and who mourn her with me.

I found in her letter case this passage written in her own hand: "My father and my mother have abandoned me, but the Lord has taken pity on me."

(my trans.)

Excerpt 2

21 Juillet 1799

J'ai perdu cette enfant chérie, objet de mon intérêt, de ma tendresse, et de ma seule distraction. Elle me rappelait sans cesse celui qui l'avoit tant aimée. Sa perte m'est toujours présente, et rien ne peut ni me la rendre, ni la remplacer.

(Beauvau 150)

21 July 1799

I have lost this cherished child, object of my interest, my tenderness, and my only distraction. She reminded me constantly of him who had loved her so much. Her loss is still present for me, and nothing can give her back to me or replace her.

(my trans.)

Black Faces, White Voices
in Women's Writing from the 1820s

Doris Y. Kadish

Ourika may well be the most probing and profound French example of what Henry Louis Gates has called "the Discourse of the Black Other" (*Figures* 49). But it is neither the only such text by a woman writer nor necessarily the most representative. This essay looks at three other works written, like *Ourika*, in the 1820s; all are available in French and in English (see Kadish, *Francophone Slavery*). The first is *Mémoires de la marquise de La Tour du Pin: Journal d'une femme de cinquante ans*, which Henriette Lucy de La Tour du Pin began writing in 1820 about her life as an aristocrat who narrowly escaped death during the French Revolution. This work also describes the two years the author spent in exile near Albany, New York, where she and her husband owned a farm and a number of slaves. The second example, *Noire et blanc*, is one of several works about blacks published in the mid-1820s by Sophie Doin, a Protestant abolitionist. Doin aimed to extend the reach of the antislavery Société de la Morale Chrétienne, created in 1821, to the common people. The third instance is the short novel *Sarah*, written in 1821 by the Romantic poet Marceline Desbordes-Valmore, who, as a young actress, found herself in revolution-torn Guadeloupe when slavery was reestablished in 1802. Unlike Duras and La Tour du Pin, members of the French elite, and Doin, who was wealthy, Desbordes-Valmore stood on the social and economic margins of society.

Like Duras, these three woman writers appropriate blackness to serve their own personal, literary, or political interests, but their circumstances, reasons, and perspectives are different from those that produced *Ourika*. By focusing on female figures with whom Ourika may be compared, this essay aims to have students reflect on the place *Ourika* occupies in the spectrum of social and po-litical attitudes toward race at the time it was written.

The first of these women is Judith, from chapter 18 of La Tour du Pin's *Jour-nal d'une femme de cinquante ans*. The La Tour du Pin family purchased Judith as a slave in 1794. An initial observation about the difference between Judith and Ourika concerns agency, that is, the extent to which these two black figures play a role in determining the terms of their existence in a white world. Duras presents Ourika as wholly dependent on decisions made for her by benevolent whites: decisions concerning her rescue from slavery, her education in France, the inappropriateness of marrying beneath her station, and her inability to inte-grate fully as an adult into French society. In contrast, La Tour du Pin chooses to call attention to circumstances that grant a significant degree of agency to Judith (204–05, 254–55). In *Journal* the author explains that it was the prevail-ing practice in the northern United States for a mistreated slave, like Judith, to request a new owner. Despite the objections of Judith's master, La Tour du Pin, who wishes to acquire Judith, prevails, reminding the owner that he cannot refuse to sell a slave who wishes to be sold. But it is not only the white woman who knows the workings of the slavery system and the rights of blacks: Judith is aware of her rights and tells her cruel owner directly that she wants a new master. In response to Judith's request, "il l'avait battue au point de la tuer et . . . elle en était encore malade" 'he had beaten her almost to death and . . . she was still ill from the effects of it' (205; *Memoirs* 255).[1] By emphasizing her own as well as Judith's role in acquiring a new owner, La Tour du Pin proposes an al-ternative narrative in which blacks and whites cooperate in mitigating the cruel conditions of slavery.

Other notable differences between La Tour du Pin's and Duras's accounts arise from parallels that La Tour du Pin establishes between whites and blacks, such as the importance of manual labor as a means of survival in the New World—ad-justing to a new culture, finding the means to support a family, illness, the death of children. Through cheerful industriousness, we are encouraged to believe, black women such as Judith can manage, as does the author, to maintain an orderly household, to help run a viable farm, and to engage in other productive agricultural and domestic activities. Whites must abandon the luxurious habits of an earlier time of privilege and set an example for their black workers. An-other quality that Judith and La Tour du Pin share is their desire for freedom. In describing her family's preparations to return to France in 1796, the author constructs a parallel between her own liberation from exile in America and the liberation from slavery of her black slaves. In a touching "tableau larmoyant," she depicts Judith, "tomba[nt] sur une chaise en sanglotant" 'falling onto a chair, sobbing' (232; 282), amazed to learn that M. de La Tour du Pin has authorized his wife to grant their freedom: " 'Is it possible? Do you mean that we are free?' I answered: 'Yes, upon my honor, from this moment, as free as I am myself' " (232; 282–83 [these words appear in English in the original text]). Unlike Duras and other members of her French salon culture, La Tour du Pin recognizes blacks here as real persons, not exotic others. The phrase "as free as I am" indicates the common condition of the black slave and her white mistress, who must receive authorization from her husband to dispose of his property. Both women exist in a patriarchal system in which freedom is relative, not absolute.

How, then, do *Ourika* and *Journal d'une femme de cinquante ans* compare with respect to their authors' attitudes toward blacks? Although La Tour du Pin and Duras were both liberals who sought a mediating ground between the right and left during the restoration, *Ourika* is ultimately more conservative in its sympathetic attitude toward the salon culture in which it was first read aloud and its ancien régime setting (hence, undoubtedly, Louis XVIII's well-known description of it as an "Atala de salon" 'Atala of the salon' [Lescure vii]). In contrast, La Tour du Pin is highly critical of the way of life of the old nobility, including its patronizing attitude toward blacks. She does not hesitate to say that when she was in the salon of Mme de Beauvau, who raised the real-life model for Duras's Ourika, the woman "ne se lassait pas de voir les bras noirs de cette petite autour de mon col; cela m'ennuyait à mort" 'could not get enough of seeing the black arms of this child wrapped around my neck; that bored me to tears' (387; my trans.). Nor does she refrain from presenting Judith in *Journal* as ugly, although she concedes that her lack of beauty "n'empêchait pas son mari d'en être fou" 'did not prevent her husband being madly attached to her' (205; 255). Unwilling to transform real black women into romanticized, fictional models, La Tour du Pin disapproved of the "mélange de vérité et d'invention" 'mixture of truth and invention' in Duras's novel, stating that "Ourika toute véritable était plus intéressante" 'the real Ourika was more interesting' (387; my trans.).

Doin, author of *Noire et blanc*, also presents a black woman character, Nelzi, who invites comparisons and contrasts with Ourika; indeed, it seems conceivable that Doin may have read Duras's novel and sought to respond to it. Black, orphaned, and removed from their African origins, Nelzi and[Ourika are sensitive, intelligent girls who fall in love with handsome French scions of distinguished families, both named Charles.]Both girls receive an education thanks to the benevolence of whites, to whom they are profoundly devoted. As they reach maturity and envision lives as adult women, both encounter societal pressures because of their race. The discovery that prejudice exists in French society drives the plot in both Duras's and Doin's stories. How the two female characters will live their lives as black women in early-nineteenth-century France constitutes the principal question that the narratives seek to resolve.

Significant differences between the two black protagonists exist, however. Whereas Duras represents Ourika deploring her black skin, having internalized the prejudice of white French society, Doin describes Nelzi's physical attractions admiringly through Charles's eyes:

> Ses yeux ne sont-ils pas beaux, grands, expressifs? Ses dents ne sont-elles pas admirables? . . . Son teint même il a son brillant, ses nuances. . . .

Cette taille est parfaite, ses contours sont gracieux; il règne dans toute sa personne une aisance, un attrait piquant. . . . O Nelzi, Nelzi, toi aussi la nature t'a parée de mille charmes!   (101–02)

Aren't her eyes beautiful, large, expressive? Aren't her teeth admirable? . . . Even her color has its glow, its nuances. . . . Her figure is perfect, her curves are graceful. Her whole person is endowed with a poise, a piquant beauty. . . . Oh Nelzi, Nelzi, nature has adorned you too with a thousand charms!   (my trans.)

The two black protagonists' attitudes toward the revolutionary events in Saint-Domingue also differ. Ourika, who sees those events through the eyes of whites with a stake in the colonial economy, condemns them; hers is the perspective of the colonizer. In contrast, Nelzi, who lives through the events, refrains from taking the side of either whites or blacks. Her concerns are with physical survival; her perspective is that of the colonized. Another difference concerns agency. Whereas Ourika is a victim of society's prejudices against blacks, Nelzi, like La Tour du Pin's Judith, is an empowered figure. It is she who is responsible for rescuing her master from the rebels and for obtaining their passage to America.

It is also possible to read *Noire et blanc* against the backdrop of French and Haitian history in the 1820s. Such a reading can help dramatize the "non-dit" of Duras's novel—that is, the historical context in which it was written but which it chooses not to acknowledge. Nelzi's rescue of her white master corresponds to the drama of dealings between Haiti and France in the years leading up to the recognition of Haitian independence in 1825 and its unification under the rule of the mulatto leader Charles Boyer. Like those two countries after the Haitian Revolution, Nelzi and Charles living together in exile do not fully realize the depth of the affective and moral bonds that unite them. A turning point in their personal relationship that parallels the public events of 1825 occurs when Charles is summoned to return to France to reclaim his uncle's fortune on the condition that he marry his cousin. Although Charles comes close to succumbing to the expectations of his class and abandoning Nelzi, a benevolent French-woman intervenes to bring the couple back together, in sharp contrast with Mme de B.'s friend, who deepens the divide separating Ourika from Charles. Charles's public recognition of his love for Nelzi emblematizes France's public recognition of Haiti's independence and the lasting bonds of friendship, mutual interest, and loyalty that unite the two countries. Nelzi, like Boyer, fights to cement her ties with France in the person of her beloved Charles. Moreover, like Haiti, Nelzi is an apt student, to whom Charles teaches subjects that will make her an equal intellectual partner.

Noire et blanc presents two people of different races, each contributing to the common good of their partnership—a model for how abolitionists envisioned Haiti and France cooperating in the future. Nelzi demonstrates the heroism of the successful Haitian Revolution in her courageous rescue of Charles, whereas he embodies the civilizing factors of education and religion that Doin sees as the positive legacy of the French colonizing mission. At the close of the novel, Charles and Nelzi will presumably marry. But their physical union is not what matters to Doin. Although she does not explicitly rule out the possibility of mixed-race children, as Duras does in *Ourika*, neither does she choose to dwell on interracial marriage as a means of bringing forward a next generation, as did the more radical abolitionist Henri Grégoire (232–33, 247–48). As the title of Doin's story indicates, black and white ultimately remain separate. But the separation in no way implies hostility or indifference. On the contrary, by locating shared authority between whites and blacks in the most private space, the family unit, *Noire et blanc* articulates the primacy of racial equality, commitment, and loyalty as the bases of the future moral and political ties between France and Haiti.

Students need to know that abolitionists did exist in the 1820s, that their views differed from Duras's, and that *Ourika* is not, strictly speaking, an abolitionist text. The relation between *Ourika* and a work such as *Noire et blanc* does not indicate, however, that Duras and Doin represent two opposing poles on the spectrum of social and political attitudes toward race in the 1820s. Instead, I view them as occupying positions between the extremes on that spectrum. And although Doin clearly stands to the left of Duras, I would invite students to explore the ways in which the two texts are ultimately more similar than different.

It may seem surprising that the third woman with whom Ourika can be compared—Desbordes-Valmore's Sarah—is white. Orphaned and abandoned, Sarah is raised by a wealthy benefactor, Mr. Primrose. She receives the same privileged education in the Primrose home as Ourika does in Mme de B.'s salon. And she loves Edwin, the son of her benefactor, with whom she was raised, in much the same way that Ourika loves Charles. For Sarah, as for both Ourika and Nelzi, it is at the threshold of adulthood that societal pressures based on race precipitate the drama enacted in the story. Convinced by the evil overseer Sylvain that she is herself a slave, Sarah experiences the same feelings of isolation, exile, and rejection as Doin's and Duras's black characters.

The author of *Sarah* depicts those feelings and links them to a black perspective in an indirect way. The prefatory section of *Huit femmes* titled "Le retour en Europe" presents an unnamed frame narrator, who recounts how her mother died in the Caribbean islands, how she strove to return to Europe, and how she heard stories about natives of the colonies. One is the story of Sarah, the main section of the book. The frame narrator describes herself in a way that points toward the real author. Both were in the same place (Pointe-à-Pitre, Guadeloupe), at the same time (1802), under the same circumstances. Sarah's story is recounted by the frame narrator's companion, Eugénie. A multilevel narrative and authorial pattern thus reach from the actual author through the semiautobiographical frame narrator to the fictional embedded narrator Eugénie. This structure prepares the way for the reader to see the central character Sarah as an extension of the series of feminine figures in the frame.

In the novel, Sarah also becomes linked to the former slave Arsène, who narrates his own and Sarah's past lives. The thematic bonds among the frame narrator, Sarah, and Arsène are strong; and thus Arsène's resistance against racial pressures is implicitly linked to them. All three have lost their mothers, and that loss is the primary cause of the alienation and estrangement from which they suffer. Displaced geographically at a young age, the three are forced to adapt to life among strangers. Their stories place them on or near water: the frame narrator en route to Guadeloupe, Sarah on the boat that brings her to the Primrose plantation, Arsène transported from Africa. The result of these thematic bonds is again that meaning passes along the narrative chain, and, through association, all the narrative participants are linked to one another and to Arsène's condition as a former slave. Accordingly, antislavery positions developed in the novel that derive from Arsène's status as an eyewitness to the horrors of slavery attach to Sarah herself as a victim of a related fate:

> Ses yeux erraient sur les bords de la mer, où quelque nègre, traînant un fardeau à l'ardeur du soleil paraissait y succomber comme lui, et comme lui, peut-être, envoyer à sa patrie absente un soupir de regret et d'adieu. Il plaignait l'esclave, tous les esclaves. (27)

> His eyes wandered along the seashore where some black man, weighed down by a heavy burden in the burning heat of the day, seemed, like himself, to send a sigh of regret and farewell to his homeland as he succumbed to his fate. He pitied this slave, all slaves. (my trans.)

Another major difference between Sarah and Ourika concerns Ourika's submission to patriarchal societal conventions: the position of the doctor as frame narrator in Duras's novel emblematizes his superiority as a male figure of authority. Furthermore, Charles's inability or unwillingness to recognize Ourika as a potential mate indicates his commitment to preserving the purity of the aristocratic lineage to which he belongs and that is passed along to his male child. Charles's value system, which he shares with Mme de B., is never contested or undermined in *Ourika*. In contrast, Desbordes-Valmore offers a maternal ethic of caring as an alternative to patriarchal values of authority and privilege (Boutin 80). That ethic stands against what Hélène Cixous describes as the masculine ethic of the *propre*—what is "clean," "morally right," and "specific to the self"—that forms the conceptual common ground of both propriety and property (my trans.). Desbordes-Valmore rejects the *propre*, relegating patriarchal notions of possession to the cruel plantation overseer Sylvain.

In contrast, Arsène functions as Sarah's substitute mother, embodying a feminine ethic of caring that ultimately prevails over Sylvain's masculine proprietary ethic. Similarly, Sarah's real father, who appears at the end of the story, has no desire to possess wealth. When he gives his property to his daughter, it is not what Cixous calls the masculinist gift of reciprocity but rather a feminist one of generosity. Although Sarah marries Edwin, whose father bears a "proper name," it is a name stripped of the property that formerly legitimized its privilege. With the inheritance of her nameless father, who has disavowed his privileged social status, Sarah and Edwin face their future as a liberated, compassionate colonial class.

Is *Sarah* more progressive than *Ourika* with respect to race? We learn from her biography that Desbordes-Valmore knew the condition of oppressed people firsthand and that memories of her experience in the French colonies at the time of the slave revolts were long lasting. *Sarah* and her other writings also show how she called into question the patriarchal foundations of race, class, and gender inequities in French society of her time. But unlike Doin or Duras, she does not make addressing race issues her primary intention. *Sarah* adopts a mode of sentimental writing in which sympathy for blacks plays a role but in which class inequality is a predominant theme. This mode propels the formerly excluded to center stage, thereby celebrating their humanity. By foregrounding the importance of the voice of the heart and nature, *Sarah* illustrates how essential humanity transcends social hierarchies. Sentimental writing can thus reach a popular audience unreceptive to Enlightenment discourses of reason and argument. It represents the misfortune that occurs when a villain causes harm to a member of the family and ends with a leveling of social classes: "It is when social barriers are transgressed, when some kind of *déclassement* occurs, when a shift down the social ladder takes place, that true sentimental epiphany is provoked" (Denby 96). *Sarah*, unlike *Ourika*, has a happy ending. But it is one in which class barriers alone are transgressed. The racial boundaries that the abolitionist Doin advocated crossing remain fixed in both Desbordes-Valmore's and Duras's works.

Ourika, then, is neither an abolitionist text nor the most progressive work by a woman writer from the 1820s. Reading *Ourika* in the broader context of *Noire et blanc* and *Sarah* liberates Duras's novel from the heavy burden it has often been made to bear as the only representation of blacks by a woman writer in early-nineteenth-century France.

NOTE

[1] His reaction recalls the fate of the runaway slaves in Jacques-Henri Bernardin de Saint-Pierre's *Paul et Virginie*, a seminal nineteenth-century work about slavery. Bernardin's slaves, like Ourika, are objects of the benevolence of whites: Paul and Virginie, who, despite their good intentions, deliver the slaves back to their original cruel master.

Ourika and Women's Literary Tradition in France

Chantal Bertrand-Jennings

The turn of the nineteenth century has been described as "le sacre de l'écrivain" 'the consecration of the writer' (Bénichou; my trans.). This statement, however, certainly cannot apply to the woman writer. In fact, for her, the period following the French Revolution was more like a deconsecration, since women's rights underwent a drastic regression. Women's influence in cultural exchanges waned, and more than ever women were relegated to the private sphere. Indeed, in *De la littérature*, Germaine de Staël identifies the woman writer of that period as "une paria" 'a pariah' (2: 341; my trans.). In her first novel, *Delphine*, Staël firmly defends the rights of all women; she protests their situation by exposing the tyranny of contemporary social mores in an unjust society. Staël's second novel, *Corinne ou l'Italie*, tells the tale of a brilliant, sensitive woman's suffering and death at the hands of a society for whom "genius" was incompatible with "feminine." Staël's essay *De l'Allemagne* asserts, "[L]a gloire elle-même ne saurait être pour une femme que le deuil éclatant du bonheur" 'For a woman, glory itself necessarily entails the shattering demise of happiness' (2: 218; my trans.). Staël, therefore, perceives women's unhappiness and diminished role in the arts as a deplorable but incontrovertible misfortune of the times. It is in this light that students should be encouraged to consider *Ourika*.

Students should also consider *Ourika* in a long tradition of women's fiction dating back at least to the seventeenth century. Readers of Claire de Duras's novel, like those of Madeleine de Scudéry, are led to believe that the female protagonist's worth ought to be measured not by birth but by merit. *Ourika* shares the most affinity with Mme de Lafayette's groundbreaking novel *La princesse de Clèves*. Both the princess and Ourika suffer psychological torments and must make a heart-wrenching decision before seeking refuge in a convent, where they soon die. If the milieu described in *Ourika* is less grandiose than that in Lafayette's fiction, it is no less refined in its aristocratic customs. Both novels are centered on the heroine's mental anguish; both are characterized by an elegant style and a concise simplicity. Yet the two are more dissimilar than similar. Ourika is a young black woman rescued from slavery and adopted by a French noble family; the princess is a white woman of the highest social rank. Moreover, in Duras's novel the question of prejudice supersedes that of sentiment. These significant differences make *Ourika* a far more socially engaged work than *La princesse de Clèves*. But Ourika appears to lack agency in comparison with Zélia, the heroine of Françoise de Graffigny's *Lettres d'une Péruvienne*, who, by actively subverting the marriage plot, defines her own *bonheur*.

The tradition of women's novels of sensibility privileges the private sphere, especially matters of the heart and marriage. Nonetheless, one can argue that women's fiction has always had a social connotation, for the private is always political. Identity building for women, through marriage and social relations, impinges on the political; for example, Olympe de Gouges in *L'esclavage des nègres* and Staël in *Mirza* take up the defense of rejected, marginalized, black-skinned protagonists. Yet in *Ourika*, Duras is the first to dwell, not on slavery per se but on the profound psychological consequences of intolerance and prejudice. Her novel can therefore be considered a study of alienation caused by difference.

Around the turn of the nineteenth century, female novelists often denounced the shallowness and hypocrisy of high-society mores (Bertrand-Jennings, *Un autre Mal* 45–61). In so doing they shared a trope familiar to all female writers, who were often more sensitive than their male counterparts to the plight of women and the downtrodden. These early-nineteenth-century authors use fiction to chastise the cruelty of public opinion for excluding any woman who does not abide by its rules. Usually, an innocent and virtuous heroine becomes the persecuted victim of, and is excluded by, a corrupt and hypocritical society, precisely because, through her honesty, sincerity, and lack of artifice, she unwittingly defies the constraints imposed on persons of her sex. These authors object to social discrimination that encroaches on the happiness of their heroines and often prevents unions of inclination in favor of arranged marriages based on class, convenience, or family matters. Prejudices can be based on rank (Genlis's *Mademoiselle de Clermont*), related to a previous marriage (Krüdener's *Valérie*), or caused by physical infirmity (Gay's *Anatole*) or paternal tyranny (Cottin's *Amélie Mansfield*). Unlike the heroes of the Romantic *mal du siècle*, such as François-René de Chateaubriand's René, these writers' characters do not rejoice in their exclusion. Rather, they plead for social integration. Rejection due to difference was thus a theme already broached by earlier female novelists. The originality of Duras's novel stems from the fact that Ourika is excluded from society because of a difference in skin color.

What strategies does Duras use to inscribe the idea of difference onto every level of her novel? Students should consider the narrative structure, the symbolic dimension of time and space, and the tribulations of the female-gendered black subject (Bertrand-Jennings, *D'un siècle* 27–58).

Narrative Structure

Ourika has a frame narrative, and the typography used in the MLA editions of the text and translation appropriately highlights its two narrative levels. The main story is told in the first person by a young black nun who is dying of grief after having confided in a medical doctor, hoping for recovery. But it is the doctor's narrative (italicized), also in the first person, that frames and surrounds the nun's tale, as if to authenticate it. The doctor also briefly interrupts Ourika's story to comment on the evolution of the nun's illness (DeJean 33; Fowles 33–34). He is a white Frenchman, a graduate of the prestigious medical school in Montpellier, who now practices in the capital. He is a worthy ambassador of science and, as such, inspires in the reader a confidence and consideration that the young black woman could not command on her own, thereby lending credence to her tale.

Time and Space

Ourika's fate is sealed at the novel's first page. The flashback technique whereby the doctor tells the story of a woman who has already died adds a dimension of irrevocability to the text. Moreover, the setting of the novel's opening scene, a ruined cloister strewn with tombs, casts a macabre atmosphere on the doctor's first meeting with Ourika. The nun's despondent words, as well as the negative early diagnosis pronounced by the physician and his presentiment of her death, add to the sense of inescapability of the heroine's destiny (5; 5). The sadness that permeates the story and the gloom of the heroine's fate are enhanced by the pathetic fallacy contained in the text's closing lines: "elle mourut à la fin d'octobre; elle tomba avec les dernières feuilles de l'automne" 'She died at the end of October, with the last of the autumn leaves' (45; 47). Falling leaves, a natural phenomenon, suggest that her death too is natural, inevitable, necessary. Indeed, except for a brief moment when Ourika walks with Charles in the forest at Saint-Germain (25; 26), she is always confined: from salon to convent to, it is suggested, tomb. These are womblike enclosed spaces, the epitome of the private sphere. There is no room for Ourika in the public sphere.

The Female-Gendered Black Subject

The modalities of the inscription of the first-person black female subject are significant. In the frame surrounding the nun's narrative, both the doctor's and Ourika's subject pronouns remain unchanged while the exact opposite happens to the voice of the heroine in the framed narrative. Representing as it does the authority of science, the doctor's designation of himself has no reason to fluctuate. Not so for the black female narrator.

In the nun's account, the heroine is, at first, a passive object. At age two she is bought out of slavery by the chevalier de B. and becomes the object of a violent abduction and appropriation, torn from her native land despite her cries, to be offered as a gift to Mme de B. The infant is but goods bartered. She then constructs herself into a strong and solid entity under the watchful eye and loving guidance of her substitute mother within the confines of that lady's salon. Gifted, witty, remarkable, Ourika becomes possessed of all the accomplishments of persons of her sex and station, admired and applauded by her benefactress's friends and confident in her charm and demeanor as a black girl (7–10; 7–10). At that time in her life she is totally blind to what society considers her natural inferiority; she so completely identifies with the aristocratic class in which she has been brought up that she harbors contempt for those who do not share Mme de B.'s distinguished bearing (8; 8).

When the girl reaches adolescence, however, she is made aware of the singularity of her destiny by a conversation she overhears between her adoptive mother and the emissary of the outside world (public space), the marquise. That lady is the harbinger of her society's prejudices, which appear natural even as the text designates them abhorrent. She makes explicit to Ourika what her adoptive mother knows all too well but has not had the heart to tell her: no man of noble birth will marry a "négresse" 'negress' (13; 13), and her upbringing prevents her finding happiness in an arranged marriage below her rank. The message that marriage is a woman's only possible chance of acquiring a social identity is implicit in the text. Having become aware of her real status, the subject undergoes a crisis during which she experiences herself as "the other" that all see in her, an object of revulsion and pity. She has learned that her fate is "sans remède" 'can't be remedied' (39; 40), for her physical appearance condemns her to a life of isolation and opprobrium.

This consciousness of herself as ostracized transforms Ourika's relation to the world. Thus begins a process of reification, of painful self-deprecation that makes Ourika avoid her reflection in mirrors and even see herself as having "[les] mains noires . . . d'un singe" 'monkey's paws' (15; 15). Here the subject has been devalued to the point of becoming an "it," an animal, an object of scorn and aversion. In the salon of Mme de B., dressed in exotic costume and seated at the feet of her benefactress, Ourika was also adopting the posture of a household pet (8; 8). When she comprehends her real position in Mme de B.'s household, she complains of having been but "un jouet, un amusement pour ma bienfaitrice" 'a toy, an amusement for my mistress' (12; 12). For a while she hopes that the French Revolution might bring her the equality it has proclaimed. But Ourika soon realizes that this supposed equality does not extend to her (18–19; 19–20 [nor did it extend to women in general]). Ourika has by then removed all the mirrors from her bedroom; indeed, her self-hatred compels her not to leave even her head and hands unclad for fear that any part of her black skin might be visible (27; 28).

When the marquise announces to Ourika that her chagrin is in fact caused by Ourika's hopeless love for Charles (her adoptive mother's grandson), the young woman at first denies it, then comes to doubt herself. Finally, she becomes convinced of her forbidden passion for him. Her melancholy degenerates into despair and, ultimately, a malady from which she cannot recover. She feels "étrangère à la race humaine toute entière" 'cut off from the entire human race' (15; 16). The disintegration of her personality is symbolized by the splitting of the subject into an "I–she/Ourika" (especially in the original French text). The narrator can no longer say "I," for this "I" is not accepted in its difference (32; 33).

After Charles's marriage to Anaïs and the birth of their son, Ourika deplores her loneliness and desires for herself a family and happiness comparable to theirs (32–36; 33–37). She longs to have "ma place dans la chaîne des êtres" 'a place in the chain of being' (41; 43) and to play her prescribed feminine role:

to marry and have children. Here Duras departs significantly from previous novelists like Graffigny, Tencin, and Charrière, whose heroines tend to subvert the marriage plot (Trousson, Introduction). She finally turns to God, for "tous les cœurs sont égaux devant ses yeux" '[a]ll hearts are equal in His eyes,' and opts to enter a convent (DeJean 43; Fowles 45). Mme de B.'s admission, "Je vous ai fait tant de mal en voulant vous faire du bien" 'I've done you so much harm in wishing to do you good,' explicitly puts into question her benevolent paternalism (45; 46).

Having opened with the subject "I," the nun's narrative closes on a "you" ambiguously addressed to Charles, who seems to have usurped the place reserved for God in the future nun's prayers. Yet there are only two references to the possibility of Ourika's passion for Charles. The first, when a mysterious voice within convinces her she is guilty (42; 43), happens only after she has vehemently denied it to the marquise. One might argue that by then she is in such a weakened state of mind that she has become susceptible to another's influence, especially one she fears. The second concerns the puzzling "vous" 'you' that ends Ourika's narrative. Nevertheless, the rest of the text points to her sisterly or even maternal feelings toward Charles (28; 29); Ourika never expresses jealousy toward Anaïs. Could the heroine be displacing her guilt from race to love? Is it less painful to die for love than as a member of a proscribed race?

In the frame narrative, the black female subject, now a sick and dying nun, can again say "I" without wavering. She seems to have regained the entirety and certainty of her status as subject, for she has admitted and accepted her guilt in having "brisé l'ordre de la nature" '[upset] the natural order of things' (13; 14), and she has also recognized the need for expiation. She has been effectively muted, however, for she is heard only as quoted by the doctor, whereas in the main narrative she appears to be speaking in her own voice. The text, therefore, seems to be implying that Ourika's selfhood can only be restored if she is seen as culpable, repentant, and removed by death from a society where she does not belong. Neither reason (the marquise and Charles) nor religion (the priest and his advice) nor even science (the doctor) can cure Ourika, whose malady originates in others' intolerance of her difference.

Her plight might well be construed as emblematic of women's experience at the beginning of the nineteenth century in France. After a period of contentment during childhood, there came an awakening, during adolescence, to a radical difference from men. This deviance from the (male) norm, inscribed in their flesh, condemned women to social powerlessness and to the misery of exclusion from the public sphere.

Prejudices of race, class, and gender are inextricably woven together in *Ourika* and leave the heroine in a hopeless situation. As a woman she is destined to marry. As a black woman, she must marry a man of lower rank. As an aristocratically raised young lady, she cannot marry below her rank. Hence her doom.

Students should be urged to reflect on the universal value of *Ourika*'s message, for the novel sheds light with great accuracy and compassion on the psychological experience of any form of alienation. Alienation is a process of self-deprecation, self-loathing, and self-destruction resulting from the internalization by the victimized subjects of others' prejudiced gazes and negative value judgments. It also entails the helplessness of the victims, their collaboration with their denigrators in their own reduction to an inferior status, and in their ultimate submission. Across almost two centuries this brief novel speaks to concerns that remain topical to us and to our students.

Telling Stories of Melancholia: *René* and *Ourika*

Kari Weil

After years of teaching Claire de Duras's *Ourika* in French departments, I recently taught it in a course called The Outsider, as part of the humanities curriculum at an art school. The course focused on the experience of being or of being made into an outsider, or other, for moral, sociocultural, physical, or psychological reasons. As aspiring artists and writers, my students tended to consider themselves as outsiders and were quick to identify with characters who might be similarly defined. Even these students, however, were discriminating and only admired or sympathized with "activist outsiders," like Michel from André Gide's *L'immoraliste* or Renée from Sidonie-Gabrielle Colette's *La vagabonde*, who appear to have chosen their outsider status because of some personal or political agenda. Ourika is anything but an activist, and thus most of the class was frustrated with and critical of her. "Why doesn't she find something to be happy about?" "Why does she linger in her depression?" they all fretted, except for one student (I'll call her Leah), an African American woman who had been adopted as an infant by a progressive, educated, white family. We learned about Leah's past on the first day of class when I asked each student to describe an experience of being an outsider. The word seemed to describe most of her life as a teenager and young adult, despite what she recognized as a privileged upbringing with loving parents. For this student, Ourika's story was her story, not only because of the similarities of the circumstances of cross-racial adoption, but also because of the psychological hold of the feelings of alienation, against which both women seemed powerless to fight.

While I was thrilled to see Leah, who had not been much of a reader, take so strongly to Duras's novel, I was also troubled by the way her sympathy for Ourika's torment seemed to make her into an outsider in our class and thus alienate her once again. What I discovered was that the class had inadvertently devalued and marginalized the suffering that Leah identified with. In so doing, most students gave a clear but unsympathetic answer to the question concerning sympathy that Ourika raises in the novel, whether "les chagrins inspirent plus d'intérêt par leurs résultats ou par leurs causes" 'the results or the causes of unhappiness inspire the most sympathy' (DeJean 26–27; Fowles 27). Ourika is led to believe, as was Leah, that "unreasonable" suffering inspires little sympathy. Indeed, insofar as Leah's sympathy for Ourika appeared unreasonable, she was silenced, much as Ourika had been silenced. Ourika, in fact, was silenced a second time, by the Romantic literary canon that dismissed the novel. To my dismay, my class had repeated that double silencing by privileging one kind of alienation over another and thereby reinforcing the dominant view of the insider.

Thus I address here a question raised both in the novel and in the class response to it: How and why do certain positions of alienation become empowering? What allows some to fashion a life story that enables them to move on, and what silences others or brings them to narrate a life story that hastens their death? My answer leads students through both feminist and psychoanalytic theory, especially as the two come together, to understand how the *mal du siècle*, a malady of melancholia, may be experienced differently by men and women.

Psychoanalytic theory demonstrates the importance of thinking through one's relation to the past, especially for those whose experience of alienation stems from a sense of estrangement from the past. "[C]'est le passé qu'il faut guérir" 'it's the past we must cure' (4; 5), says Ourika's doctor, and her ailment indicates the difficult process of repatriation after the French Revolution, experienced by émigrés like Duras and François-René de Chateaubriand. In particular, melancholia, the name that the doctor gives to her ailment and that Théophile Gautier says was invented in its modern form in Chateaubriand's *René* (4), is theorized as the sickness of being stuck in the past. But Ourika's and René's experiences (like Duras's and Chateaubriand's) are very different, and a comparison helps show the gendered manifestations of melancholia.

Feminist theory reveals the particular difficulty women and certain minorities have of fashioning a new relation to their pasts in part because women's biological links to the past (as well as to the future) are said to take precedence over any intellectual disaffection or disidentification with it. Women, moreover, have lacked the authority, if not the right of authorship, to make acceptable sense of their experience and, through its representation, put it behind them. A "feminine" malady (Waller, *Male Malady*), the *mal du siècle* is constructed, perhaps like Romanticism itself, as a stage that must be passed through or grown out of; its very gendering reifies the opposition between those who are outsiders by choice and those who are outsiders by force and have little possibility of moving on.

Both Ourika and René exhibit symptoms similar to those described by Sigmund Freud in his 1917 essay "Mourning and Melancholia." He distinguishes between these two responses to loss by describing melancholia as a "pathological disposition" (243). The pathology results from an inability to sever an attachment to a past love object. Instead, through unconscious mechanisms of identification with or incorporation of that object, the attachment is turned toward some apparently lost part of the self. Melancholia and mourning are reactions to the loss of a loved object—either a person or "some abstraction which has taken the place of one, such as fatherland, liberty, an ideal, and so on" (243), and both are painful kinds of work by which the ego deals with that loss. Melancholia, however, differs from mourning, Freud suggests, in the way external loss is transformed into internal abasement. The ambivalent feelings of reproach that may have been felt for the object are now directed toward the self. "In mourning it is the world which has become poor and empty; in melancholia it is the ego itself" (246). Indeed, melancholics are not consciously aware of what they've lost, and this inability to explain the cause of their suffering only exacerbates a sense of worthlessness and helplessness. Melancholia thus entails the same symptoms of guilt and hopelessness that are today associated with clinical depression. I retain the term *melancholia* here, however, because of its specific link, through mourning, to a lost, if unknown, past.

The loss of Amélie in *René*, like that of Charles in *Ourika*, stands in for a much larger, if unacknowledged, loss. But whereas René is enabled, after the death of Amélie, to produce a narrative that will allow him to mourn his past and proceed to his chosen future, Ourika is prohibited from even claiming Charles as a lost love object. Moreover, the loss of loss that he represents leaves Ourika stranded between his past that she wants but is not allowed to claim and an African past she comes to know only through its distorted, French representations.

The story that René finally relates in the New World to his adopted fathers is evidence that the work of mourning has achieved its goal, freeing him from his past enough to make his memories tellable. The story becomes the vehicle for his insertion into his new family and into a history where the female role, and the femininity he both identified with and feared, is effaced. Relation through narrative takes the place of relation by birth, creation for procreation. What psychoanalytic theory does not account for, however, is the extent to which the success of René's story is determined by the sociocultural situation of its reception. The consolation that René finds among the Indians is achieved through his position of cultural dominance. Chactas's blindness betrays the increasing difficulty for the "civilized savage" "[de]cherch[er] sa route" 'to find his own way' (146 [Regard]; my trans.) as well as his dependence on René, the European, for remembering and knowing his own past. As René substitutes his own, European past for that of the Indian, we see the European exile's complicity with the spread of French imperialism and the destruction of France's cultural others.

This ambivalent but ultimately destructive relation between France and its others is foregrounded in *Ourika*, where the story is told from the point of view of the exiled woman who has no other, no one to hear her story with a sympathetic and nonjudgmental ear. The confessional frame of *René* is reversed: rather than the Frenchman recounting the reason behind his chosen exile to his colonized others, it is the Senegalese woman telling the story of her imposed exile in France to a Parisian doctor, the voice of French authority whom Ourika fears may find it "déraisonnable" or 'doubt [her] reason' and thus have little sympathy for it (DeJean 5; Fowles 6).

Two opposed ideologies of assimilation are set into play to render Ourika's story at cross-purposes with itself. The beginning of her story reads like support for the policy of assimilation that justified French expansion into Senegal and that, while promoting belief in the superiority of French culture, also claimed that education was all that separated France from its others—savages can be civilized, as we saw with Chactas.

"To speak means . . . above all to assume a culture," Frantz Fanon writes in *Black Skin, White Masks* (17), and in relation to her perfect assumption of the French language and culture, Ourika's race appears only a matter of surface, like the exotic dress she wears. Lacking memory—or even knowledge—of her origins, Ourika's earliest experiences in Mme de B.'s household give her no sense of her difference: "rien ne m'avertissait que ce fût un désavantage" 'There was nothing to warn me that the color of my skin might be a disadvantage' (DeJean 9; Fowles 9). Her upbringing and education make her into the perfect protégée of her mistress, with whom she identifies, as she does with Mme de B.'s grand-son Charles: "Depuis si longtemps il comptait sur moi, que mon amitié était pour lui comme sa vie, . . . il savait bien qu'en me parlant de lui, il me parlait de moi, et que j'étais plus *lui* que lui-même" 'To him, my companionship was like existence itself. . . . He knew very well that when he talked about himself, he talked about me. I was closer to him than he was to himself' (26; 26).

And yet, while Africans and Indians may both be savages in the French imagination, only the latter are permitted to be "noble" (Liebersohn 756–57). Ourika's near-perfect assimilation, her admired elegance and grace may distin-guish her from the more popular European depiction of the Negro as physically deviant, but these qualities also form the basis of what she will painfully come to see as her "blindness" and "error": "sans le savoir, je prenais un grand dédain pour tout ce qui n'était pas ce monde où je passais ma vie" 'without realizing it, I acquired a sharp contempt for everything that didn't belong in that world. *My* world' (DeJean 8; Fowles 8). This disdain will inevitably turn inward as she becomes the abject object of this world.

Here, too, one can see how *Ourika* can be read as both building and cri-tiquing psychoanalytic models of individuation. Oedipalization is said to be the result of the father's "no" that forces the child out of the mirror stage, out of a dyadic relationship with the mother, and into assuming a separate and sexed subjectivity. A similar "no" is pronounced in Duras's story by the marquise, who shows subjectivity as gendered and gender as inflected by race. Her "no," in fact, is to miscegenation, to Ourika's love for Charles (and by extension for her adopted mother), which Ourika is forced to see, like incest, as a crime against "l'ordre de la nature" 'the natural order of things' (13; 14). Ourika's reaction is an instantaneous recognition of the ideological significance of blackness:

> [L]'éclair n'est pas plus prompt: je vis tout; je me vis négresse, dépen-dante, méprisée, sans fortune, sans appui, sans un être de mon espèce à qui unir mon sort, . . . bientôt rejetée d'un monde où je n'étais pas faite pour être admise.   (12)

> Lightning does not strike more swiftly. I comprehended all. I was black. Dependant, despised, without fortune, without resource, without a single other being of my kind to help me through life. . . . I was . . . cast out of a world that could never admit me.   (12–13)

Whereas according to oedipal models, the father's "no" forces his children to take on alternative identities and loved objects, the marquise's words force Ourika to disidentify with the only family and culture she has ever known with-out providing alternative possibilities for identification. The marquise's "no" is the cause of Ourika's melancholia; it forces Ourika to take up the "proper" side on the sexual divide and on the racial divide, even though that leaves her no grounding for constructing her own past or identity.

Duras's protagonist thus illustrates the alienation that takes place through the "epidermalization" of inferiority that Fanon analyzes more than a hundred years later. In *Black Skin, White Masks*, he examines the particular "being for others" that is experienced by the black man who is forced to see himself and his body not only as an object but as a black object: "Mama, see the Negro, I'm frightened" (112). Defined by the white world, his blackness evokes images of savagery or cannibalism or slavery that are utterly foreign to his own experience but that force him to disidentify with blackness. Yet even as he is forced to see with white eyes, and from the point of view of European culture, he can neither be seen nor see himself as white. As Fanon suggests, the situation for the black woman entails a further level of alienation because of the way in which she is immediately associated with illicit sexuality. "It is an honor to be the daughter of a white woman. That proves that one was not 'made in the bushes'" (46n5). The result for the black woman is an all-out attempt at "a kind of lactification," a concerted effort to "whiten the race" (47).

Gender and race thus work together to produce the particular, incurable form of melancholia that is Ourika's. René's sickness leads him to seek out new cultural identifications and so cure himself of the femininity of his melancholia. Ourika, however, is brought to hide her sexuality and her race, deceiving herself, as she admits to her confessor, by putting away all the mirrors in her room and covering all sight of her skin beneath long-sleeved, high-necked clothes; gloves; and a hat with a veil (DeJean 27; Fowles 28). The disdain for other cultures that she had unknowingly learned as a child now turns inward, bringing her to hate herself as the other but also preventing her from finding affinity with other oppressed groups. Attracted by the talk of emancipation, she has the "illusion" that there exist others like her. Hearing of the Saint-Domingue massacres, however, she gains only the "honte d'appartenir à une race de barbares et d'assassins" 'shame of belonging to a race of barbarous murderers' (20; 21).

While Ourika's desire for Charles may be read as the desire for some illusory, preoedipal past, he also represents the future that such a past would make viable and that her blackness denies her—family, future, and a desire that was perceived as wholly "naturel" 'nothing . . . forced' (25; 26). Ourika's desire for and identification with Charles can be explained by what Judith Butler posits as the need to "institute a disidentification with a position that seems too saturated with injury or aggression, one that might, as a consequence, be occupiable only by the loss of viable identity all together" (100). As the only black woman in a world of white aristocrats, Ourika has no viable identity that is not injurious. When Charles becomes engaged to a woman of his society, Ourika is denied the one identity readily open to women—that of wife and mother—and as a black woman she is condemned, indeed rendered criminal, for desiring that identity. Having no outlet for her desire, Ourika, like Amélie and so many French heroines, retreats to a convent, there to preserve her prohibited illusions and thus her melancholia. She pleads, "Laissez-moi aller, Charles, dans le seul lieu où il me soit permis de penser sans cesse à vous" 'Let me go, Charles, to the one place where I may still think of you day and night' (DeJean 45; Fowles 46).

Ourika's terminal illness may be read as the affliction imposed by a social order that denies her a place but perhaps also as a heroic refusal to submit to an order that demeans otherness and denies it a place in the transmission of history. That abjection is enabled through the work of mourning, understood as a healthier relation to loss, although effected through a less open relation to alterity. Ourika is not allowed to overwrite her origins, inscribed as they are on her own body, even though she never actually remembers them.

A reasonable story about pain, Chateaubriand and Duras illustrate, is one that mourns difference by getting rid of it. Such a story René can tell, even in exile, but Ourika cannot. René need never question whether he will be understood or pitied (even Souel's harsh words at the end mask "un cœur compatissant" 'a sympathetic heart' [144; my trans.]). On the contrary, his torment becomes an aesthetic privilege, granting special status to the rock where he sat at sunset and inspiring future writers and artists to imitate his melancholy pose. But Ourika has no one with whom to identify in the universe of the novel, and in my classroom no one wanted to identify with her. Perhaps it was for this reason that Duras did not publish her story for a long time, saying that her writing "liked solitude" (Pailhès 290).

As my experience with Leah showed me, however, Duras's novel also invites company, and we must teach it so that its sympathetic readers do not become alienated. When I teach *Ourika* again, I will ask students to think about what might make stories like Ourika's and Leah's more tellable, what might allow their forms of alienation to become a more secure place from which to fashion a story they can live with and pass on. More important, I will ask how we might learn from Duras's text to hear and read differently so that the aesthetic privilege of insiders' stories and histories will not bring us to silence or discount those like Ourika's. In Ourika's story, students can learn to hear an alternative aesthetics of an embodied reason that connects to difference and heterogeneity, rather than one that represses it.

Ourika and the Reproduction of Social Forms: Duras and Bourdieu

Dorothy Kelly

In my courses on nineteenth-century literature, a major theme that I pursue with students is what Mark Seltzer describes as the discovery "that bodies and persons are things that can be made" (3). In these texts, the authors' explorations of physical and social construction ("physical construction" in the sense of evolutionary theories from transformism to Darwinism) make their representations of identity formation—of gender, race, and class—particularly compelling. Claire de Duras's *Ourika* provides a remarkable case of the representation of social construction, because the author makes visible the mechanisms that define Ourika's place in a system in which gender, race, and class are interrelated.

To understand the ways in which social identity might be constructed, students read Pierre Bourdieu's *Masculine Domination* before reading *Ourika*. *Masculine Domination*, one of Bourdieu's shortest and most accessible but still challenging texts, provides students with a set of tools to help them describe Duras's representations. Bourdieu defines the formation of social identity (gender identity specifically) as a process that structures bodies and minds, a social education that slowly embeds identities through a long process of conditioning. The result is the *habitus*, as Terry Lovell defines it: "ways of doing and being which social subjects acquire during their socialization" (27); here emphasis must be placed on both being (identity) and doing (ways of acting). The socialization that has shaped the self has created dispositions that then provide the subject with an array of possible actions in a given situation.

Duras's tale of a black female child's exceptional upbringing in the aristocracy, a kind of aberrant programming, makes visible Bourdieu's *habitus* as a combination of inculcation, practice, and rules. In fact, Bourdieu and Duras pursue similar strategies in their representations of social construction: Bourdieu uses certain structures of Kabyle culture to inform those of his own society; Duras makes strange the workings of French culture by importing into it a stranger from another place and race. Ourika's training to be a French aristocratic woman grants her a distinguished "disposition" and develops her aristocratic "taste" (words used by both Bourdieu and Duras) through her immersion in elite society, or through "habitude," as Ourika calls it (*habitude* evokes, of course, *habitus*):

> Le bon goût est à l'esprit ce qu'une oreille juste est aux sons. Encore toute enfant, le manque de goût me blessait; je le sentais avant de pouvoir le définir, et l'habitude me l'avait rendu comme nécessaire.   (DeJean 8)

> To possess good taste is like having perfect pitch in music. Even as a small child, bad taste offended me. I could sense it before I could define it, and habit made good taste an essential requirement of my life.   (Fowles 8)

This world is her world; as she says, "Je ne connaissais pas autre chose" 'I knew no other way of life' (8; 8).

That she fits so well into this world, that she has so thoroughly incorporated its principles, makes strange her subsequent exclusion from it and puts into question the basis for that exclusion. Her exclusion in turn makes strange the fact that she was allowed entry into this closed society in the first place. Her race and place of origin make her so different that, in a certain way, she is allowed to be a kind of beloved family pet (as Julien Sorel is later described twice by Stendhal in *Le rouge et le noir*). Thus it is Ourika's strangeness, and her lack of place in France's rigid class structure, that allows her access to upper-class life—it would be hard to imagine that a lower-class white woman would be granted the same opportunity. The conjunction of the ways in which Bourdieu and Duras make social structures seem strange can lead students to an appreciation of the social revelations made by Duras's text, as well as to a way of thinking about what it means to be a man or a woman, black or white, in society.

Two sets of questions can help guide students as they read Duras after having read Bourdieu. The first concerns the role of biological reproduction in the text and the possible relation between it and Bourdieu's ideas about the reproduction of social forms. The second set of questions addresses the technique of making strange: Ourika has mastered the rules of the aristocratic society in which she lives, but she learns rather late what it means to be black and thus that she has a different predetermined role to play. What is the effect of this late *prise de conscience*, and how might Bourdieu give us a way to think about it?

Biological reproduction plays an important role in Bourdieu's analysis because, there, culture becomes disguised as nature, as exemplified in Kabyle society:

> Far from the necessities of biological reproduction determining the symbolic organization of the sexual division of labour and, ultimately, of the whole natural and social order, it is an arbitrary construction of the male and female body, of its uses and functions, especially in biological reproduction, which gives an apparently natural foundation to the andocentric view of the division of sexual labour and the sexual division of labour and so of the whole cosmos. (23)

Teaching Duras through Bourdieu, instructors may find it strategically useful to focus on the role of reproduction to bring out the way this supposedly natural female function is culturally determined. Society denies Ourika a role in sexual reproduction, and this denial constitutes her crisis, which begins during what resembles a coming-of-age party, when she is fifteen. This very odd party functions as a kind of social ritual that Ourika performs. It is a theatrical performance, and she wears African clothing and dances a *comba* from her country; thus she represents her origin as other. This ritual is both physical, which exemplifies Bourdieu's bodily acquisition of culture, and cultural, because she mimes or performs stories and texts that have informed her about her heritage:

"je devais représenter l'Afrique. On consulta les voyageurs, on feuilleta les livres de costumes, on lut des ouvrages savants sur la musique africaine" 'I was to represent Africa. Travelers were asked for advice, books of costumes were ransacked, and learned tomes on African music consulted' (DeJean 10; Fowles 10). Her role is performed also in the sense of J. L. Austin's performative, because it will make visible and real, it will call into being, her identity as an outcast young black woman, an identity she assumes shortly after the ball when she sees just what she is in her society. The marquise's discourse makes clear that Ourika cannot reproduce biologically in her social world: "Qui voudra jamais épouser une négresse?" 'What kind of man would marry a negress?' (13; 13). Thus she learns that she will not be granted a real place in the class in which she was raised. The black mourning cloth donned by her male dance partner performs her status in a symbolic way: she will be denied a white, noble partner, and the mourning associated with the black *crêpe* will now be her grief over her social death.

Ourika's arrival at womanhood and the denial of a role for her to play in sexual reproduction make visible the elements of her subaltern identity:

> [J]e *vis* tout; je me *vis* négresse, dépendante, méprisée, sans fortune, sans appui, sans un être de mon espèce à qui unir mon sort . . . bientôt rejetée d'un monde où je n'étais pas *faite* pour être admise.   (12; my emphasis)

> I comprehended all. I was black. Dependent, despised, without fortune, without resource, without a single other being of my kind to help me through life.   (12; The English translation does not include the verb *to see* nor the suggestion of being "made.")

At the time when she becomes able to reproduce biologically, society denies her a role in biological reproduction and thereby controls the symbolic reproduction of its own social forms, forms that do not allow black, nonnoble women real access to upper-class French society. Biological reproduction reproduces social forms, as Bourdieu says: "to (re)produce the agents is to (re)produce the categories . . . that organize the social world" (44). This symbolic social reproduction can be clarified for students through Bourdieu's book, much of which investigates how social structures continue to be reproduced even when they are visibly prejudiced:

> I have always been astonished by what might be called the *paradox of doxa*—the fact that . . . the established order, with its relations of domination, its rights and prerogatives, privileges and injustices, ultimately perpetuates itself so easily . . . and that the most intolerable conditions of existence can so often be perceived as acceptable and even natural.   (1)

For Bourdieu, two principal means of the reproduction of social forms are the institutions of marriage and the family, which aim to pass along and increase

bolic and real capital of the family in masculine-dominated societies
(......). As he says, "The social order functions as an immense symbolic machine tending to ratify the masculine domination on which it is founded" (9).
No matter how exceptional Ourika is, how well brought up and educated, she
cannot escape the social machine that defines her as a nonaristocratic black
woman—a person with no social or economic capital, nothing to give to any
prospective family.

Before her initiation rite, she lived in a world that was undifferentiated by
sex or class, predominantly a woman's space without race, where her skin and
sex did not exclude her. And it is this nondifference that makes strange the sudden imposition of difference and that makes the difference itself seem to be
arbitrary and symbolic—her skin color (which she describes as "le *signe* de ma
réprobation" 'the brand of shame' [DeJean 15; my emphasis; Fowles 16]) as it
combines with her female sex. The sudden and strange change points out the
arbitrary and unjust nature of her social exclusion: it is not based on her innate
inferiority, because she has perfected her behavior in her social world. Based on
her skin color, it is a belated enforcement of the already existing and arbitrary
social assignment of meaning to skin color and birth.

Duras's emphasis on Ourika's successful learning of culture shows us that
Ourika's identity as a black woman is grounded not in nature but rather in arbitrary cultural definitions that parade as nature. One sentence is particularly
interesting in its use of the word *nature*, a use that should seem strange to
today's students. The marquise says that because Mme de B. has raised Ourika
in aristocratic society, Ourika has "brisé l'ordre de la nature" 'flouted her natural destiny,' yet her subsequent words show that this nature is really a social
construction:

> [La philosophie] ne peut rien contre les maux qui viennent d'avoir brisé
> l'ordre de la nature. Ourika n'a pas rempli sa destinée: elle s'est placée
> dans la société sans sa permission; la société se vengera.   (13)

> Reason may help people overcome bad luck. But it's powerless against
> evils that arise from deliberately upsetting the natural order of things.
> Ourika has flouted her natural destiny. She has entered society without its
> permission. It will have its revenge.   (14)

Duras's representations are revolutionary in that they anticipate Bourdieu's call
for a "dismantling [of] the processes responsible for this transformation of history into nature, of cultural arbitrariness into the *natural*" (2). Duras's revelation of the arbitrariness of social definitions that claim to be based in nature
ultimately reveals the workings of the social machine.

Here students can reflect on the ways in which the role of sight in the text
becomes a symbolic act of revelation. Through the process of making strange,
so that Ourika and the reader move away from blindness to see Ourika's place

in society, Duras makes us see how social power works. Indeed, Ourika sees the disdain on other people's faces (she is shown her place in the social world, determined by social law) as her own face (the arbitrary place of skin color where social law is grounded): "J'étais poursuivie, plusieurs jours de suite, par le souvenir de cette physionomie dédaigneuse; je la voyais en rêve, je la voyais à chaque instant; elle se plaçait devant moi comme ma propre image" 'For days on end I was haunted by its sneering face. I saw it in my dreams, in every waking moment. It stood before me like my own reflection' (DeJean 28; Fowles 29). Once Ourika is able to see her skin color, she sees her place in the social order. Her former "illusions" (14; 14) about being an integral part of her society enable us to see that society's supposedly natural laws are themselves illusions.

After looking at this function and result of Ourika's vexed social education, at the role of nature in the text, and at the rites and rights of reproduction, one can then ask students to think about Bourdieu's idea of the symbolic violence of culture, visible in the real physical and emotional suffering of Ourika. Since she has been created by the culture in which she continues to live, Ourika cannot choose to free herself from it, and, in a sense, she does not even consider the possibility that things could change (except for a short time, during the French Revolution). She cannot see being a real part of anything outside it; for instance, she could not return to Africa. She does not reject her society; rather, she mourns the fact that she is not able to be included in it. She sees herself as subaltern, she understands and accepts her situation, and this perception is extremely painful to her.

Ourika expresses the violence of her feelings when she realizes that Charles will marry another, an aristocratic white woman, and that she herself will be forever alone, forever excluded from that happiness: "Cette affreuse pensée me saisit avec plus de violence qu'elle n'avait encore fait" 'This terrible thought gripped me with more violence than ever before' (32; 33). And when she realizes that she loves Charles, the voice of conscience inside her, the voice formed by her society, tells her that her love is criminal: "Et cependant, je ne sais quelle voix crie au fond de moi-même, qu'on a raison, et que je suis criminelle" 'But all through this, a mysterious voice cried deep in my heart: [the marquise] is right, I am guilty' (42; 43). Bourdieu calls this effect symbolic violence, the helpless, painful, seemingly necessary submission to domination. To escape her fate, Ourika needs a successful revolution, a transformation of the society in which she lives.

If in the text Ourika's subordination is made visible to her, Charles is strangely blind to Ourika's situation. He even says to Ourika at one point that he wants to be able to share as much with his wife as he is able to share with her, unaware that this might be painful to her (30; 31). Ourika later notices how easy it is for him to accept the excuses she makes to hide her problems (34; 35). His blindness to her untenable position is understandable because for him it has always been that way: there is no revelation for him, it is just everyday life. Charles's attitude seems to figure what Bourdieu describes as the unconscious nature of domination itself (37). She is a black woman, and her place in society is not a surprise to him in any way: that is her place. His privileged place in the world does not need to be justified; as Bourdieu shows, the androcentric vision is neutral, invisible, and all of the physical and social order is organized in accordance with it (9, 24). In the light of Charles's identity as white male aristocrat, it is interesting that Bourdieu says that masculinity is like a kind of nobility (60).

Finally, one should look at the role of the French Revolution in the text. At one point, it did offer to Ourika the possibility of a transformation of her society, when "des hommes distingués" 'clever men' put everything into question (DeJean 18; Fowles 19). Yet as soon as the revolution begins to threaten the "intérêts intimes de chacun" 'the private interests of the individual' (19; 20)—what Bourdieu might call the individual's symbolic, social, and material capital—it becomes a battle, and once it is over, the same social order remains in place. It is after the revolution that Charles marries and reproduces; his son will carry on the family line and, symbolically, the social order. The important final question for students and teachers is just what kind of revolution might be able to dismantle these unjust and tenacious social structures of domination that continue to exist today.

Ourika's *Mal*

Mireille Rosello

The Doctor's Story

Ourika is the story of a doctor who tells the story of a young nun who has told him her story. Ourika's narration is meant to help the physician find a cure for her: she is a patient whose symptoms are difficult to interpret. Yet, despite his efforts and patience, he cannot save Ourika. She dies shortly after finishing her tale of woe. The doctor's account is not as clearly goal oriented, and therefore its failure or success is difficult to assess. We are not sure what the point of his story is: does he seek to express regret at the patient's death? confess his own failure? state a truth? denounce a social phenomenon? Nor do we know exactly to whom he tells the story. What is immediately obvious, however, is the overwhelming number of references to illness and *mal*. How are we expected to read the doctor's account?

Let us pay attention to the different meanings of the word *mal* in French, which can refer to illness but also to pain and even evil. Let us explore the hypothesis that the doctor functions not as a medical professional but as the conveyor of a story and that Ourika is not sick but relegated to a position where the only way for her story to survive is to pretend that she is.

The only approach that we, as readers, have to the cloistered nun is through the doctor's story. The word *approach*, with its geographical implications, suggests that the frame orients us toward a certain entry point into an imaginary universe. The presence of doctor and patient, of disease and death, opens up a universe dominated by health and malady, cures and antidotes, and forces us to concentrate on such issues. In other words, the space of the story we will read is infused from the start with meaning, value, and semantic substance.

Margaret Waller suggests that "*Ourika* is one of the earliest examples of the pathologizing of emotion of literature" (Introduction xv). If we remain aware of *Ourika*'s narrative structure, however, we may wish to keep in mind the difference between a story about pathologies and the pathologizing of the story. If our approach pathologizes, we may wish to ask ourselves what latitude is left to the subject that we have not yet reached but merely approached. Indeed, emotions are not the only elements that are pathologized and criminalized in this text. Students may notice that we have not yet mentioned Ourika's race, an omission that should alert us that something in our language, worldview, or narrative grammar is disposed either to disregard or to conceal actively what would otherwise be an obvious factor and the reason the heroine is ostracized.

The doctor (whose medical training will not be the most relevant part of his identity) will have to understand something about the past that a form of violence has rendered incomprehensible yet deadly. He will have to become both a student and a historian, the equivalent of Jacques Rancière's "ignorant schoolmaster," who was a well-known contemporary of Claire de Duras. Exiled from France to Louvain, in a land whose language he did not speak, he could no longer talk to or understand his students. As a result, he could no longer teach. All he could do was "émanciper" 'emancipate' his students by showing them how to learn and, more important, by freeing them from him (14; my trans.).

Ourika's story owes its survival to a doctor who, like the ignorant schoolmaster, renounces his professional expertise. Unknowingly perhaps, he reinvents his profession and his function. First, he approaches his patient from a new and unknown perspective. Even before reaching her, he acknowledges his ignorance: "Je n'avais jamais vu l'intérieur d'un couvent; ce spectacle était tout nouveau pour moi" 'I had never before seen the inside of a convent, and it was therefore an entirely new experience for me' (DeJean 3; Fowles 3).

Second, he lets race enter his story: "je fus étrangement surpris en apercevant une négresse" 'I had a strange shock. I was looking at a negress' (4; 4). He sees Ourika for who she is even before he talks to her. Before being introduced to his patient, the doctor recognizes that she is no abstraction: he sees a black body and acknowledges that he was not prepared for such an encounter. He does not hide his surprise from himself or from the reader. For Ourika, the revelation of her blackness was more than a shock: it was a profound trauma for which she was completely unprepared, since everyone had carefully avoided the subject in her presence. She eventually tells the doctor how the consequences of her skin color were bluntly revealed to her. Unseen behind a lacquer screen, she overheard Mme de B. and the marquise talk about her (11; 11). At this moment Ourika discovers that she has no social existence, at least not as a subject or as an interlocutor. She has in fact never existed as an autonomous human being. Seeing herself through racist eyes is a brutal point of no return; she can never go from knowledge back to innocence. Suddenly, she loses the ability to talk about what matters most. This process of identification or social formation is not gradual; she is literally dumbstruck: "l'éclair n'est pas plus prompt" 'Lightning does not strike more swiftly' (12; 12). In a single stroke, Ourika is estranged from the company of human beings in whom she could confide. Alone, she can talk only to herself ("à chaque instant je me répétais, seule! pour toujours seule!" 'Again and again I repeated that phrase: alone, always alone'), until the late arrival of the special interlocutor who is able to frame her story without silencing her (14; 15).

The Doctor's Diagnosis

The young doctor from Montpellier who tells Ourika's story is not the first doctor to be consulted; immediately after Ourika's traumatic discovery of her isolation, Mme de B. had sent for Doctor Barthez (14; 15). It is worth comparing the two physicians. The young doctor from Montpellier approaches both Ourika

and the past as a humble, ignorant person who must first learn. And his pre-
ferred way of learning is to listen to Ourika, to her language and to her stories.
As he nears Ourika in the convent garden, he comments that the path is made
up of tombstones that literally pave the way toward her. The dead are helping
him find his way through this unknown territory. He also notices that whatever
was written on the stones is no longer legible. And yet, having observed that the
past is in ruins and undecipherable, he will still suggest that the only way for his
patient to get better is to cure the past (4; 5). For him to help her to do so, he
explains, "je ne puis le guérir sans le connaître" 'I must know it first' (4; 5).

In other words, it is the past that is sick, not the patient, and he is the first
to notice it. Yet, as Ourika's tale unfolds, we discover that Ourika has always
used the word *sick* to a cover up for something else, something that she cannot even name. It is a sort of *mal* that she is convinced is incurable; its main
symptom is that she cannot describe its symptoms. She is now aware that she is
a black woman, but this recognition is no secret. There is nothing to reveal that
is not already plainly in view; in her case, knowing involves no agency and no
power, no possibility even of talking about the reality of racism. Duras depicts a
character who instantly internalizes all the prejudices of class, sex, and race but
does not have a language to describe the wrong that she suffers.

The Doctor's Examination

Ourika can articulate neither her grievances nor her desire. She neither accepts
the unacceptable nor imagines a space where resistance could be formulated.
One reason no remedy is appropriate is that Ourika is not ill. Instead, she treats
her life-altering discovery (and its sickening social consequences) as something
that she must hide so that the motif of illness appears immediately, as a way to
cover up the open secret: "je dis que j'étais malade; on le crut" 'I said I didn't
feel well. I was taken at my word' (14; 15).

Yet the first doctor Mme de B. sends for is not taken in by the lie that protects
the system. "Mme de B. envoya chercher Barthez, qui m'examina avec soin, me
tâta le pouls, et dit brusquement que je n'avais rien" 'Mme de B. sent for Doctor
Barthez, who examined me carefully and took my pulse, and then announced
curtly that I was fit as a fiddle' (14; 15). Barthez interprets only Ourika's body.
He does not talk to her, he does not listen to her. He speaks only when he has the
result of an examination that entails no questions and that requires no follow-
up. According to Ourika, that first and last encounter has no effect. She receives
no treatment, and, perhaps more important, she is not even identified as a patient (etymologically, someone who suffers).

The text, however, does not dismiss Barthez as incompetent, despite his curt
bedside manner. It is important that his failure to help Ourika not be considered an isolated incident. The novel questions the entire medical profession and
the decision to involve a doctor at all. Barthez is chosen by Mme de B., whose

recommendation, from within the text, suggests that he represents the best of what medical science can offer, at that time, to the community of aristocrats. And yet nothing happens. The narrator knows that she is and is not "fit as a fiddle" but also knows why she chooses to pretend to need a doctor.

The body that can be examined, observed, is fit. For contemporary readers, *fitness* evokes recreational sports and health. For slaves, *fit* meant capable of hard labor. Frantz Fanon maintains that people who had been physically and mentally brutalized by colonization could not hope to be "rescued" by doctors who were members of the colonial regime. In the light of this observation, Barthez's approach appears highly problematic: how could he not be the guardian of the "natural" hierarchy between races? Is his examination of Ourika's body different from the practice of plantation owners who checked muscles and teeth to ascertain a slave's health and strength? Nevertheless, Barthez does tell a truth that no one wants to hear. If we look at the French original, we may note the ambiguity of the diagnosis and the silent irony that sneaks into Ourika's repetition of his words: "je n'avais rien," she says (14), which means both "there was nothing wrong with me" and "I had nothing, I owned nothing, nothing belonged to me."

The Patient's Suffering

Ourika is not sick, but she is suffering from what I propose to call an anomalous subjectivity. Even when she thinks of herself as a human being, the text warns us that she is more like a curiosity: "Mme de B. . . . donna un bal dont ses petits-fils furent le prétexte, mais dont le veritable motif était de me montrer fort à mon avantage" 'Mme de B . . . gave a ball—ostensibly for her grandsons, but really to display me, much to my advantage' (10; 10). Ourika seems unaware of the tensions she reveals. Mme de B. puts on a show whose object is her toy, her pet. In French, the etymological connection between the words *montrer* ("to show") and *monstre* ("monster") is still audible. Ourika is *montrée*—that is, displayed, exhibited; the only difference between a circus animal or a Hottentot Venus and Ourika is that Ourika says "I," which should make her position of enunciation unrealistic. Her anomaly is that she speaks like a subject although she is treated as a nonsubject.

Indeed, the very first lines of Ourika's framed story show both her awareness as subject and her passivity as object: "Je fus rapportée du Sénégal" 'I was brought here from Senegal'; M. de B. "m'acheta" 'bought me' and "me donna à Mme la maréchale de B., sa tante" 'gave me to his aunt, Mme la Maréchale de B.' (7; 7). Of course it would be absurd to criticize M. de B. for having saved Ourika from the Middle Passage, but the novel shows us that he has done so by acting like a capricious god whose power over an anomalous half-toy, half-human creature is absolute. Ourika, an educated woman, knows full well that she is, and has always been, a toy that is cherished but that can never be free.

She has been given a life that allows her to imagine what could have been had she been treated as a human being. She knows that no matter what she says, thinks, or does, she has never moved of her own accord.

The Doctor's Role

It is only death that liberates Ourika from her anomalous subjectivity; it allows her to fall, not from grace, but like an "autumn lea[f]": the doctor closes her story with an epitaph that returns Ourika to the "nature" that she has supposedly betrayed. Her now motionless body is no longer the prisoner of racist myths. Death, paradoxically, sets her in metaphorical motion: "elle tomba avec les dernières feuilles d'automne"—a nuance that does not appear in John Fowles's translation: 'She died at the end of October, with the last of the autumn leaves' (45; 47).

Her death is witnessed by someone who can speak and be heard: the ignorant doctor. Critics have pointed out that the presence of the white doctor risks disempowering Ourika. Nathaniel Wing says:

> One cannot fail to observe . . . that the male narrator indirectly repeats the displacement of the black and the woman that takes place in the main narrative. The woman's voice does not "speak for itself" directly, but is repeated by a male representative of patriarchal order.   (84)

Yet this doctor is really less a doctor than a translator who is patient and painstaking and who puts himself in Ourika's place (the convent). It is because he comes back several times, because he becomes a friend, that Ourika finally talks to him. He does not save her. As a doctor, he is not successful. But as someone who listens to Ourika's voice, he is finally able to construct her as something other than a passive toy. We may describe his activity as a form of literal sympathy: unable to save her, he now suffers with her and becomes a conduit for her tale instead of the provider of a cure. His framed narrative protects Ourika from being dismissed as an anomalous subject, an object that produces only noise and that cannot feel pain.

The Meaning of Mal

The secret that no one ever wants to talk about is not Ourika's skin color but the fact that she was taught a language and a universalistic worldview that preclude thinking of oneself as both same and different. A black subject does not exist. Neither Ourika nor the doctor nor Duras seems capable of writing into the story a fate or destiny that would accept that a slave is a human being who can liberate him- or herself. No narrative voice imagines that freedom could be claimed rather than granted.

The twenty-first-century student has listened to other stories and may remember other rebellious characters, such as Toussaint Louverture or Solitude, from André Schwarz-Bart and Simone Schwarz-Bart's *La mulâtresse Solitude*. But to be a rebel, one has to be able to say "I" in ways that remain beyond Mme de B.'s comprehension. As a result, Ourika never becomes a social agent; she remains a distressed bundle of emotions and thoughts, forced to forever mourn her inability to become a subject. Ourika teaches the doctor that, as an acknowledged subject whose words are heard, he alone is in the position to articulate the fact that she has been wronged and that she is not sick. Ourika was tormented to death by what she is finally able to call "cette société cruelle qui me rendait responsable du mal qu'elle seule m'avait fait" 'this merciless society that declared me guilty of a crime it alone had committed' (DeJean 28; Fowles 28–29). At this point, we may finally be able to understand the other meaning of the word *mal*: Ourika clearly means "harm" and not "disease." Ourika has the doctor tell us that if one is forced constantly to put blackness under erasure, then "I am black" is the opposite of "I am."

The Literary Frames of *Ourika*, Then and Now

Adrianna M. Paliyenko

A poignant narrative that elaborated on the true story of a Senegalese girl and her encounter with colonialism in late-eighteenth-century France, *Ourika* was an overwhelming success in the 1820s. However profound the chord struck by what John Fowles calls the "first serious attempt by a white novelist to enter a black mind" (Foreword xxx), Claire de Duras's novel did not regain the popularity it first enjoyed until the late twentieth century. Now widely circulated and studied, *Ourika* has become a privileged point of entry into the colonial past for students in programs advancing the integration of French and francophone studies at various levels of the curriculum. *Ourika* powerfully engages French colonial history and invokes the Romantic chapter of literary history. To approach the story with the aim of understanding the cultural forces operative in the world in which Ourika ultimately finds no room to maneuver requires a "historically enlightened reading" (Kadish, "Cultural Diversity" 155). The narrative of fatal exile re-created by Duras also invokes a transnational tradition of Romanticism and thus passes on the universally resonant theme of solitude with the singular accent of a black woman isolated in a white man's world.

How can we guide students to read *Ourika* in context while enabling them to hear Ourika speaking to them about a world of prejudice and its discontents still very much alive? To situate Duras's novel in the historical frame of Romanticism we take our literary cue from Duras and consider the implications of her text's opening with an epigraph from the English poet Lord George Gordon Byron. This point of departure enables us to glean meaning from lessons in literary history that overlap with Duras's literary engagement with history in *Ourika*.

In this essay, I consider the curricular integration of *Ourika* at a small liberal arts college: in an intermediate course designed to instruct students in the art

of critical analysis and in two upper-level courses, one focused on cultural legacies of nineteenth-century France and another treating the nineteenth-century epidemic of passionate discontent.[1] In both intermediate and upper-level
courses, *Ourika* reveals the traditions of literary and social Romanticism and the
history that produced them, while capturing for a new generation of readers the
public life of prejudice and its psychological impact. To feel "étrangère à la race
humaine tout entière" 'cut off from the entire human race' as Ourika did (De-
Jean 15; Fowles 16) is to be alone in a world that defines differences spawned
by class, race, or gender as signs of inferiority, instead of accepting these differences as part of humankind's rich cultural heritage.

The Literary Frame of Romanticism

"This is to be alone, this, this is solitude!" This epigraph, from the second canto
of Byron's *Childe Harold's Pilgrimage*, figures prominently in English on the
title page of the original 1823 edition of *Ourika*, just below the one-word title in
capital letters (Scheler 12). In an age of "Byronomania" (Cardwell 4), one can
imagine that the elite among whom the novel initially circulated readily placed
the excerpt in its literary context. Students today—whose visual literacy may
surpass their literary competence—need to discover anew what openings Duras
created for the reception of *Ourika* by choosing a transnational intertext. The
connections to be drawn between Byron and Duras form the basis of a fundamental lesson in literary history: the influence of the Byronic hero on French
Romanticism. To promote collaborative learning and directed use of the Inter-
net among students who study *Ourika* from various perspectives, I assign the
task of placing the excerpt from Byron in context.

A Google search for the exact phrase produces not the stanzas from *Childe
Harold's Pilgrimage* but a poetic text entitled "Solitude." Directed next to locate
the precise source of the text from Byron, students discover no poem by that
title. The initial reference to "solitude," however, is the lead students follow
as they peruse the general index of Byron's *Complete Poetical Works*. This research yields the principal Romantic theme of solitude in society and the text in
its literary context, canto 2 of *Childe Harold's Pilgrimage*, stanzas 25 and 26:

> To sit on rocks, to muse o'er flood and fell,
> To slowly trace the forest's shady scene,
> Where things that own not man's dominion dwell,
> And mortal foot hath ne'er or rarely been;
> To climb the trackless mountain all unseen,
> With the wild flock that never needs a fold;
> Alone o'er steeps and foaming falls to lean;
> This is not solitude, 'tis but to hold
> Converse with Nature's charms, and view her stores unroll'd.

But midst the crowd, the hum, the shock of men,
To hear, to see, to feel and to possess,
And roam alone, the world's tir'd denizen,
With none who bless us, none whom we can bless;
Minions of splendour shrinking from distress!
None that, with kindred consciousness endued,
If we were not, would seem to smile the less
Of all the flatter'd, follow'd, sought and sued;
This is to be alone; this, this is solitude!   (52)

The different paths students take to discover the text in context provide the means for generating a lively discussion about research methods in upper-level French studies classes. In my intermediate class, where students learn what questions to ask of various types of texts, both printed and visual, the detective work they conduct to locate Byron's text prepares their understanding of the master narrative of Romanticism in which Duras inserted her own framed narrative, or story within a story. What key thematic strand is pulled into play in *Ourika* from the epigraph that harks back to the musings of the brooding Byronic hero who wanders the earth in isolation? Put another way, how does Byron express what is and what is not solitude? The answer to this question, students discover, requires a close reading of the two stanzas to comprehend poetic spins on unfamiliar words and to reconstruct Byron's thought.

The kernel phrase "This is not solitude" and its mirror opposite, "this is solitude" are essential points from which to read the text against the grain. This strategy allows students to recognize how the thematic movement from stanza 25 to 26 pivots on a binary opposition constructed between nature and society. Undergraduate students unfamiliar with the term *pathetic fallacy* at the core of Romanticism may not appreciate fully the speaker's sense of personal connection with a sentient nature and estrangement from an indifferent society ("But midst the crowd . . . / . . . / With none who bless us, none whom we can bless"). This brief treatment of Byron's text reveals the social provenance of the alienation experienced by Duras's Romantic heroine but not the historical context that determined Ourika's particular sense of solitude: "Qu'importait au monde qu'Ourika vécût? Pourquoi était-elle condamnée à la vie? C'était donc pour vivre seule, toujours seule! jamais aimée!" 'What did the world care whether I lived? Why was I condemned to exist? Unless it was to live alone, always alone, and never loved' (DeJean 32; Fowles 33).

Byron: Duras's Mirror or Foil?

That the Anglophile Duras chose to foreground Byron is not altogether surprising, especially given her admiration of the English poet recorded in epistolary exchanges (see Duras's letters to Rosalie de Constant reproduced in Pailhès 456, 466). It is possible that the feeling of banishment voiced by Byron's hero, whether self-imposed or imposed by an external force, mirrored the isolation from society that Duras felt as a young girl living in political exile in London from 1793 to 1808. Like other members of the French aristocracy, she and her mother sought refuge from the Terror, during which her father perished. It is useful to specify the circumstances surrounding Duras's period of exile and thus begin to frame the historical backdrop of her novel for students without, however, advocating literary biographism as an approach to reading *Ourika*. The historically grounded predicament on which Duras invites readers to reflect in *Ourika* clearly goes beyond her life story.

The epigraph raises other questions about how to situate Duras's novel in literary history. Separated from the text, this paratext relates *Ourika* to Romanticism but not exclusively to the French literary tradition. The ambiguous positioning obviates comparisons of Duras's heroine to François-René Chateaubriand's and Benjamin Constant's Romantic heroes. Yet pairing *Ourika* with *René* (1802) or *Adolphe* (1816) to examine different creative expressions of passionate discontent (as I do in one advanced course) or with Prosper Mérimée's "Tamango" to develop literary aspects of the French colonial archive (as I do in another) allows students to address questions about the literary traditions to which *Ourika* belongs. Is the eponymous heroine Ourika thoroughly Romantic in the canonical sense of the term? Does she suffer from the "vague des passions" 'waves of sentiment and passion' that Alfred de Musset later identified as "la maladie du siècle" 'sickness of our entire age' (78; my trans.)? If not, what is the source of her melancholy? What difference does her race make? Duras's selection of Byron is not only clever as a literary choice but also astute when considered in colonial context. By placing her narrative in a transnational Romantic tradition of literary activism, Duras could also subtly suggest the dynamism of British abolitionism (in contrast to French apathy) at the time.

Historicizing the Frame of Romanticism in Ourika

> Croiriez-vous que, jeune comme j'étais, étrangère à tous les intérêts de la société, nourrissant à part ma plaie secrète, la Révolution apporta un changement dans mes idées. . . . J'entrevis donc que, dans ce grand désordre, je pourrais trouver ma place; que toutes les fortunes renversées, tous les rangs confondus, tous les préjugés évanouis, amèneraient peut-être un état de choses où je serais moins étrangère.   (DeJean 18–19)

> Young as I was, ignorant of the intrinsic selfishness of society, nursing my secret wound in silence . . . you won't find it hard to believe that the Revolution brought a change in my views of life. . . . I sensed that at the end of this great chaos I might find my true place. When personal destiny was turned upside down, all social caste overthrown, all prejudices had disappeared, a state of affairs might one day come to pass where I would feel myself less exiled.   (Fowles 19; first ellipsis in orig.)

To the literary framework drawn from Byron, Duras adds a historical border—the aftermath of the French Revolution—that complicates the meaning of Ourika's retrospective account of her life in Paris during the revolutionary period. Her personal drama intensifies during the radical persecution of the aristocracy known as the Terror (1793–95). Though composed from 1821 to 1822, during the restoration, *Ourika* also reaches back to the colonial echo of the revolution, since the European example inspired a similar struggle for freedom from oppression in the French colonies. Students studying Duras's novel from the literary perspective set forth by Byron need to ponder the significance of the postrevolutionary setting for the doctor's frame narrative.

To address the implications of the cultural moment evoked in Duras's Romantic narrative, students must familiarize themselves with the political extremes of the long French Revolution (1789–99). I direct students to a Web site that offers a detailed timeline of the revolutionary period (Mannière). We reconstruct in class the principal lines along which Ourika's revelation of her past progresses, including the specific dates that punctuate her narrative (20 June 1792, 10 Aug. 1792, 1793, 1794, 1795). Students then juxtapose references to measures taken by colonial authorities to delimit slaves' freedom with Ourika's dream that from such disorder would spring a new social order that would erase color prejudice.

This sociohistorical framework seems to create a point of identification between the white aristocratic author and her black heroine, both displaced by power struggles and political shifts beyond their control. The question, as Nathaniel Wing reminds us, is, What type of reading does one perform by equating gender and race? A shift to the colonial arena along the axis of "[l]es massacres de Saint-Domingue" '[t]he Santo Domingo massacres' complicates how Ourika may function as a mirror to Duras (DeJean 20; Fowles 21). Both the "Black Terror"—the massacre of whites during the initial slave revolt in Saint-Domingue (modern-day Haiti) in 1791—and the "White Terror" haunted the minds of those who lived well after Duras's Romantic generation. But of whom is Duras speaking when she borrows the voice of Ourika to revile "une race de barbares et d'assassins" 'a race of barbarous murderers' (20; 21)? Does Duras filter this colonial memory through Ourika's European-educated mind to expose the racial thought of her time? Or, bearing in mind the cause of abolition that began to regain ground in the 1820s, is Duras attempting to reveal "the psychological effect of white racism on a black person" (O'Connell 52)?

This doubling in the character of Ourika, which positions her between races, is not only the expression of her inner experience of racism. As my former student Jacqueline D. Mourot says, *Ourika* is also a literary reflection of the ever-present colonial past that still determines how we understand ourselves as members of the human race:

> What struck me about this text was Ourika's fatal reaction to her blackness and all of the interdictions that being black entailed. It pained me

that she avoided mirrors and covered her arms not to bear witness to the color of her own skin. I remember empathizing with her to a certain degree, in that I was a black female at a majority white college and dreamt of accomplishing and seeing many things. Yet a part of me questioned whether these desires would be denied me at some point just because of my skin color. I was angry for her, with her, at the unfairness of society. Yet I longed for her to accept herself as she was and to show those around her the error of their ways.

To converse with Ourika is not only to hear the heart's desire of her Romantic cousin Byron, who longed for a place in society, but also to confront the pathos of social oppression that even now binds the entire human race.

NOTE

[1] Syllabi and resources for these courses discussed here may be found at the following Web sites: http://www.colby.edu/personal/a/ampaliye/FR252/index.html; http://www.colby.edu/personal/a/ampaliye/FR356/index.html; http://www.colby.edu/personal/a/ampaliye/FR358/index.html.

Ourika as an Inversion of the Pygmalion Myth

Damon DiMauro

Given Claire de Duras's lucid and well-crafted prose and given the inherently compelling nature of questions of identity, I find I can introduce *Ourika* to foreign language readers by the end of a second-semester intermediate course. Students are also usually prepared to engage the text as a reversal of the Pygmalion story, at least in some rudimentary way. They might have firsthand knowledge of the Ovidian fable, or they might have had exposure to one of its latter-day avatars, such as *My Fair Lady*. Advanced students, however, are perhaps better equipped to profit from the rich collateral information necessary for a truly rewarding investigation of the subject. For to teach *Ourika* as an inversion of the Pygmalionist enterprise is to undertake an excursus into late-eighteenth-century art, literature, and philosophy.

It is no small advantage that the eponymous heroine herself, at the opening of her narrative, draws attention to the figure of Galatea, thus authorizing this particular pedagogical approach:

> Me sauver de l'esclavage, me choisir pour bienfaitrice Mme de B., c'était me donner deux fois la vie: je fus ingrate envers la Providence en n'étant point heureuse. . . . et la fable ne nous dit pas si Galatée trouva le bonheur après avoir reçu la vie. (DeJean 7)

> Rescued from slavery, placed under the protection of Mme de B.—it was as if my life had been twice saved. I have shown ingratitude to Providence by being so unhappy since. . . . The myth doesn't say whether Galatea was given happiness as well as life. (Fowles 7)

Like Pygmalion's adored statue whom Venus brings to life, as related by Ovid in the *Metamorphoses*, so Ourika characterizes her improbable change of personal circumstances as being granted life anew. Still, Ourika tellingly remarks that Ovid's account fails to mention whether the sculptor and his animated creation did live happily ever after. It is this subtle note of contrast that sets the stage for the present *via negativa* exploration of the Ovidian analogy.

A contrastive line of inquiry can first be approached with students by recourse to simple etymology. Ourika, set apart in society by the pigment of her skin, is the absolute antitype of Galatea, who is traditionally associated with the purest white. Indeed, according to Ovid, Pygmalion carves his maiden of surpassing beauty out of "snowy ivory" (83). In the original fable, however, the statue remains nameless; the ascription of "Galatea" to Pygmalion's animated statue is a later, eighteenth-century addition (Reinhold). The name signifies "milk-white" in Greek (from *gala* ["milk"]). When Ourika later decries her fate, namely that she will be utterly bereft of family ties—"moi qui jamais ne devais être la sœur, la femme, la mère de personne" 'I was never to be a sister, a wife, a mother myself' (DeJean 17; Fowles 17–18)—etymology plays a double role, since "Galatea" connotes not only whiteness but lactation or motherhood as well.

The fable of Pygmalion and his statue turned flesh was often used in Enlightenment France as a powerful metaphor for human creativity; it also served as a symbol of latent eroticism. Artistic representations were legion. Among the painters who tried their hand at the subject were Jean Raoux, François Lemoyne, François Boucher, Louis Lagrenée, Jean-Baptiste Deshays, Laurent Pécheux, Jean-Honoré Fragonard, Jean-Baptiste Regnault, and Anne-Louis Girodet. The marble composition by the sculptor Étienne Maurice Falconet, *Pygmalion aux pieds de sa statue qui s'anime* (1763), deserves special mention, since Denis Diderot praised it highly (*Salons* 245). On the musical front, more than a dozen operas and ballets were created between 1700 and 1800 (Coulet, "Présentations" 10–11). Jean-Philippe Rameau's *Pygmalion*, composed in 1748, had an enduring success, with some two hundred performances at the Opéra and at court. In the domain of letters, François-Thomas de Baculard d'Arnaud's *Liebman* and Nicolas-Edme Rétif de la Bretonne's *Le nouveau Pygmalion* took a more ominous, if not deviant, turn. In *Liebman*, the protagonist raises a girl from infancy in total isolation in the hopes of becoming a second Pygmalion to whom his creation will owe her entire existence. In *Le nouveau Pygmalion*, the main character adopts a young orphan, has her raised by a surrogate, but later falls in love with and weds his ward.

The device of quickening marble also enjoyed popularity among the philosophes. In their effort to combat religious creationism, they espoused instead naturalist theories concerning the transmutability of matter and the concept of the sense-soul. By way of analogy, the figure of Galatea was particularly appealing to them, since, as an adult born tabula rasa, she could be used to verbalize how external stimuli were received and the senses successively awakened. The Pygmalionist influence appears notably in Étienne Bonnet de Condillac's *Traité des sensations* and in Diderot's *Entretien* with Jean d'Alembert. There is, however, perhaps no finer example of Enlightenment "sensationalism" than André-François Deslandes's philosophic tale, *Pygmalion, ou la statue animée*, in which the main character muses about the relation between mind and matter while sculpting an effigy of Venus. Before his eyes, the statue gradually becomes a living soul, acquiring first the power of movement, then thought, then speech.

While Duras would certainly have been aware of the Pygmalion myth's rich eighteenth-century heritage, I have established elsewhere that two works in particular informed her *Ourika* (190–91). These are Jean-Jacques Rousseau's *Pygmalion*, literature's first melodrama, and Stéphanie Félicité de Genlis's *Pygmalion et Galatée, ou la statue animée depuis vingt-quatre heures*, a play conceived as a sequel to Rousseau's *scène lyrique*. While Rousseau's rewriting of the fable centers on the sculptor and his emotions, Genlis's focuses on the statue's perceptions after being released from her marmoreal state. Thus Ourika's initial question about Galatea's happiness after coming to life is precisely the dimension Genlis endeavors to examine in her drama.

As a pedagogical aside, and depending on the skill level and major of the students, I suggest that individual or group presentations be assigned on Enlightenment renditions of the Pygmalion myth. The object is to prepare students to observe how Duras, in portraying Ourika as a Galatea in reverse, will play off these previous representations. Art students might present contemporary painting; musicians could introduce a period opera or ballet; philosophy students might give an oral presentation on Condillac or Diderot; literature students could treat Rétif's novella, Rousseau's melodrama, or Genlis's play. The groundwork must be laid for earlier reworkings of Ovid's tale, since there are some key moments in *Ourika* that the instructor will want to highlight.

Ourika begins her story by relating the circumstances that brought her to France, almost as an object of mercantile exchange. Though Ourika's account confirms her initial reified state, her adoption is reckoned a kind of rebirth—hence the reference to Galatea. In the household of her benefactress, Ourika's existence takes form:

> Mes plus anciens souvenirs ne me retracent que le salon de Mme de B.; j'y passais ma vie, aimée d'elle, caressée, gâtée par tous ses amis, accablée de présents, vantée, exaltée comme l'enfant le plus spirituel et le plus aimable. (DeJean 7)

> My first memories are of Mme de B.'s drawing room. I spent my life there, loved by her, fondled, spoiled by all her friends, loaded with presents, praised, held up as the most clever and endearing of children.
> (Fowles 7)

The word "salon," which John Fowles renders as "drawing room," has obvious artistic connotations. There is something in the rhythm of the original passage as well, with its heavy punctuation compounded by the number of consonantal stops and acute accents, that suggests a sculptor's chisel. This imitative device is not without parallel to musical renditions of the time in which repeated notes were used to represent the chippings of Pygmalion's chisel (DiMauro 193).

Moreover, in a manner reminiscent of Enlightenment treatises in which the statue's sentience and cognition are progressively awakened, Ourika here comes to life, assimilating the ideals and values of the urbane and refined society grouped around Mme de B. During these formative years, Ourika lives in an almost osmotic relationship with her adoptive mother, who, in turn, takes pains to provide Ourika a first-rate education, complete with voice, painting, and language lessons. Ourika is cast in the very mold of her benefactress, modeled in every respect upon the image of a French noblewoman.

The crowning moment in Ourika's young existence comes when Mme de B. hosts a ball to show off her adoptive daughter's talent and "grâce" 'natural grace' (DeJean 10; Fowles 10). In the dance of the four continents, Ourika represents Africa. Her partner must wear "un crêpe sur son visage" 'a mask of black crepe' to play his part (10; 10)—a disguise that Ourika does not need. As a black Galatea, she thus appears fully unveiled, like a finished work of art, put on public display. Similarly, the unveiling of the statue just before its animation figures prominently in period adaptations of Ovid's myth, such as Rousseau's melodrama (103–04). In addition, Ourika now reveals herself to be completely alive. She discovers that she is instinctively capable of expressing a wide range of human emotions. The analogy here with Rameau's opera-ballet is compelling; for, at its close, the Graces complete Love's transformation by guiding the Statue in the various figures of the dance. A chain of increasingly dynamic dances ensues and is meant to evoke the Statue coming to life (44–57).

But an overheard conversation between Mme de B. and the marquise soon dissipates Ourika's illusions and plunges her into a downward spiral of anguish and despair. Ourika learns she is unmarriageable and has no place in society. If in the canonical Pygmalion myth, Venus takes pity on the infatuated sculptor and brings his creation to life, the marquise has the opposite effect. As society's self-appointed mouthpiece, she becomes an agent of death. The marquise will appear again at the denouement of the novel as the *dea ex machina* to deal the final blow to Ourika's fragile psyche. But now, in a moment of searing lucidity, the eponymous heroine perceives her true condition and objectified state:

> [J]e vis tout; je me vis négresse, dépendante, méprisée, sans fortune, sans appui, sans un être de mon espèce à qui unir mon sort, jusqu'ici un jouet, un amusement pour ma bienfaitrice, bientôt rejetée d'un monde où je n'étais pas faite pour être admise.　　　　　　(DeJean 12)

> I comprehended all. I was black. Dependent, despised, without fortune, without resource, without a single other being of my kind to help me through life. All I had been until then was a toy, an amusement for my mistress; and soon I was to be cast out of a world that could never admit me.　　　　　　(Fowles 12–13)

Ourika's newfound self-consciousness has its counterpart in eighteenth-century representations of Galatea, but from the opposite standpoint; in them a sudden awakening to life and emerging selfhood is portrayed. Nearly every painter of the theme chose to capture that precise instant when the marvel occurs, when the statue becomes flesh and descends from her pedestal. Lyric and prose adaptations also centered on this moment.

According to the marquise, Ourika has somehow violated "l'ordre de la nature" 'the natural order of things' (13; 14) by not accepting her station in life: "elle s'est placée dans la société sans sa permission; la société se vengera" 'She has entered society without its permission. It will have its revenge' (13; 14). It is as if this black Galatea has dared to step off her plinth. Henceforth, it will be the views and attitudes of a prejudiced and class-bound society that mold Ourika in its image, forcing her back onto her pedestal; in other words, her role in the world will be severely circumscribed by the forces of race, class, and gender. Her narrowly defined place is ultimately symbolized by her seeking refuge in a convent, where the frame narrator first finds her alone on a bench, in the innermost recesses of this secluded retreat. And Ourika is also transformed within by society's sneering gaze. As she comes to see herself through the distorted lens of bigotry, she can no longer bear to look upon her body, compulsively covering and veiling herself. In the end, when she dons a nun's habit and thereby remains perpetually covered, Ourika appears much like a veiled statue. In stark contrast, nearly every pictorial representation of Galatea in European art features her scantily clad or nude.

The psychological disintegration that Ourika undergoes after being confronted with her *négritude* can be retraced step by step. In a reversal of the Enlightenment philosophic tales that used the artifice of giving sensation to stone to study emerging life, Duras's novel systematically analyzes what transpires in the psyche of a victim of injustice and oppression. Society's rejection has a definite physical effect on Ourika, too. In contrast to the mythological Galatea, who is brought to life, Ourika loses her vitality as her acute mental distress renders her melancholic and listless, leading to actual illness and death. It is as if this black Galatea is forced not only to remount her pedestal but to revert to stone as well. Indeed, the cloister where she eventually takes refuge is an austere and lifeless place. The doctor takes due note of the petrified surroundings: "Une religieuse m'introduisit dans ce cloître, que nous traversâmes en marchant sur de longues pierres plates, qui formaient le pavé de ces galeries: je m'aperçus que c'étaient des tombes" 'It was to these cloisters that I was conducted by a sister. I noticed, as we went through them, that the long flagstones with which they were paved were in fact tombstones' (3; 3).

Charles plays a particular role in Ourika's plight. Like her benefactress, Charles is a Pygmalion figure, to the extent that Ourika initially perceives him as life-giving. But Charles does not reciprocate her feelings. When he meets the wealthy and well-born Anaïs de Thémines, he decides to marry this mirror image of himself. His conception of love, in which the ideal partner is the reflected image of the self, owes something to the legacy of the Pygmalion myth. Moreover, Charles's desire for his soul to be transposed into his bride-to-be recalls period treatments of the theme, most notably Rousseau's *scène lyrique* (110):

> Quelque-fois je crois sentir que mon âme tout entière va passer dans la sienne. . . . [Q]uand elle rougit, je voudrais me prosterner à ses pieds pour l'adorer. . . . Que je la rendrai heureuse! Je serai pour elle le père, la mère qu'elle a perdus: mais je serai aussi son mari, son amant! Elle me donnera

son premier amour; tout son cœur s'épanchera dans le mien; nous vivrons
de la même vie.   (DeJean 31–32)

Sometimes it's as if my whole being enters hers. . . . If anything makes her
blush, I want to fall at her feet and adore her. . . . I want to be everything
that makes her happy. The father and mother she lost. But I'll be her
husband too, her lover. I'm the very first man she's ever been in love with,
she'll pour her feelings into mine, we shall be one life.   (Fowles 32)

Even Charles's eagerness to worship at blushing Anaïs's feet is an oblique reference to Pygmalion, for in nearly every visual representation of the myth, the
sculptor is depicted in rapt adoration at the foot of the stone figure the moment
the miracle occurs. And, just as in traditional accounts the newly animated statue
is completely dependent on Pygmalion, who, as her maker, is father, mother,
spouse, and lover all rolled into one, so too does Charles want to be the center
of Anaïs's universe. It is at this point in the narration that Ourika, confronted
with the image of Charles's unbounded happiness as well as her own unbearable
sense of loss, experiences a crisis from which she will not recover.

To ascertain the larger significance of Ourika's inverse metamorphosis, we
return to Genlis's *Pygmalion et Galatée*, where the author emphasizes the reactions of the woman, rather than those of the sculptor, after she has been freed
from her marmoreal domain. In Pygmalion's absence, Eurinome, a former slave,
methodically introduces Galatée to the woes of the human condition—pain,
danger, pride, greed, injustice, inequality, hypocrisy, ambition, war, hate. When
Pygmalion finally returns, Galatée informs him that she now understands the
harsh realities of the temporal order and will never again know pure happiness.
Genlis's drama is didactic and religious: despite the evils associated with earthly
existence, there still remains hope for an afterlife. Since Galatée's soul is immor-
tal, she belongs ultimately to God. Happiness is to be found not in the embrace
of her lover but in returning to her true maker.

In a similar fashion, the archetypal pattern found in *Ourika* of innocence
overturned by the revelation of a hostile world, which results in grief, withdrawal, and death, goes back to the fall from Eden. Ourika's plight represents
that of fallen humanity in an unjust and imperfect world. Although she happens to be the victim of racism, which, with its heritage of slavery, stands as the
most pernicious of social ills, her particular suffering encompasses all forms of
isolation, ostracism, and oppression. The message of Duras's text does seem
to contain a strong otherworldly strain. And Ourika's final turning to God has
been carefully prepared in the text. She states on one occasion, "j'essayai de me
vaincre, de trouver en moi-même une force pour combattre les sentiments qui
m'agitaient; mais je ne la cherchais point, cette force, où elle était" 'I tried to
conquer myself, to find some strength inside me to combat these feelings that
tore me apart. But I didn't look for this strength where it truly resides' (36; 37).
The strength of which Ourika speaks is found in a higher power: "je ne sais quel

mouvement me portait vers Dieu, et me donnait le besoin de me jeter dans ses bras et d'y chercher le repos" 'Some instinct drove me toward God. I felt the need to throw myself into His arms and find peace there' (43; 44). In hearing her prayer, the Christian God, whom she has now significantly begun to call her "Créateur" (38; Fowles's translation does not refer to a creator [39]), proves to be the true life giver and her sustaining force. At last Ourika does find rest for her soul. The notion has its roots in a famous phrase from Augustine's *Confessions*: "You [God] have made us for yourself, and our heart is restless until it rests in you" (3).

Duras and Hugo: An Intertextual Dialogue

Kathryn M. Grossman

One fruitful approach to teaching Claire de Duras's *Ourika* (1823; composed in 1821–22) is to place the novel in its literary context while emphasizing its particular originality. Scholars agree that Duras's work responds to François-René de Chateaubriand's version of *le mal du siècle* in *René* (1802). But it also reframes the first version of *Bug-Jargal* (1820), Victor Hugo's tragic tale about slavery, friendship, and revolution, composed when the author was sixteen and published two years later in *Le conservateur littéraire*, the literary journal founded by Hugo and his two older brothers, Abel and Eugène. A comparison of the two novels enhances students' ability to grasp the issues that inform Duras's text and the techniques used to develop them: first-person and embedded narratives, the themes of exile and race relations, psychological realism, and social and political commentary, including reflections on both slavery and *la condition de la femme*. Hugo's subsequent revisions to his novel following the independence of Haiti in 1825 may likewise constitute a reflection of and on Duras's best seller. This dialogue illuminates the complex literary debate surrounding *Ourika*—one rooted in some of the most critical sociopolitical issues of the day.

Narrative Strategies

From Antoine-François Prévost's *Manon Lescaut* (1731) through *René* to *Ourika*, first-person narratives helped ensure the premier status of the French psychological novel. Des Grieux's tale of devotion to, and suffering for, the unfaithful Manon enables the reader to accept his "unmanly" passivity and rich emotional life. René's lyrical diction and yearning for the infinite make his blind egotism easier to bear, to the point that, rather than condemn him for his uselessness, as Chateaubriand had intended, an entire generation ended up identifying with him. And Duras's use of the first person helps her white bourgeois reader see the world both vividly and unexpectedly through the eyes of the marginalized black female protagonist. By "catching" and then modifying René's *mal du siècle* (see Bertrand-Jennings, "Condition" 41; Waller, *Male Malady* 19), Ourika also enlightens the reader about far more concrete—and widespread—forms of existential dislocation than that of her literary predecessor.

At the same time, the composition of *Ourika* within two years of the appearance of Hugo's *Bug-Jargal* suggests that *René* may not be the only nineteenth-century intertext. Purportedly aspiring at fourteen to be "Chateaubriand ou rien," the young Hugo concocted a first-person story set in far-off Saint-Domingue (later Haiti) during the slave rebellion of 1791. Hugo's embrace of the historical novel, following Sir Walter Scott's invention of the genre in the 1810s, finds its echo in Duras's reflections on the same era in France. Although

neither text luxuriates in local color or historical detail, both display the historical self-consciousness that characterizes Scott's work. Hugo's melancholy narrator, Delmar, a captain in the revolutionary army, recounts to the other soldiers
gathered under his tent the tragic tale of his youth in the colonies—a scene
mirrored in Ourika's woeful disclosures to her doctor regarding her life as a
displaced Senegalese raised in France. Delmar's "sombre désespoir" 'gloomy
despair' (378; 246)[1] adumbrates Ourika's "long et violent chagrin" 'prolonged
and acute melancholia' (DeJean 4; Fowles 4), since each evokes the paradise
lost of youthful innocence and precious relationships. In reliving the progressive disintegration of both protagonists' emotional and sociopolitical worlds, the
reader is able to empathize with their uncommon sense of internal and external
catastrophe.

While students often recognize this classic narrative strategy on their own, they
are less frequently aware that Ourika's and Delmar's tales use additional framing devices. Indeed, students are sometimes surprised when I ask them, "Who
is telling the story?" As with *Manon Lescaut* and *René*, I point out, *Ourika* constitutes an embedded narrative—in this case a medical doctor's story about his
encounter with a dying nun (3–6, 33, 45; 3–6, 33–34, 47). The technique is present in *Bug-Jargal* as well, first through the presence of the soldier Thadée, who
testifies to the veracity of Delmar's recollections, and second through Delmar's
subsequent account of the slave Bug-Jargal's revelations about his kingship
(371; 237–38).

Rather than simply encourage students to appreciate the elegance and complexity of the framing structure, however, I challenge them to reflect on the
ramifications of having one person relay another's story. As feminist critics have
noted (see, e.g., Massardier-Kenney 192), the voice of the white male doctor in
Ourika covers the black female protagonist's, potentially rendering her voice
as invisible as her suffering in a society dominated by his analogues. Here, the
embedded tale can be deemed at least somewhat suspect (see Booth 149–65).
Similarly, Hugo's benighted narrator appears less than reliable when we consider his inability to decipher the many clues to his friend Pierrot/Bug-Jargal's
true identity offered by the text—clues abundantly apparent to the reader.
(Delmar's entourage twice encourages him to tell them the story of "Bug-Jargal,
autrement dit Pierrot" 'Bug-Jargal, otherwise known as Pierrot' [355; 220].) We
view the sublime outlaw Bug-Jargal only secondarily, through his unenlight-
ened, conventional white friend allied with the slave-owning powers that be.
Bug-Jargal's situation in the text is much like that of Ourika, who speaks to us
through a representative of the society that oppresses her not only as a person of
color but also as a woman in postrevolutionary France (see Bertrand-Jennings,
"Condition" 40–42).

For students who have read *René*, the restrained style of both *Bug-Jargal*
and *Ourika*—published some twenty years later—may come as a surprise. It
is important to remind them that the 1820s marked a transitional period in
the evolution of French aesthetics. With the triumph of the nascent Romantic

movement far from assured (after all, the neoclassicists continued to dominate the Académie Française into the 1840s), it is entirely understandable that writers such as Hugo (b. 1802) and Duras (b. 1777) would adhere to traditional artistic principles, if not share similar artistic tastes. In this way, the young ultraconservative Hugo, raised by a royalist mother, could belong in 1820 to the same literary generation as the aristocratic Duras. By the time *Ourika* appeared three years later, Hugo had gone over to the gothic side with his first full-length novel, *Han d'Islande*.

Race Relations

The correspondences between *Ourika* and *Bug-Jargal* are evident not only in the novels' narrative style and technique but also in their content. The exploration of race relations—an issue only tangential to *René* (though not to its sister text, *Atala* [1801])—plays a major role in both works. The nephew of a slave owner, Delmar is directly implicated in the social ills associated with such dealings. Whereas his uncle's "long habitude de despotisme absolu [lui] avait endurci le cœur" 'heart had been hardened by a longstanding habit of absolute despotism' (356; 221), he and his cousins had tried to relieve in secret "des maux que nous ne pouvions prévenir" 'the ill-usage we could not prevent' (356; 221). This open-minded attitude leads him to befriend one of the slaves, "[un] homme singulier connu . . . sous le nom de Pierrot" '[a] remarkable man . . . known . . . by the name of Pierrot' (356; 222), who prevents Delmar's uncle from murdering another laborer on his plantation. But if the colonial master seems cruel, the slave uprising in August 1791 shows that evil is not the realm of one race alone. Having set fire to the plantations where they worked, "[les rebelles] y laissèrent en partant des traces de leur cruauté; tous les blancs furent massacrés ou mutilés de la manière la plus barbare" '[the rebels] left many a trace of their cruelty: all the whites were massacred or mutilated in the most barbarous manner' (361; 227). Amid the carnage, Pierrot stands out for saving the uncle's family, thereby signaling yet again his *différence*. Yet anger and prejudice prevent Delmar from seeing in the man who ceaselessly calls him *frère* the magnanimous rebel chief, Bug-Jargal, who repays the torture of his father (an African king), the prostitution of his wife, and his own enslavement not with vengeance but with mercy. The young man fails at every turn to grasp the big picture, to glimpse in the other his moral superior, and so to ensure the survival of his own savior.

Rescued as a toddler from slavery and raised in a loving white household in Paris, Ourika has lived an experience that at first might seem the antithesis of Bug-Jargal's. But, just as Delmar displays a decided lack of foresight and imagination regarding his friend, Ourika's adopted mother, Mme de B., fully educates Ourika without making any provisions for her future. When Ourika overhears the marquise ask Mme de B., "que deviendra-t-elle? et enfin qu'en ferez-vous?" 'But what next? . . . what do you intend doing with her?' (DeJean 12; Fowles

12), she realizes that her happy childhood is leading nowhere. "Pour la rendre heureuse, il eût fallu en faire une personne commune; je crois sincèrement que cela était impossible" 'To have made her happy I'd have had to try to turn her into a common servant. I sincerely believe that could never have been done' (13; 13), Mme de B. declares. Perhaps Ourika will be able to rise above the singularity of her situation because of her natural superiority. But the marquise replies, "Ourika n'a pas rempli sa destinée: elle s'est placée dans la société sans sa permission; la société se vengera. . . . [J]e désire son bonheur, et vous la perdez" 'Ourika has flouted her natural destiny. She has entered society without its permission. It will have its revenge. . . . I want her happiness, and you are destroying it' (13; 14). Because her achievements result from nurture rather than nature, Ourika will never find an appropriate place in society or a companion who is her equal. In a white-dominated world, her race works against her as surely as it does against Hugo's exceptional black protagonist.

As with Bug-Jargal, Ourika's sense of self is further complicated by the aftermath of the French Revolution. Bug-Jargal must associate with infernal colleagues like Biassou in the slave revolt of 1791; Ourika, finding potential "semblables" 'others like myself' in the blacks affected by the abolitionist movement (20; 21), is soon disabused:

> Les massacres de Saint-Domingue me causèrent une douleur nouvelle et déchirante: jusqu'ici je m'étais affligée d'appartenir à une race proscrite; maintenant j'avais honte d'appartenir à une race de barbares et d'assassins.   (20)

> The Santo Domingo massacres gave me cause for fresh and heartrending sadness. Till then I had regretted belonging to a race of outcasts. Now I had the shame of belonging to a race of barbarous murderers.   (21)

The echoes of *Bug-Jargal* in *Ourika* are nowhere more evident than in this recollection in Duras's text of the violent attacks on the colonialists and their families witnessed by Delmar. In both instances, the failure of white liberal ideals contaminates the notion of confraternity for the black characters as well.

Paradise Lost

Ourika's grief is thus compounded by multiple losses as she is ejected from the pleasures of childhood into a dead-end adulthood: her mother dies (from unspecified causes) when she is an infant; she is torn from her African village at two and transported to a faraway land; the marquise's conversation with Mme de B. precipitates "la perte de ce prestige qui m'avait environnée jusqu'alors" '[the] loss of the till-then-unshaken sense of my own worth' (14; 14), along with the loss of her hopes for the future; she is bitterly disappointed not only by the "fausse philanthropie" 'false notion of fraternity' (19; 20) of the white revolutionaries but also by the savagery of members of her own race; and her emotionally intimate bond with Charles, Mme de B.'s grandson, is broken when he marries another woman. She feels exiled from her country, her family, her race, and even herself, "étrangère à tout" 'ostracized [from everything]' (16; 17). Her psychological horizons are severely limited, not just because she retains no memories of her previous life in Senegal but because she lacks hope for what is to come.

At one point, a false nostalgia for the life as a slave she escaped overcomes Ourika, and she regrets that she was not allowed to fulfill her destiny:

> Eh bien! je serais la négresse esclave de quelque riche colon; . . . mais j'aurais mon humble cabane pour me retirer le soir; j'aurais un compagnon de ma vie, et des enfants de ma couleur, qui m'appelleraient: Ma mère! (38)

> What did it matter that I might now have been the black slave of some rich planter? . . . But I would have a poor hut of my own to go to at day's end; a partner in my life, children of my own race who would call me their mother. (39)

The delusional nature of her wish—to which Bug-Jargal's tale of horror serves as an excellent corrective—suggests that she risks becoming *aliénée* ("mentally disturbed") in her alienation.

The climactic crisis occurs immediately thereafter, when the marquise declares that all Ourika's suffering ensues from a doomed love for Charles. Accepting for the first time her own possible complicity, if not culpability, in her misery, the protagonist embraces a final form of exile by entering a convent. Though students may view this step as yet another sad episode in her life, Ourika clearly indicates otherwise. Her quest for a sense of belonging is wholly satisfied by her belief that "tous les cœurs sont égaux" 'All hearts are equal' in the eyes of God (43; 45), who has given her "l'humanité toute entière" 'all mankind' as a family (44; 45). The nun is sister, mother, and daughter to all who need her, a person both useful and, she repeats, happy. In the end, hers is a tale of paradise found.

When asked, students are nearly unanimous in finding Ourika's melancholia to be better justified than René's. They also see the parallels between her self-imposed exile in the convent and that of René's sister, Amélie. In *Bug-Jargal*, on the other hand, it is not the eponymous hero but his white counterpart who is depressed, again for reasons that students consider well founded. Delmar's idyllic island paradise is consumed by flames; his misreading of Bug-Jargal's actions indirectly causes the death of his friend, an extraordinary hero; and he ends up, in a form of exile, campaigning with the revolutionary army in nations far from his Caribbean home. In some ways, his trajectory anticipates Ourika's, in that he leaves his native country (in this case, France) at an early age and bonds in his new home with a "brother" of another race—and, like Ourika, Delmar experiences the breaking of this bond as a personal catastrophe.

But what of Bug-Jargal? He, too, loses his happy homeland, as well as his wife and father; he is "vendu à différents maîtres comme une pièce de bétail" 'sold to different masters as one sells a head of cattle' (371; 238); and the last of his children die in Saint-Domingue at the hands of whites. Fueled by righteous anger, he does not fall into self-pity or despondency or vengefulness. Instead, he seems to follow a finely tuned moral compass that requires him to do whatever he can to help others—even "enemies" like Delmar's uncle. Remarkable self-assurance seems to follow him everywhere, even in prison or on his way to certain death.

In some ways, then, we might say that Ourika reworks traits of both Hugolian heroes, beginning her tale as Delmar's analogue and finishing it as Bug-Jargal's. Her evolution from passive, uncomprehending victim to active "sœur de la charité" 'nun' (44; 45; literally, "sister of charity") combines aspects of the two characters in a highly original manner. Beyond depicting Ourika as someone who, like Bug-Jargal, learns to transcend her situation, Duras re-creates Hugo's famous *mélange des genres* through the literary "miscegenation" of imbuing a physically black woman with a culturally white psyche. Hugo plays his two protagonists off each other to achieve a dramatic effect; Duras places the struggle within her protagonist. The psychological realism of Delmar, who experiences a series of awakenings in his perception of Pierrot/Bug-Jargal, also infuses Ourika's character as she deals with revelations regarding her race, her love for Charles, and her religious vocation. The psychological irrealism of Bug-Jargal passes into her ability, despite her many afflictions, to die happy. Hugo's Romantic doppelgänger achieves stunning unity in Duras's more neoclassical rendition.

In conclusion, let us remember that intertextual resonances work two ways. That Duras's novel went into multiple printings in 1824 could hardly have escaped the notice of the former literary critic of *Le conservateur littéraire*. Literary rivalry for Hugo suddenly extended beyond Chateaubriand to embrace a new, more contemporary, figure. The expansion of *Bug-Jargal* in 1825 (published in 1826) to roughly three times its original length enabled Hugo, among other concerns (see Grossman 59–110; Bongie), to improve on aspects of his work better addressed by Duras's. Thus the exquisite satire of self-serving revolutionary rhetoric in *Ourika* is echoed in *Bug-Jargal* in repeating scenes of colonial and insurgent hypocrisy alike. The critique of false confraternity in both writers enhances the portrayal in each of what constitutes genuine human affinity.

By the same token, Duras's devastating indictment of *la condition de la femme* in postrevolutionary France—an issue virtually absent from the first *Bug-Jargal*—might help account for the role of Marie in the second version. The fiancée of the white protagonist, rechristened Léopold d'Auverney, is not just the passive screen on which Delmar/d'Auverney and Bug-Jargal inscribe their desires; she also reflects the situation of all women of the age whose fate depends on male perceptions and decisions. (One might add that the second *Bug-Jargal* closes the narrative, as in *Ourika*, through further embedding, while the overall aesthetic of the novel changes to incorporate far more romantic local color.) The many echoes between the second *Bug-Jargal* and *Les misérables* (1862) suggest that the question of women's status continues to haunt Hugo for many years to come—and that he comes fully to grips with the problem only in limning the characters of Fantine and the young Cosette, each a "slave" in her own right. From this perspective, *Ourika* appears as an important intertext not only of *René* and of the two iterations of *Bug-Jargal* but also of Hugo's later masterwork. In evoking the anguish of women, both black and white, in postrevolutionary France, Duras awakens and attunes the reader to the more politically powerful voices that will one day be raised on their behalf.

NOTE

[1] This and all subsequent quotations from *Bug-Jargal* are from Jean Massin's edition and Chris Bongie's translation.

Exile according to Ourika and Julia

Dawn Fulton

The field of francophone studies tended initially to restrict itself to the purview of literature produced outside hexagonal France in the second half of the twentieth century. As the recent rise in interest in literature of migration, particularly in *"beur"* literature and film, has dissolved some of these spatial boundaries, the expansion of disciplinary consideration to works produced before 1950 has proved to be equally worthwhile, especially as a pedagogical strategy for encouraging comparative reflection. The theoretical work emerging from francophone studies not only allows us to assess French texts from the Renaissance or the Romantic period as foundational to postcolonial works in French but also brings attention to some of the thematic and ideological resonances between colonial French writings and recent literature that would otherwise be overlooked.

In the classroom, a pairing of texts from colonial and postcolonial periods can offer an effective introduction to the concerns and approaches of francophone studies while encouraging students to think historically about the corpus. Reading Claire de Duras's *Ourika* in conjunction with a late-twentieth-century francophone novel such as Gisèle Pineau's *L'exil selon Julia* permits discussion of key topics of francophone studies like exile, cultural assimilation, and national identity. Such a pairing might be integrated into a course organized around one of these themes, a general introductory French and francophone literature course, or a course framed by the question of *le regard de l'autre*, treating canonical examples of exoticism in French literature along with colonial or postcolonial reversals of this gaze.

Ourika is an early example of a reversal that exploits the culturally unfamiliar subject to critique French society. While *Ourika* offers this exterior vision as imagined by a European writer, *L'exil selon Julia* offers the perspective of a writer who is a cultural and racial outsider in metropolitan France. Pineau was born in Paris in 1956 to parents from the French Overseas Department of Guadeloupe and later spent twenty years living and working in Guadeloupe before returning in 2000 to Paris. Her numerous books for children, adolescents, and adults examine in various modes the relationship between France and its former colonies in the Antilles. In the autobiographically inflected *L'exil selon Julia*, Pineau explores the cold welcome received by a Guadeloupean family living in postwar Paris. The eponymous Julia is the young narrator's grandmother, reluctantly displaced from her native Guadeloupe to the unfamiliar *métropole* late in life. The novel's tale of exile, then, is anchored to this juxtaposition of Caribbean grandmother and French metropolis, and it is Julia who supplies the culturally external view of French society.

By hinging the comparison of Duras's and Pineau's novels on each author's use of the external gaze, the class can focus on three topics: the idealized vision of the French nation presented in each text, the consequent subversion of this

image, and the related appraisal of the link between education and colonial ideology. As a first step, students can research the image of France as a morally and
culturally superior territory; they can explore, for example, the concept of the
mission civilisatrice ("civilizing mission") that undergirded the French colonial
enterprise and the political and psychological ramifications of departmentaliza-
tion in 1946 in the Caribbean. From there, students can consider how France is
conceived in *Ourika* as a protective space where a Senegalese child can be saved
from slavery: "Me sauver de l'esclavage, me choisir pour bienfaitrice Mme de
B., c'était me donner deux fois la vie" 'Rescued from slavery, placed under the
protection of Mme de B.—it was as if my life had been twice saved' (DeJean 7;
Fowles 7), Ourika declares. Similarly, in *L'exil selon Julia*, the narrator's father,
Maréchal, impulsively forces his mother to join the family in Paris in the belief
that he is rescuing her from an abusive marriage: this is "sa dernière chance de
sauver sa manman" 'one last chance to save his Manman' (*L'exil* 22; *Exile* 9).
The religious overtones of this "saving mission" echo those of *Ourika*; indeed,
the chapter announcing Julia's arrival in France is entitled "Deliverance," and the
young narrator and her family members see themselves as "ses sauveurs" 'her
saviors' (39; 18).

The self-image generated by this particular vision of the French nation is
in each text a critical aspect of the dynamic between savior and saved. Asking
students to consider the passing reference Ourika makes in the novel's opening lines to the Pygmalion myth (DeJean 7; Fowles 7) can generate a critical
evaluation of the relationship between Mme de B. and her exiled protégée. Students might examine instances in which the paternalism that underwrites M. de
B.'s rescue of Ourika from slavery also infuses the education of this avid young
student, particularly in the dance scene where Mme de B. resolves to display
her brilliant creation for all Parisian aristocracy to see. Here, still blissfully ignorant of her fate, Ourika revels in this culminating moment in her education
(10; 10–11). As Ourika's description astutely points out, the audience's desire
to please Mme de B. with an enthusiastic response reveals the extent to which
Ourika's "success" stands first and foremost as an indication of her mistress's
talent and benevolence.

In a striking parallel to the image of Galatea, Pineau's Julia appears in sculpted
form, the product of her son's unconscious fantasies of heroism. In the dream
that incites Maréchal to take Man Ya, as the family calls her, with him to France,
he superimposes himself onto a national narrative of salvation:

> Le général de Gaulle lui est apparu étreignant une Marianne de pierre
> soustraite à la malédiction de Hitler. . . . Enchaînée, bâillonnée, meurt-
> rie, humiliée, Man Ya est une Marianne aussi, ou plutôt une idole afri-
> caine—parce que noire et taillée dans un bois d'ébène comme il en a vu
> au Sénégal.   (*L'exil* 41)

> General de Gaulle has appeared to him, clasping a stone Marianne, sym-
> bol of the French Republic, rescued from Hitler's curse. . . . Chained,

gagged, beaten, humiliated, Man Ya is a Marianne too, or rather an African statuette—because she is black and carved in an ebony wood like wood he saw in Senegal.   (*Exile* 19)

Like Ourika, Julia is a passive object crafted by the imagination of her savior, a creation that reinforces the heroic self-image produced by association with the French nation's claim on moral and cultural superiority. The images of Julia and Ourika as sculpted manifestations of successful "civilizing missions" serve to strengthen their saviors' inscription into a national narrative of heroism.

The moral division between France and its colonies on which this self-appointed heroism depends, however, proves in both novels to be a false one. Rather than the promised land of salvation, France for Ourika is a land of exile and bitter disappointment, ultimately more painful to bear than the life of slavery that she was supposedly spared (DeJean 38; Fowles 39). Similarly, in Paris Julia thinks of nothing but her native Guadeloupe, despite the violence that awaits her there, and she becomes increasingly ill and depressed the longer she is separated from her home. What further betrays the false dichotomy between French civilization and colonial barbarity is the physical confinement to which both women are subjected in the *métropole*. Ourika's and Julia's experiences in France are almost entirely restricted to the domestic sphere, a testament to the tenuous nature of the protection offered by the French territory.

A critical moment in each novel underscores the dubiousness of this salvation, since it is through a disruption of the carefully guarded interior space that each woman gains crucial insight into her place in French society. For Ourika, this disruption comes in the form of the infamous marquise, whose callous assessment of Ourika's condition discloses a plain reality from which Mme de B. and her family had carefully shielded their protégée (11–14; 11–15). In Pineau's novel, the defining moment is an unplanned departure from the space of the home when, protecting herself from a sudden rain with her son's military coat, Julia attempts to find her grandchildren at their school and attracts a small crowd. As in *Ourika*, the encounter is a clear and unequivocal indication of society's rejection:

> Le village entier nous dévisage. Des yeux en quantité, effarés. Pourquoi les gendarmes? A cause du képi de l'armée, du manteau militaire? Pourquoi ces visages graves, ces grands airs offusqués? Man Ya n'a pas voulu outrager la France, seulement barrer la pluie. Elle n'a pas vu le mal qu'il y avait à marcher en manteau militaire dans les rues d'Aubigné.
> (*L'exil* 98)

> The whole village is staring at us. Lots of eyes, alarmed. Why the police? Because of the army cap, the military overcoat? Why these solemn faces, these grand outraged airs? Man Ya did not intend to insult France, only to keep off the rain. She did not see what wrong there was in walking through the streets of Aubigné in a military overcoat.   (*Exile* 51)

More than wearing a French military coat, of course, Julia's "crime" is the racial otherness that is compounded by her inability to speak French, prompting the police to seek explanations elsewhere: "Nous n'entendons pas son langage. Si vous parlez le français, LE FRAN-ÇAIS!, dites-nous comment il se fait qu'elle soit en possession de ce manteau et de ce képi de l'armée française?" 'We do not understand her language. If you speak French, FRENCH!, tell us how she comes to be in possession of this overcoat and this kepi belonging to the French army?' (99; 51). Despite her French nationality, the juxtaposition of Julia's black skin with the military uniform produces an image as incoherent in the postwar *banlieue* as the genteel, educated black woman does in prerevolutionary Paris. This incoherence and the rejection that necessarily follows reveal that the image of France as an idealized space of salvation can be maintained only in a strictly delimited domestic sphere.

Yet one important point of divergence between the two novels is the fate of the exiled heroine. Despite the solace Ourika claims to have found in the alternative isolation of the convent, the incoherence of her existence as a Senegalese woman living as a French aristocrat torments her to her death. Julia, however, finally returns to her native Guadeloupe at the novel's close and enacts a triumphant reunion with her homeland. To parse this distinction with students, instructors can introduce a discussion—or a sequence of discussions—on cultural assimilation. Returning to the Pygmalionesque underpinnings of the relationship between Ourika and Mme de B., students can focus on the pedagogical strategies used by Ourika's benefactor in the creation of her African Galatea. Particularly when viewed through Ourika's eyes, the education offered by Mme de B. provides a clear path toward assimilation (DeJean 9; Fowles 9). Ourika also reveals the melding of education and imitation, since her profound admiration for her benefactress blurs the line between instructor and instruction: "[E]n la voyant, en l'écoutant, on croyait lui ressembler" 'Watching her, listening to her, people began to feel they resembled her' (8; 8). The rescued slave will thus successfully complete her education by becoming her benefactress, by becoming a member of the French aristocracy. Ourika's tragic end, of course, is a result of the fact that this transformation produces a monster, a socially impossible being.

Pineau's Julia exhibits none of Ourika's propensity for imitation. Instead, her interaction with the *métropole* is marked by a nearly complete refusal of its cultural meaning, a persistent comparison to her home that exposes everything her current landscape lacks. In opposition to her grandchildren, whose education in the French school system represents a painful encounter with metropolitan racism, Julia stubbornly refuses to practice her French, and the written language the children attempt to teach her in turn meets a formidable impasse: "[É]criture et lecture ne trouvent pas une place où se suspendre en elle" '[R]eading and writing find no place to attach themselves to in her' (*L'exil* 133; *Exile* 69). Julia would like to reward the children's efforts, but her lifelong suspicion of written documents and her acquisition of survival strategies in the absence of formal education are unyielding: "Il est trop tard, je suis trop vieille. Les lettres ne veulent pas se faire connaître" 'It is already too late, children. I am already too old. The letters don't want to let themselves be known' (133; 69).

It is this recalcitrance that enables Julia to retain a crucial connection to the language, chronology, and natural landscape of her home, her physical displacement notwithstanding. On her return, after a six-year period of exile, humiliation, and hostility, Man Ya regains her humanity and her rightful role as the educator of her grandchildren, deciphering the Caribbean landscape for their unaccustomed eyes:

> Elle nous montra les feuilles et fleurs, nous les nomma. Pour notre apprentissage, elle ouvrit la terre de ses mains et planta des graines, enfouit des jeunes tiges. Nous étions à son école. Et les petites lettres si faciles qu'elle ne savait écrire, l'alphabet infernal, lui demandèrent pardon pour l'avoir tant de fois criée grande couillonne, imbécile, illettrée.　　(305)

> She showed us leaves and flowers and told us their names. To teach us, she made holes in the earth with her own hands and planted seeds, buried young stalks. We were at her school. And the little letters, so easy, that she could not write, the infernal alphabet, begged her pardon for having called her "Ignorant!" "Imbecile!" "Illiterate!" so many times.　　(165–66)

Insistence on the pedagogical model in this scene underscores the extent to which Julia's comparatively successful return depends on its opposition to metropolitan education. The Caribbean grandmother presents not an absence of language or education, as the *métropole* would view her, but an alternative education, a knowledge of language, sights, sounds, and text as complex as any other. Pineau thus exposes the conditions under which Julia was labeled illiterate as particular rather than universal.

When studied alongside the story of Ourika's encounter with a late-eighteenth-century incarnation of French education, Pineau's novel can prompt students to assess the phenomenon of French universalism in a comparative framework and consider the challenge posed by racial difference in both settings. As a conclusion to this discussion, students might examine a phrase that has become synonymous with French colonialism: "Nos ancêtres les Gaulois" 'Our ancestors the Gauls,' the inaugural phrase in French history textbooks, repeated by colonized subjects across the globe, that succinctly demonstrates the ideological link between education and cultural assimilation. By considering the ways in which this sentence captures the dynamics of power in both *Ourika* and *L'exil selon Julia*, students can appreciate the historical basis of the important ties between French and francophone studies.

Ourika in the History Classroom

Sue Peabody

A history course can profitably use fiction—specifically, historical fiction—to engage students in a critical analysis of the relation among historical context, representation, and time. I define historical fiction as a work in which the action is set at least twenty-five years before the moment when the work was written. A crucial period of distancing must take place between the action of the novel (or short story) and the author's setting it to page. Twenty-five years is admittedly arbitrary, but, as a convenient marker of generational shift and perhaps hindsight, it seems to work.

Historians have often found it more problematic to assign *Ourika* in college history classes than have their colleagues in literature and the humanities for several reasons. First, until fairly recently, questions of race have been marginal to mainstream French historiography (Peabody and Stovall). Fortunately, this marginality is changing as historians explore the important connections between the French and Haitian revolutions as part of a wider project of Atlantic history. Second, history curricula typically maintain a strict divide between the ancien régime (early modern period) and revolutionary-modern France. As departments increasingly switch from Western civilization to world-history models of instruction, there is more room for a text like *Ourika*, which straddles both chronological and geographical divides.

A third reason why historians generally have been reluctant to assign *Ourika* until now may have to do with the ambiguous status of the novel as a teaching tool in the history classroom. Some of these objections can be easily addressed. The complaint that novels are make-believe and that students will never learn the facts of history by reading fiction is something of a straw man. Most contemporary historians have already made the "linguistic turn" (Toews 879) and understand that there are ways to interrogate fiction that reveal much about a novel's culture and time. A more practical objection is that fiction takes too much time and that reading novels takes time away from reading important works by historians; yet a short work like *Ourika* (read in English translation) avoids this problem. Today's students can be sophisticated with regard to visual imagery, deciphering elements of propaganda, and so on, but few seem to find time to curl up with a long novel, much less a carefully argued historian's tome, and wrestle with unfamiliar vocabulary or engage with arguments and debates about the past. But teachers need not sacrifice quality for quantity. Carefully chosen articles and short works of fiction—like Claire de Duras's *Ourika*—can be an excellent way to draw students into the historical debates surrounding people in a particular time and place.

Using historical fiction in a history classroom can be challenging, however, since historical fiction represents three distinct moments in time: the historical past (the setting of the novel), the time period in which it was written (reflecting the novelist's preoccupations), and the time in which it is read (the reader's present). For students to read historical fiction fruitfully in a history class, the distinction among different historical moments must be made clear. I expand on this necessity through three analogies: fiction as window, fiction as prism, and fiction as mirror.

Fiction as Window

Through a window, we observe the world beyond; through historical fiction, a historical era. Duras's *Ourika* describes the life of a character on the eve of and during the French Revolution. We access that world through the character of Ourika, but she is not just a fictitious creation. Ourika was a real woman, and the chevalier de Boufflers—Duras's M. le chevalier de B.—a real man, the son of the marquise de Boufflers, who had been the mistress of King Stanislaus I of Poland. Records show that a six-year-old girl from Senegal arrived in France in 1786 in the company of the chevalier de Boufflers, then governor of the French colony of Senegal ("Avis"; "État"). (Although French law prohibited the entry of all people of color into France since 1777, the ban was poorly enforced, particularly regarding nonwhites in the entourage of the elite.) On his arrival in Paris, Boufflers arranged for the girl's baptism as Charlotte Catherine Benezet Ourika.

We can compare the historical Ourika with other black people in France during the ancien régime. Since the early seventeenth century, French merchants on the Atlantic coast had engaged in trade with Africa, the Americas, and, to a lesser extent, societes bordering the Indian Ocean. They established colonies in Canada, the West Indies, West and East Africa, and India and participated in the slave trade to supply laborers for the lucrative sugar, indigo, and tobacco industries. The French established a trading post in Senegal in 1638 and became active in the transatlantic slave trade in the late seventeenth and eighteenth centuries. In the 1763 treaty that concluded the Seven Years' War, the French government gave up Canada and India to the British but retained the highly productive Caribbean colonies and Senegal to supply the plantation colonies with slaves. Throughout the eighteenth century, French planters and merchants traveled back and forth across the Atlantic, frequently accompanied by their enslaved servants. At any given time, there were several hundred blacks in the landlocked capital city of Paris. We know of their presence because the king issued several laws requiring the registration of all blacks in the kingdom, culminating in the notorious Police des Noirs of 1777, which prohibited the further entry of all blacks into France. This law paralleled the institutionalization of racist hierarchies in France's colonies, which defined people of color (*gens de couleur*) as inferior to whites and prohibited them from specific trades, from wearing the same clothing styles as members of the white elite, and from marrying whites (Peabody).

The census records generated by the Police des Noirs allow us to learn that, although Ourika was not the only black child in Paris in the late eighteenth century, her situation was in many ways unusual. Most blacks came to France as enslaved domestic servants and had been born in a Caribbean colony or a French trading settlement around the Indian Ocean, not West Africa. Most were male and, by the end of the eighteenth century, their average age had increased from sixteen in 1762 to twenty-one in 1789. Like the far more numerous white servants, these black immigrants were clearly near the bottom of the social ladder; however, their scarcity and their appearance (exotic to French eyes) made them highly valued as status symbols for the French elite. French masters exaggerated this exoticism by dressing them in turbans (not an indigenous dress style for West Africans) or dress livery uniforms (Boulle 161–62).

The character Ourika's experience of the French Revolution allows us a window into the revolution in Europe and its relation to the Haitian Revolution, in the Caribbean. The unfolding story of the French and Haitian revolutions is complex, and the details need not concern us here. Students of *Ourika*, however, should be informed of the key turning points of the two revolutions, particularly as they affected the status of free people of color and the emancipation of slaves. First, as the National Assembly convened to represent the grievances of the Third Estate, many free men of color—the sons and heirs of white planters, privy to an elite education in France and possessing great wealth, including slaves—demanded rights of citizenship and representation equal to those of whites. The revolutionary government eventually recognized equal political representation for free men of color, but meanwhile thousands of slaves had risen in revolt in Saint-Domingue, France's richest colony, in August 1791. Then the Spanish and English armies attacked the French colonists of Saint-Domingue, each trying to take advantage of the crisis to gain control of the wealthiest colony in the world. When representatives of France's fragile revolutionary government arrived in the colony from Paris in 1793, they tried to shore up their position by offering freedom to the slaves, many of whom had already claimed their freedom by force. Paris ratified and extended this general emancipation to all slaves in the French empire on 4 February 1794.

Meanwhile, by mid-1794 the Terror was in full bloom in France. The novelist, speaking through the fictional Ourika, describes how Ourika's aristocratic mistress lived in hiding for months, protected by anonymous friends in high places (DeJean 23–24; Fowles 24). Maximilien de Robespierre, the zealous leader of the Terror, was executed on 28 July 1794, thus ending the widespread imprisonment, trials, and executions of French aristocrats and Robespierre's political opponents.

Five months later, the historical Ourika appeared before a Parisian notary on 15 December to make a formal declaration of her emancipation in front of seven witnesses. By now she was about fourteen years old, and her guardian was a Parisian named Jean Nicolas Deal. The record mentions a "generous" but anonymous person who bestowed on her nine thousand livres to be used as a lifetime annuity ("Avis").

According to a list of her effects, Ourika died just six years later, on 28 January 1800, at the home of Citoyenne Beauvau in the Faubourg St. Honoré outside Paris, where she had lived with her guardian, Deal ("État"). Apparently Mme de Beauvau had been paying Ourika's living expenses, but these were in arrears.

The scarce traces of Ourika in the historical record thus confirm the rarity of her position as a black girl amid Parisian aristocratic society. Her predicament as a young woman without a dowry and no clear marital prospects for the class into which she was raised is also real. Students need to know that marriages in the late eighteenth century were not based on romantic love but rather were arranged by parents to solidify class and social networks. Her race, but especially her lack of a dowry, prevented Ourika from an arranged marriage in elite society.

Let me extend the metaphor of the window a bit further. Sometimes we come across aspects of the past that, because they are unfamiliar, make it hard to understand what is going on. These are, if you will, smudges on the window of history. There are, for example, key words in *Ourika* that, through their very unfamiliarity and opacity, provide excellent jumping-off points into understanding the era. We can ask students to pay attention to this unfamiliar vocabulary so that we can provide them with more historical background. The following terms might well take us further into the historical period in which the novel is set: "Ursulines" 'Ursuline order' and "les préjugés" 'anticlerical prejudices' (DeJean 3; Fowles 3), "un quadrille" 'a quadrille' (10; 10), "des enfants nègres" 'mulatto children' (13; 13), the grand tour (17; 18), salons, and revolutionary culture (18–20; 18–20).

Fiction as Prism

My second category for the analysis of historical fiction is the prism. A prism bends and distorts the light that passes through it. The key here is to help students realize that the story of the revolution is being told not only from the point of view of a fictional character, but—perhaps more important—from the point of view of a novelist writing twenty to thirty years after the events. As the MLA editions' introductory essays make clear, *Ourika*'s author was no mere disinterested observer. She had lived through the revolution and viewed it as a member of the liberal, enlightened aristocracy.

Claire de Duras was born in 1777 and was thus only a few years older than Ourika. Like most aristocratic daughters, Duras received her education at a residential convent. The Jacobin Reign of Terror guillotined Duras's father, the comte de Kersaint, in December 1793, just a few weeks after the executions of Marie Antoinette and Olympe de Gouges, when Claire was sixteen years old. Claire and her mother then fled into exile, first to Philadelphia, then to Martinique (a French slave colony under English occupation from 1794 to 1802), and finally to London, where Claire met and married Duke Amédée-Bretagne-Malo Durfort de Duras in 1797. After the birth of their two daughters, Félicie (1798) and Clara (1799), Claire and her family returned to France in 1801, one year after the death of the historical Ourika. Despite her success as a writer and *salonnière* in the restoration court of Louis XVIII, Duras suffered from bouts of depression and died in 1828, five years after the publication of *Ourika* (Crofts).

Duras's biography suggests several points of connection between her personal history and the novel's story. The author could well have met the historical Ourika before Duras fled France, and her exile in Martinique probably exposed her to colonial racism, sharpening her awareness of racial exclusion. But Duras could not have witnessed Ourika's death in 1800; the novel's imagination of Ourika's dawning realization of her isolation and her experience of racial prejudice is purely a work of fictive sympathy, not historical reportage.

Ourika contains many passages in which the fictive Ourika editorializes on the revolution with the hindsight shared by Duras and many of her contemporary readers. In the novel, the Senegalese Ourika dismisses the French revolutionaries as hypocritical and the execution of King Louis XVI as "ce grand crime" '[an] outrage' (DeJean 21; Fowles 22). Students need to learn to read these passages critically, as evidence of Duras's bias, borne of her personal loss during the Reign of Terror.

Historians point directly to this problematic as the biggest obstacle in their adoption of the novel for classroom use. Alyssa Sepinwall puts the problem of using *Ourika* in a course on the French Revolution especially well, explaining that *Ourika* "purports to be an African woman's voice, but is instead that of a white aristocrat in the post-revolutionary era." John Savage makes a similar point:

> [T]he main challenge in teaching [*Ourika*] is also the reason it's so interesting: on one hand, students may have an expectation that the subject matter means it will be a progressive story that reveals the openness of French views about race. In fact it's at least partly a conservative diatribe

about how the Revolution and rights talk [have] left people disappointed and ruined because they expected things they couldn't have (or that weren't "natural").

By setting the novel in the context of Duras's life experience, students can be more critical of its portrayal of French history.

Fiction as Mirror

Finally, I want to explore the impact of the present moment on the reading of historical fiction: using historical fiction as a mirror. Students bring their own experiences to the reading of any text. A truly effective history lesson should not only instruct students about the events of the past but also ask them to reflect on how they have been shaped by their historical context. Thus I conclude with a discussion of how we, as subjects of history, experience some of the important trends of our time. I might begin a discussion by asking students whether they have lived through a period of political turmoil akin to the French Revolution. (Few American undergraduates have, but recent immigrants or soldiers may have witnessed such upheaval.) Have students experienced isolation or prejudice based on assumptions about who they are? How does society shape the limitations—or opportunities—that we experience in our lives? Through these kinds of questions literature facilitates transformational classroom discussion.

Students might find it interesting that, unlike in the United States, recent thought in France, particularly on the left, has been resistant to explicit discussions of race. Since the French Revolution, successive republican governments have deliberately omitted racial designations in their censuses, drivers' licenses, or any other official documentation: France is officially color-blind. In fact, some progressive French intellectuals find the whole idea of race and multiculturalism to be distasteful and unworthy of serious inquiry. It's as if the French believe that by avoiding the mention of race, they have gone beyond it. Yet, as any person of color can tell you, racial discrimination persists in France today. Even white French people may be able to recognize the pervasiveness of racist assumptions if you ask them whether a black man or woman could ever be the president of France.

Yet racism in France is not the same as racism in the United States. Whereas American racism arises out of the need to justify the past—the taking of Native American lands, the enslavement of Africans—and out of present anxiety over waves of immigration from many parts of the world, the history of racism in France is tied to its colonial and imperial past, especially the migration of its former colonial subjects into the French nation or *métropole*. Historically, the French have tried to minimize the assimilation of former colonial subjects by holding to rigorous criteria of citizenship. For a colonial subject to become a French citizen, she or he must embrace all aspects of French culture through education and through cultural transformation. There are parallels, of course, with certain aspects of American racism, like movements to codify a national tongue, but French racism has been structured on cultural exclusion, not the color bar (Chapman and Frader).

Ourika has a great deal to recommend it for the study of race, gender, and politics in the period of the French Revolution and its aftermath. Yet, historical fiction's prismatic effect—the distortion between the novelist's position in history and the events that the novel describes—make it a particularly challenging tool for the instruction of history. The problems presented by this effect are not insurmountable—indeed, they can permit a more sophisticated and nuanced unpacking of how texts relate to their historical contexts—but they require teachers to distinguish among the functions of the historical novel as window, prism, and mirror.

Ourika in the French Civilization Class

Scott M. Powers

The French civilization course poses a number of challenges to instructors. The most immediate challenge may be to teach in a coherent fashion the broad and diverse subject matter, which spans several centuries and includes France's social, political, economic, and aesthetic history. Another challenge is the temptation to present French civilization solely in a positive light. As a rule, textbooks designed to introduce France to students of the anglophone world extol the culture's great contributions to Western society, including Enlightenment principles of democracy, artistic movements such as impressionism, and the invention of cinema. At the same time, they often ignore the underside of French history, notably the evils of colonialism. For instance, Ross Steele's widely used *Civilisation française en évolution I* briefly mentions colonialism and the slave trade, but only to paint the picture of a prosperous and mighty French economy with a global presence (29, 342, 365). In fact, the omission of any discussion of colonialism from French civilization textbooks is somewhat of a paradox, as the French first employed the term *civilisation* in reference to its colonialist mission to "civilize" the world.

To help students in the French civilization class synthesize the vast array of topics covered in the course, make connections among disciplines, and voice a critical perspective on French history, I have turned to *Ourika*. This short literary depiction of the misfortunes of a young African woman living in France during the Terror gives students the opportunity to review what they have learned about various political regimes, the French Revolution, and class structure. The novel's treatment of Ourika's intimate and social life, in the context of national turmoil, enables students to identify the relations among the individual, the social, and the political. Insofar as the heroine is a foreigner living inside the *hexagone*, *Ourika* also anticipates key issues of postcolonial France, including the assimilation of immigrants. Finally, the novel encourages students to think critically about troubling aspects of French civilization, because Ourika's psychological condition of insecurity, self-hatred, and despair mirrors that of Africans who grew up under French colonialism. Here I propose ways in which the French civilization instructor can use *Ourika* to aid students in acquiring a more informed perspective on French civilization. Doing so involves opening debate on the very nature of the course, including the appropriateness of the term *civilization* in the course title.

Since *Ourika* recounts the life of aristocrats who lived through the Terror, a logical time in the semester to introduce the novel is after the study of the class system of the ancien régime and the French Revolution. Because of the novel's brevity, I have found two seventy-five-minute class sessions sufficient to engage students in classroom activities that range from summarizing the plot to critiquing the notion of civilization.

In preparation for the first day, students are assigned half of the novel and given questions that encourage reflection. I ask students to identify the various subject positions that Ourika occupies and to consider the different ways in which she can be considered a marginal voice in French society. In class, students share their lists, which include answers such as *"négresse,"* "Senegalese," "woman," "orphan," "adolescent," and "aristocrat." A brief review of the history of French patriarchy, the gradual ascendancy of the bourgeoisie as a socioeconomic class and political force, and the homogeneous ethnic population of early nineteenth-century France helps students emphasize Ourika's marginality.

Another preparatory question asks students to consider ways in which Ourika's marginal status in French society affects her adolescence and adulthood. In class, I modify the question slightly by asking students to imagine themselves in the role of the doctor to whom Ourika recounts her story and to present their diagnosis of Ourika's *maladie*. A variation is to ask students to explain—by referring to examples from the text—Ourika's remark, "[M]on malheur, c'est l'histoire de toute ma vie" 'The story of my unhappiness is the same as the story of my life' (DeJean 5; Fowles 5). Reflecting on Ourika's adolescence, students come up with a variety of reasons for the heroine's sadness. Most can be attributed to her exclusion from French society.

To assist students in identifying a critique of the "civilizing" process in *Ourika*, instructors can point out that literature can be approached on many levels. A novel can be read as a portrait of the society in which it was written. It can also be read as a subversive text that calls into question dominant social norms, customs, and ideologies. The subversive nature of *Ourika* can be appreciated through textual analysis of passages that describe the heroine's assimilation into French society. To begin this analysis, I have one student read aloud the passage describing Ourika's education, which endowed the adopted girl with the knowledge and qualities of a French aristocrat. Ourika claims to have received "une éducation parfaite" 'a girl's perfect education,' a general nurturing of "le jugement" 'judgment' and "[l']esprit" 'intellect.' She has acquired "tous les talents," including those of singing, painting, and conversation, as well as fluency in English and Italian (9; 9). It is appropriate at this point to indicate the striking resemblance between Ourika's education and a main objective of nineteenth- and twentieth-century French colonialism—to educate, or "civilize," "les sauvages."

As part of a larger critique of France's civilizing mission, the novel questions Ourika's ostensibly ideal education, partly through foreshadowing; Ourika contrasts her instruction with her bleak future: "Hélas! je ne prévoyais pas que ces douces études seraient suivies de jours si amers" 'Alas, I didn't know then that these innocent studies would ripen into such bitter fruit' (9; 9–10). As this passage suggests, Ourika's education is linked to her subsequent mental anguish.

Other passages question Ourika's education by juxtaposing the knowledge that she acquires with her ignorance regarding her social destiny. Students working in small groups can be prompted to identify a series of binary opposites in select passages and to comment on their role in the text. Ourika's education is described as "prolonge[ant] [s]on *erreur* et autorisa[nt] [s]on *aveuglement*" 'prolong[ing her] mistaken view of existence and ma[king her] blindness natural' (10; 10; emphasis added). I have students compare this description of Ourika's education as the cause of her "blindness" with a subsequent passage in which, overhearing a conversation concerning her unpromising future in French society, Ourika claims finally to "see": "je vis tout" 'I comprehended all' (12; 12). Ironically, it is the information that is deliberately withheld from her formal education that Ourika understands as the cure for her "blindness." In yet another passage, Ourika describes her education: "Il y a des illusions qui sont comme la lumière du jour; quand on les perd, tout disparaît avec elles" 'There are illusions like daylight. When they go, all becomes night' (14; 14). This unexpected association between light and illusion constitutes another example of the subversive nature of the novel. A textual analysis of these passages, in which students are asked to comment on the unconventional use of opposites such as light and darkness, knowledge and ignorance, highlights the text's critique of an initially idealized French upbringing.

The judgment that Ourika passes on her education is linked to the frustration she feels toward her inability to assimilate in French society. No matter how French she has become, French society will not allow her to lead the life of a French woman, because of the color of her skin. Ourika is faced with the reality that she will never be able to marry a Frenchman or start a family of her own. This paradox of French civilization becomes all the more disturbing as the text highlights the fact that Ourika's civilizing cannot be undone and that she is condemned to live the life of an outsider. The harsh realities of the Atlantic slave trade (in which the French were major participants), as well as her "rescue" and relocation to France at age two, have made it impossible for Ourika to return to her family (15; 16). Moreover, Ourika's French upbringing and education have made it difficult for her to identify with the oppressed colonized (20; 21).

In preparation for the second class session on *Ourika*, the instructor may ask students to write out short answers about what they believe the term *civilization* means. A related question could ask students to identify the defining characteristics of French civilization. In answering, students should be encouraged to reflect on the course thus far. As students are solicited to share their responses in class, many will refer to French art, architecture, and literature—elements that one typically associates with French culture and that are the primary focus of French civilization textbooks. Students will also likely mention a variety of other components that make up a civilization, such as its economy, its politics, and its social classes. Because it is less common for students to associate the term *civilization* with anything negative, I encourage a more critical assessment of French history by asking the class to make a list of any negative consequences of civilization that they can imagine and to consider the novel's conclusion in their response.

In discussing the meaning of civilization, I observe that both etymologically and historically, the term is linked to the verb *civiliser*. In fact, *civilisation* was a term first used during the Enlightenment to refer to a specific civilizing process, in which all peoples naturally evolve from savagery to a "civilized" state. As a corollary, societies already "civilized" should help "barbarous" nations along the path toward civilization through the hierarchical transmission of culture (Swenson 324, 343).

The analysis by J. Swenson is helpful in preparing to lead a class discussion on the notion of civilization: he presents several definitions of *civilization*, the most pertinent for this discussion being the eighteenth-century French one that divided the world into societies that live in light and others that remain in darkness (330). This dualist view of the world justified France's colonial expansion, and, for influential thinkers and politicians such as Montesquieu, Mirabeau père, Rousseau, Condorcet, and Robespierre, the terms *civilisation* and *civiliser* implied power relations of "domination and exploitation . . . of one class or society upon another" (323–24, 348).

Although Ourika is raised in France in the eighteenth century, in some ways her education is an example of the type of so-called civilizing process that took place in French colonies during the nineteenth and twentieth centuries. She is Senegalese and yet is raised to speak, act, and think just like a young French woman. A paradox of France's civilizing mission lies in the fact that no matter how successful a foreigner such as Ourika may be in becoming French, French society will always view the person as a foreigner. As a result, Ourika begins to loathe the color of her skin and to see herself as ugly and unloved (DeJean 15; Fowles 15–16).

To help explain Ourika's condition and, by extension, the condition of the colonized, I introduce to the class issues raised by twentieth-century francophone writers. An important reference is Frantz Fanon's *Peau noire, masques blancs*, which describes the feelings of insecurity and state of self-hatred from which Africans suffered as a result of French colonialism. David O'Connell's article "*Ourika*: Black Face, White Mask" summarizes Fanon's thesis on the mental anguish of the colonized and applies it to Duras's novel. To explain Ourika's "psychological disintegration" (52), O'Connell cites a key passage from Fanon's work that outlines three stages in the development of the colonized psyche: "Le nègre infériorisé va de l'insécurité humiliante à l'auto-accusation ressentie jusqu'au désespoir" 'The Negro, having been made inferior, proceeds from humiliating insecurity through strongly voiced self-accusation to despair' (Fanon, *Peau noire* 68; Fanon, *Black Skin* 60). The instructor can ask students to apply Fanon's description of the colonized psyche to passages of the novel that illustrate Ourika's psychological journey from insecurity and self-accusation to despair.

At this point, I invite the class to reflect more generally on the French civilization of other peoples by considering additional negative consequences that may or may not be found in *Ourika*. I emphasize that each region, before colonization, had its own language, religion, customs, traditions, and economy. To underscore the negative effects of the imposition of French culture on other peoples, I turn to an oft cited passage of Aimé Césaire's *Discours sur le colonialisme*:

> Moi, je parle de sociétés vidées d'elles-mêmes, des cultures piétinées, d'institutions minées, de terres confisquées, de religions assassinées, de magnificences artistiques anéanties, . . . de millions d'hommes arrachés à leur terre, à leurs habitudes, à leur vie, à la danse, à la sagesse.   (20)

> I am talking about societies drained of their essence, cultures trampled underfoot, institutions undermined, lands confiscated, religions smashed, artistic creations destroyed, . . . men torn from their gods, their land, their habits, their life—from life, from the dance, from wisdom.
> (*Discourse* 43)

Not only does French colonial civilization destroy other civilizations, it *decivilizes* both the colonized and the French:

> Il faudrait d'abord étudier comment la colonisation travaille à *déciviliser* le colonisateur, à l'*abrutir* au sens propre du mot . . . à le réveiller aux instincts enfouis, à la convoitise, à la violence, à la haine raciale, au relativisme moral.   (11)

> First, we must study how colonization works to *decivilize* the colonizer, to *brutalize* him in the true sense of the word, to degrade him, to awaken him to buried instincts, to covetousness, violence, race hatred, and moral relativism.   (35)

Statements like these suggest that to equate colonization with civilization is a French perspective, which writers such as Fanon and Césaire sought to challenge by revealing the barbarism of French imperialism. A brief presentation of Césaire's and Fanon's statements, alongside the discussion of Ourika's life—her education, her unsuccessful assimilation, her *maladie*, and her eventual retreat from society to convent life, but also the enslavement of her family by French slave traders that can be considered the origin of her deplorable state—helps students develop a critical perspective of French history.

As a follow-up assignment, I recommend giving students the choice of composition topics. A topic that requires students to do some research is the comparison of Ourika's condition, as described in Duras's novel, with that of immigrants living in France today. For material concerning the question of the successful—or unsuccessful—assimilation of immigrants and ethnic groups into French society, the instructor can refer students to French newspaper and magazine articles on the November 2005 riots. Articles published that month in *Le monde* and *Le nouvel observateur* discuss various causes of the riots, including the poor living conditions and high unemployment rates among immigrant and ethnic youth, despite their French education.

Another composition topic asks students to draw from various sources, including their textbook and the novel to give an account of both the positive and negative dimensions of French civilization, as well as to explain why the term *civilization*, in reference to French culture and history, can be considered ambiguous and problematic.

To end the classroom discussion of *Ourika* and to further relate the novel to the overall subject matter of the course, the instructor can engage the students in a debate on French Civilization as the title of the course. Is this an appropriate title? Does it accurately indicate the course content? Does it suggest a biased perspective on the topic? Do better titles come to mind? While the value of such a debate lies in the opportunity that it gives students to process their readings and classroom discussions, as well as to formulate and defend their opinions, many will challenge the title French Civilization as ambiguous, Gaulist, and limited in scope for a course whose content and goals are much broader.

Ourika in an Honors College: From Intermediate French to Comparative Literature Seminar

Jocelyn Van Tuyl

"Leave the bookstore a standing order for *Ourika*," we joke, "it's the French program's greatest hit." *Ourika*'s pedagogical versatility has indeed made it one of the most frequently taught titles at our liberal arts honors college: fourth-semester French-language students appreciate its clear prose and its resonance with today's political and social issues; students in the advanced course The French Revolution in the Cultural Imagination gain insight into matters of race, class, and gender in revolutionary France (Van Tuyl and Wallace 12); those in the comparative literature seminar Double Stories explore intertextuality through a paired reading of *Ourika* and John Fowles's *The French Lieutenant's Woman*. This essay describes two very different approaches to the novel and posits connections between the lessons learned in fourth-semester French and those in a literature seminar.

Intermediate French: Bridging Language and Literature

A wealth of historical and social commentary combines with modest length and relatively simple language to make *Ourika* an ideal first novel for French-language students. Before reading *Ourika*, our fourth-semester students complete the *French in Action* immersion program and read a number of short stories, poems, and articles from the French-language press. Building on those earlier readings, we begin our study of the novel with an introduction and review of essential vocabulary for the study of prose fiction in French: *le roman* ("the novel"), *le romancier / la romancière* ("the novelist"), *le personnage [principal]* ("the [main] character"), *la narration [à la première/troisième personne]* ("[first-/third-person] narration"), *le récit-cadre* ("the frame narrative"), and so on. As reading progresses, the instructor helps establish the literary and historical context with brief presentations on the Enlightenment and Romanticism as well as the French and Haitian revolutions.

A primary goal is to facilitate literary understanding while reinforcing and expanding students' knowledge of vocabulary and grammar. The first line of Ourika's narrative, "Je fus rapportée du Sénégal" 'I was brought here from Senegal' (DeJean 7; Fowles 7), provides the basis for a perfect integration of lexical study and literary analysis. After reviewing the French verbs *porter*, *apporter*, *rapporter*, and *emporter*, which describe carrying or bringing inanimate objects, and comparing them with their counterparts that refer to human beings (*mener*, *amener*, *ramener*, and *emmener*), students are prepared to discuss what Ourika's choice of verb implies about her self-perception: her words mark her as an object or possession rather than an autonomous human subject. When asked to interrogate the prefix Ourika appends to the verb, students discover that *rapporter* assumes that France, not Senegal, is the speaker's point of origin and reference. These insights prepare the way for further discussions of Ourika's subjecthood and identity.

A series of brief assignments makes students largely responsible for integrating the linguistic with the literary. Because discussion of the novel runs concurrently with a review of key grammar topics, several review exercises are based on the novel. An assignment on the conditional mood, for example, asks students to write present and past conditional sentences about the characters: "Si Charles n'aimait pas Anaïs . . ." 'If Charles did not love Anaïs . . .'; "Si Ourika était restée au Sénégal . . ." 'If Ourika had remained in Senegal . . .'. Ongoing assignments require students to take reading notes on recurring motifs and lexical fields, such as the extended discourse on blindness and sight: "tout prolongeait mon erreur et autorisait mon aveuglement" 'everything prolonged my mistaken view of existence and made my blindness natural' (10; 10); "une conversation . . . ouvrit mes yeux" '[a] conversation dropped the scales from my eyes' (11; 11); "je vis tout; je me vis négresse, dépendante, méprisée" 'I saw everything; I saw myself as a Negress, dependent, scorned' (12; my trans.); "mes yeux s'obscurcirent" 'everything grew dark' (12; Fowles 13); "à présent, mes yeux étaient ouverts" 'now my eyes were opened' (14; 15); "je fermais les yeux, et je croyais qu'on ne me voyait pas" 'I shut my eyes, and supposed myself invisible' (27; 28).

A two- to three-page analysis of *Ourika* is the first literary paper that students write in French. (Previous writing assignments include letters, surveys, current events pieces, and poems). To make the exercise less daunting for beginning students of literature and to underscore the importance of active reading and advance preparation, I propose topics based on the note-taking assignments:

> Analyze the extended metaphor of blindness and sight.
> How is Ourika represented by others, and how is this representation linked to Ourika's self-perception?
> What is the function of the doctor's frame narrative? How does the introduction by this white man of science influence the reader's perception of Ourika?
> How does the marquise's suggestion that Ourika's suffering stems from her "guilty" love for Charles (41; 42) and not from her skin color modify the novel's potential for social critique?

Because the paper topics call for a formal literary analysis of the novel, the final exam asks students to take an approach that is both creative and oriented toward social and political issues. The essay question sets up an encounter between Ourika and Ousmane, the black student in *French in Action* who retreats to the library in lesson 2 (Capretz et al. 9) and is scarcely seen again over the course of the remaining fifty lessons. "Imagine that Ousmane opens a mysterious door in the library reading room to find himself transported through time to Ourika's convent," the directions state, "and write a three hundred– to five hundred–word dialogue in which the two characters compare their experiences." (For students unfamiliar with *French in Action*, the topic can easily be recast as a dialogue between Ourika and any modern counterpart.) This apparently whimsical subject typically produces some very fine comparisons of what has and has not changed in race and gender relations as well as astute interpretations of the often marginalizing representation of black and female fictional characters.

Double Stories: Intertextuality and Blackness sous Rature

Double Stories: Historic/Heuristic Fictions is an advanced comparative literature seminar that explores fiction's relation to history in paired texts and works structured by various forms of doubling. From Plutarch through postmodernism, these works reveal a proliferation of doubling strategies: historical repetition, geographical duality, bilingualism, the quest and inquest structure of detective fiction, interpolated narratives, intertextuality, and the relationship of *Histoire* to *histoire*—of history to personal story. These last two categories are exemplified by the pairing of *Ourika* with Fowles's *The French Lieutenant's Woman*.

Discussion begins with the French Revolution as catalyst and metaphor for Ourika's personal conflicts. "J'entrevis . . . que, dans ce grand désordre, je pourrais trouver ma place" 'I sensed that at the end of this great chaos I might find my true place' (DeJean 18–19; Fowles 19), Ourika explains. The promise of political change—"[o]n commençait à parler de la liberté des nègres" 'talk started of emancipating the Negroes' (20; 21)—is not the sole source of hope: ironically, the shared suffering of the Terror augments Ourika's feelings of solidarity with the endangered aristocracy and attenuates her sense of social alienation. The relation between *Histoire* and *histoire* is evident in the lexical overlap between historical events and the protagonist's emotions: narrating her experience of the revolutionary Terror (22; 22–23), Ourika describes her psychological state of "anxiété et . . . terreur" 'anxiety and terror' (23; my trans.). Ourika's juxtaposition of *Terreur* and *terreur* invites comparisons with the *Histoire/histoire* binary. In both cases, French differentiates through capitalization, apparently according greater value to the capitalized, public half of each equation while nonetheless underscoring its connection to the lowercase word denoting subjective, individual experience and personal narrative.

The link between Ourika's inner life and the circumstances in which she lives is readily apparent since, as Margaret Waller observes, "Duras's heroine notes the specific social, historical, and political causes of her alienation and makes her story a vehicle for pointed social criticism" (Introduction xvi). With the introduction of writings by Fowles, we witness a turn away from social critique and toward an increasingly psychological interpretation of the heroine's alienation.

The way we begin to look at Fowles has a great deal to do with the unusual bilingual format of our literature courses. In our very small liberal arts college (approximately 725 students), courses in French and francophone literature and culture must be bilingual to serve the needs of both French speakers and the wider college population. We generally meet as a group early in the week, then break into French- and English-speaking sections for the second seminar meeting of the week. Though sometimes awkward, this arrangement has one distinct advantage: students who are reading the original French texts have at least one class a week with those who read in translation and are able to serve as authorities on lexical and stylistic matters. Giving students this authority—rather than having all clarifications come from the professor—fits well with the honors college mission: French speakers are empowered, and other students are often inspired to begin or to continue their study of the language.

After reading Doris Y. Kadish's "Rewriting Women's Stories: *Ourika* and *The French Lieutenant's Woman*," French and English speakers work together to verify the author's assertion that Fowles's translation of *Ourika* "strengthens the male medical discourse by enhancing the clinical tone of the text" (76). Although *Ourika* is, as Waller says, "one of the earliest examples of the pathologizing of emotion in literature" (Introduction xv), discussion makes it clear that the readers of the translation come away with a much stronger sense of the pathological. Knowing that the translator is the author of the novel with which *Ourika* is paired, the group is sensitized in advance to the shift from the critical, social explanation for the protagonist's alienation in Duras's novel to the psychological explanation found in *The French Lieutenant's Woman*.

Fowles's novel affords us the opportunity to interrogate many aspects of postmodern literary practice. Using Linda Hutcheon's insights on "historiographic metafiction" as background (105–23), we explore Fowles's layering of dual historical perspectives and his self-conscious use of intertextuality in *The French Lieutenant's Woman*. Much of our discussion, however, concerns the novel's implicit intertextual dialogue with *Ourika*. The class readily identifies similarities between the protagonists' situations: superior education has made each woman a misfit in society, and each is confronted with the example of happy marriage and motherhood—forms of satisfaction denied a woman in her position (DeJean 13, 38; Fowles 13, 39; Fowles, *Woman* 169). Students further note the extent to which a doctor—a white, male scientific authority—influences interpretations of the two heroines: Duras's frame narrator, who has the first and last word, colors our perception of Ourika's suffering, and Fowles's Dr. Grogan goes unquestioned when he diagnoses Sarah Woodruff with a typically Victorian malady, melancholia. The doctor distinguishes his diagnosis as "obscure melancholia"—depression for which there is no known, comprehensible, or valid explanation. "Dark indeed. Very dark," he remarks (*Woman* 156). This is our cue to investigate Fowles's exteriorizing, figurative treatment of darkness.

In the foreword to his translation of *Ourika*, Fowles asserts that "the African figure of Ourika . . . was very active in [his] unconscious" while he was writing *The French Lieutenant's Woman* (xxix). This unconscious preoccupation surfaces in the description of Sarah's skin as "very brown, almost ruddy . . . as if the girl cared more for health than a fashionably pale and languid-cheeked complexion" (*Woman* 71). Indeed, as Kadish argues, Sarah is presented as "the sensual, lower-class, darker-skinned alternative to the virginal, upper-class, white Ernestine," Charles Smithson's betrothed ("Rewriting" 84). Moreover, Sarah is repeatedly described as a "dark" or "black figure" (198, 85, 86), but these terms refer primarily to her clothing and mental state. Reading *Ourika* as the "forgotten history" of *The French Lieutenant's Woman*, students discover how blackness appears *sous rature* ("under erasure") in the 1969 novel: Ourika's black skin is replaced by Sarah's black garb; Ourika's socially and politically conditioned alienation gives way to Sarah's black melancholy—an "addiction" to suffering that the novel's medical authority presents as Sarah's choice, conveniently precluding any social explanation for the young woman's alienation (156).

It is not only social critique that is eclipsed in Fowles's novel: blackness itself is also altered past recognition. Acknowledging *Ourika*'s influence on *The French Lieutenant's Woman*, Fowles identifies the unconscious racism in his failure to see that the figure "*in* black, . . . unfairly exiled from society," *was* black (Foreword xxx; emphasis added). Lest students imagine that such biases are confined to the "ancient history" of the 1960s, I challenge the graduates of our language sequence to see the parallel between *The French Lieutenant's Woman* and *French in Action*, where the only *homme noir* ("black man") disappears from the storyline, his blackness displaced onto the white-skinned "homme *en* noir" ("man in black"), a cartoonish stalker who proves to be a harmless talent scout (Capretz et al. 511–12; emphasis added). Realizing that they have acquired their ability to read *Ourika*—or any other text—in French from a work that places blackness under erasure, students grow alert to other instances of this phenomenon and become increasingly aware that their own reading practice is historically and culturally conditioned.

Highly accessible and lending itself to a wide variety of interpretations, *Ourika* can easily be adapted to the language classroom as well as to literature seminars in French or English. Students who encounter Duras's novel more than once over the course of their undergraduate careers are never disappointed: as they discover new approaches to the material and compare their experiences of (re)reading the novel, many gain a critical appreciation of their own roles as readers of French and as interpreters of literature and culture.

Ourika in a Fourth-Semester French Language and Culture Course

David R. Ellison

The Course and Its Context

In spring 2005, I taught Claire de Duras's *Ourika* in a fourth-semester French language and culture course, designated FRE 212, at the University of Miami. The university's College of Arts and Sciences requires all students to take a minimum of three semesters of a foreign language. Those students who enter FRE 212 have satisfied that requirement, either through course work at our institution or equivalent work elsewhere; most have a genuine interest in pursuing French studies, usually as a major or a minor. For that reason, there are few problems motivating such a group or generating good classroom discussion. The linguistic level in this class varies considerably, however, which means that intensive practice in the four skills (listening, speaking, reading, writing) must always be a focus.

Of the thirteen students enrolled in my FRE 212 class, nine had completed FRE 211 at the University of Miami with a B or better, three were first-year students with superior secondary school records, and one was a transfer student who had taken the *niveau intermédiaire* in the *cours aux étudiants étrangers* at Paris 4, Sorbonne, in fall 2004. Despite these generally impressive credentials, about half the students had trouble with basic grammatical concepts and with certain aspects of essay writing. They were a genial and diverse group, hailing from various parts of the United States, two Canadian provinces, three Latin American countries, and Mozambique. Several of them spoke languages other than English, French, and Spanish, which made for interesting conversations on the topics of cultural difference and otherness. As a group, they were prepared for the fundamental themes of *Ourika*.

It is probably a commonplace to say that the intermediate level of language learning presents particular difficulties, many of them thorny and difficult to resolve. The initial enthusiasm that accompanies the ability to communicate at a basic level has worn off, the complexities of French grammar have become increasingly burdensome, the necessity of learning vocabulary at a rapid pace has imposed itself, the frustration at not being able to say what one intends to say in an accurate and differentiated way has taken hold. And, as those students who have had the opportunity to spend some time in a francophone country can attest: no one there speaks "intermediate French." The pedagogical problem, therefore, is how to make a transitional course such as FRE 212 effective and practical, as well as interesting and intellectually stimulating.

At the University of Miami, our strategy has been to teach grammar in a systematic way throughout the first three semesters so that the emphasis in the fourth semester can be on a smooth combination of the four skills, with a special concentration on reading and, especially, writing. Grammar is not neglected, but the idea is to focus on a discrete number of grammatical problems rather than provide a detailed review of what has already been covered. Further, FRE 212 needs to provide a solid bridge to the fifth-semester course, Introduction to Literary Genres (FRE 301), in which students learn to read and analyze literary texts with some sophistication while acquiring the technical vocabulary for textual interpretation.

Thus our department decided to divide the fourth semester into two distinct but related sections. During the first seven weeks, we used the text *À vous d'écrire: Atelier de français*, by Gisèle Loriot-Raymer, Michèle E. Valet, and Judith A. Muyskens, along with its workbook, and worked on the rhetorical modes of writing featured therein— such as *le texte d'information, le portrait, la description de lieu, le récit personnel, le compte rendu critique, l'essai argumentatif*. After an introductory unit dealing with the course's methodology and a few preliminary writing exercises, the following six weeks focused on each of the above units in turn. Students wrote a weekly essay in the given rhetorical paradigm and gradually grew more confident in their linguistic capacities. When I returned the papers, I gave an overview of the strengths and weaknesses I observed, not only in linguistic correctness, but also in organizational structure and in the students' adherence to the varying levels of objectivity or subjectivity implicit in modes ranging from the relatively straightforward *texte d'information* to the more intimate *récit personnel* to the more opinionated *essai argumentatif*. For the *compte rendu critique*, I challenged the students to buttress their arguments with evidence (thinking ahead to the *explication de texte* they would be learning in FRE 301); I tried to explain the relevance of the *portrait* to the seventeenth and eighteenth centuries, thereby preparing the way for its use in *Ourika*. Each time I returned the weekly papers, I provided the students with a page of *fautes typiques*, which I organized into major categories: verb tenses and usage, prepositions, problems in agreement (*accord grammatical*), anglicisms, and so on. The point was to see if, over a six-week period, there could be some reduction in typical errors through a greater awareness of the categories in which mistakes were being made. Throughout the process, I attempted to convince the class that there is an art, as well as a craft, to thinking grammatically. Whether I convinced them, following Marcel Proust's analysis of Gustave Flaubert's style, that there is such a thing as "beauté grammaticale" 'grammatical beauty' lies beyond the purview of this essay (587; my trans.).

Immediately following spring break (which divides the term neatly into two seven-week sections), the focus shifted. Instead of imitating certain modes, models, or devices, students had to confront a literary work, which itself contained elements of the rhetorical strategies they had been practicing. When reading a text as complex as *Ourika*, students necessarily encountered problems at different levels: historical, social, and political backgrounds; classical French written style; vocabulary; subtlety of psychological analysis. At the same time, however, they were prepared to recognize in the narrative movement of the text a concatenation of three of the units they had studied: *la description de lieu*, *le portrait*, and *le récit personnel*. It was most important that the first literary work many of these students were to encounter in the French language be an accessible one. If they were already sensitized to the general question of rhetorical modality, they could enter the world of the text with greater ease than they could have just seven weeks previously. Yet an overarching sense of historical context was lacking. How could I best provide this context in an informative but also entertaining way?

Ourika *in Its Context*

I decided to frame our classroom discussion of *Ourika* with the presentation and analysis of two popular films dealing with the twilight of the ancien régime: Patrice Leconte's *Ridicule* and Stephen Frears's *Dangerous Liaisons*. I saved the Hollywood simplification of Choderlos de Laclos's sexual politics and the recognizable faces of Glenn Close, John Malkovich, Michelle Pfeiffer, Swoosie Kurtz, and Uma Thurman for the final week of class, as a reward to the students for their hard work, and I focused during the first week after spring break on the cultural, geographical, scientific, and religious issues that emerge with historical accuracy as well as dramatic impact in *Ridicule*. I wanted my students to grasp not only what was at stake in the plot and primary narrative organization of the film—namely, the frustrated quest of a well-intentioned but naive provincial nobleman facing the decadence and moral nullity of the Parisian court as he tries to obtain funding for the draining of insalubrious swampland in his domain—but also the ways in which the zeitgeist of the European Enlightenment permeated this cautionary tale on the power and perils of wit (*esprit*, as opposed to the very specific *humour* of the English, as we learned to appreciate at the very end of the film).

In our classroom discussion, I emphasized the following points:

> *The eighteenth century*: a brief excursus on the Age of Enlightenment as a broad European phenomenon and a select few of its principal players in Germany and France (notably Kant, Voltaire, Diderot, Rousseau); the emerging importance of the experimental sciences; the increasingly confrontational relations between reason and religion.
>
> *Politics and society in France*: the court of Louis XVI shortly before the French Revolution; Paris and the provinces; privileges and *charges*; *esprit* in the particular context of salon society; sex, love, and power (more on this, of course, in *Dangerous Liaisons*).
>
> *Transition toward* Ourika: the problem of social inclusion versus exclusion; ideas of universality versus the particularity of individual identity and race; love and social obstacles to love.

The students enjoyed *Ridicule* very much and seemed to retain its major themes as points of reference during our five-week section on *Ourika*. For each class session students had to read no more than four or five pages of the text (I used the 1994 MLA Texts and Translations version, in the original French [DeJean]). I made it clear to them that, given the manageable assignments, they were responsible for looking up any words they did not understand, while I would provide them with certain details on the historical context, as necessary. We followed up our discussion of *Ridicule* with more systematic discussions of the question of the other (*l'autre*), with emphasis on race and gender, on the theme of seeing and being seen (being made into an object by the gaze of the other), and on the construction of identity. We talked at some length about Ourika's own political point of view, her conservatism tempered by intuitive insights into social injustices. We spent some time on those elements of the story that share in the tradition of the *roman psychologique*. On the thematic level, we focused on definitions of happiness, as well as Ourika's redefinition of *le bonheur* in the final pages of her confessional discourse.

While most of what we discussed had to do with the content of Ourika's account—her life and sufferings, her discovery of herself as other, her observations of the crucial historical turn from a dying monarchy through the political radicalism and chaos of the revolution and period of emigration to the beginnings of the Napoleonic era—I also had my students work in some detail on the various narrative strategies employed in the text: framing, anticipation and foreshadowing, acceleration and deceleration of narrative rhythm, alternating use of the *imparfait* and *passé simple*. In this sense, I tried to point out that although each text is unique, singular in its manipulations of both theme and narrative technique, each text also exemplifies general narrative laws.

Certainly one challenge I faced during this intensive five-week period of slow and close reading was that of holding my students' attention. I tried to introduce variety in the classroom discussions by asking students to debate certain propositions concerning love or happiness, sometimes in a straightforward formal way (one group of students arguing for a point, the other against), other times in a more playful way, setting up the class as a salon in which rather serious points could be discussed with varying degrees of wit (or *humour*). I continually reminded my students of what they had learned in the first part of the course and proposed as their first written assignment on *Ourika* the writing of a portrait of Ourika, including a short description of the first time we meet Ourika, her most salient character traits, her education, her interactions with Mme de B. and with Charles, and the ways in which she talks about being different.

This assignment provided a baseline for further class discussions and allowed me to find out which students were reading the text in some depth and which students were not progressing beyond a general grasp of the narrative line and dramatic situation. My goal was to encourage each student to exercise his or her reflective judgment on the text and to see the text in its moral and aesthetic complexity. As we reached the final two weeks of our unit on *Ourika*, I tried to elicit some speculative ideas from my students and to move away from questions that could be answered in a transparent way. The final assignment for the course was a three-page essay that answered a literarily complex question—a far cry from the relatively simple, imitative assignments of the beginning of the term:

> Is *Ourika* a tragedy? Consider the following points: Is Ourika a tragic heroine? Is she a victim of a closed, racist, unjust society, or does she bear some responsibility for her fate? Does the novel's ending seal Ourika's tragic destiny or offer her a promise of redemption?

I found the papers submitted on this topic to be thoughtful and, for the most part, convincing. The best students in the group wrote papers at the level of FRE 301 (which I was also teaching in spring 2005), with good moments of genuine textual analysis and attention to detail; the majority wrote solid and clear assessments; only a couple of students, while managing a workmanlike overview, remained at a far remove from the specificity of the text and would need to work on their analytic skills in FRE 301.

I had taught *Ourika* at least fifteen years ago, at Mount Holyoke College, in the context of a fourth-semester course quite similar in design to the University of Miami's FRE 212. It was a pleasure to come back to this rich and compact novel, now with the benefit of the excellent essays and notes by Joan DeJean and Margaret Waller in the MLA Texts and Translations series. Although the text can certainly be taught in various intellectual contexts and in quite differently designed courses, I think that it has particular qualities to recommend it in an intermediate course whose goal is to set up a transition from language acquisition to the study of literature and culture at the advanced undergraduate level. *Ourika*, the story of a black woman's suffering told in a confessional voice by a fictionalized black woman with emotion and insight, will elicit both emotion and insight from students today. Perhaps the greatest single quality of this important text is that it engages its readers—or, in the stronger French expression, *il accroche ses lecteurs*. It is impossible not to react to *Ourika*. Whether one is swayed by the melancholy rhetoric of the heroine and by the pathos of her self-presentation or whether, like some of my students, one finds in this discourse more than a bit of self-pity, it is, in the end, impossible to judge her badly. Built into her difference and her otherness is a combination of psychological acuity, denial, anger, passion, desire, resignation, and renewal that draws us into her universe. The novel provides an exemplary entryway into the world(s) of French and francophone literature and culture.

He Said, She Said: *Ourika* in a Gender Studies Course

Carolyn Fay

I teach Claire de Duras's *Ourika* and François-René de Chateaubriand's *René* together in a course titled He Said, She Said, which I developed at Franklin and Marshall College in 2003. Cross-listed in French and in women and gender studies, the course serves as both a survey of modern French literature and an introduction to gender criticism. The course was conceived within a women's studies program that was in the process of integrating gender studies into its curriculum, along the lines described by Beth Barila in "His Story / Her Story: A Dialogue about Including Men and Masculinities in the Women's Studies Curriculum" (35–37). Consequently, He Said, She Said does not treat French women writers as a group, the way a women's studies course might, but rather focuses on the construction and role of gender across male- and female-authored texts.

He Said, She Said presents paired readings of texts by men and women, such as Carol Singley's "Alternative Syllabi: 'Engaging Pairs.'" Each pair of texts is from roughly the same time period and is usually of the same genre. The guiding questions of the course are, What role does gender play in writing? How does writing inscribe sexual difference? The aim of He Said, She Said is not to answer these questions but rather to encourage students to explore, test, and even subvert them. As students begin to understand that gender is a social construct, they also begin to appreciate the limitations of talking about "women" and "men" as monolithic categories. *Ourika* and *René* are the ideal pair to introduce these concepts: after reading *Ourika*, students are better equipped to analyze the construction of René's masculinity; having read *René*, students comprehend how Ourika's entire story is determined by her sexual and racial difference, as well as by her status as a "cultural mulatta," to borrow Sylvie Chalaye's term (*Du noir* 181; my trans.). The dialogue between *Ourika* and *René* demonstrates that the construction of gender always intersects other categories of identity such as race, culture, sexuality, and social class.

Students are eager to participate in this dialogue as soon as they have read both texts. Undergraduate students of French are able to articulate the numerous similarities between the two texts immediately. Both consist of a first-person *récit* told within a frame narrative. Both René and Ourika are melancholy persons who recount their lives in an effort to gain solace and healing. Both characters are geographically exiled; both have an intense relationship with a sibling or siblinglike figure. Finally, both die at the end of their narratives. The interesting work is to identify the differences within these similarities and to flesh out the roles of gender and race as determinants of these differences.

To facilitate this comparative reading, I employ techniques that are designed to train students to read closely but also to consider the texts in a larger context. Before each class meeting, students are responsible for preparing answers to a series of discussion questions, starting with simple comprehension checks and proceeding to more complex questions that require students to engage critically with the texts. The questions orient students' approach to the texts and aid them in navigating difficult passages. In addition, students write weekly one-page reaction papers, in which they can comment on any aspect of the reading, ask questions, or follow avenues of thought we have not explored in class. Often I gather representative and provocative comments from these papers and use them as a basis for class discussions.

Although He Said, She Said is a discussion-based class, I do include two or three minilectures on the literary context (Romanticism) and historical background of the texts (French colonialism and the *le Code noir*). I also include a brief presentation on the African woman in eighteenth- and nineteenth-century European art. Looking at such works as Marie-Guillemine Benoist's *Portrait d'une négresse* and Édouard Manet's *Olympia* gets students thinking about ways of representing race and gender. Students are also expected to read Joan DeJean's and Margaret Waller's introductions to the MLA French edition of *Ourika*, which provide an excellent overview of the specific context in which Duras was writing. Since Waller situates *Ourika* within the *mal du siècle* vogue inspired by *René*, her remarks are a useful starting point for the comparative study in the classroom (xv).

I tend to focus on three points of comparison: narrative structure, characterization, and plot. After learning about the device of the framed narrative with *René*, students are quick to identify the framing structure in *Ourika*. Indeed, they usually comment that it is clearer in *Ourika* because Ourika's first-person narrative is presented as separate from the doctor's tale, whose text is italicized in the MLA edition and whose voice interrupts Ourika's only once. In addition, the doctor, though unnamed, is a character in his own right who functions as the supposed author of the entire text. In this way, as Chantal Bertrand-Jennings has argued, the doctor is Ourika's spokesman, a paternalistic and authorizing voice ("Problématique" 44). Moreover, the paucity of interjections or reactions on his part suggests that this is little more than a case study for him: an interesting one, but one that requires a clinical, though compassionate, distance.

The third-person frame narrative of *René*, on the contrary, emphasizes the personal relationship between René and his interlocutors, Chactas and Père Souël. The two older men prompt René to tell his story, and, although they too are quiet during the tale, René addresses them several times, which reminds the reader of their presence. At the conclusion, both Chactas and Père Souël comment on René's tale, offering comfort, admonition, and instruction. Whereas we see little of Ourika's relationship to her doctor-confessor, it is clear that René is among friends, "ses vieux amis" 'his old friends' (144 [Reboul]; my trans.). Moreover, thanks to the third-person narration of the frame, René appears to transmit his story directly to his companions. His story, compared with Ourika's, is more integrated into the surrounding narrative, just as he is more integrated into his adopted society than she. The narrative structure of each novel supports the narrative function of the hero's or heroine's story: René's tale further assimilates him into the Amerindian society, while Ourika's tale reinforces her exile from French society.

Gender plays a significant role here. In her fascinating study of melancholia in *Ourika* and *René*, Kari Weil relates the project of cultural assimilation to gender identification, noting that René's adoption of "a new family of fathers" operates through "his disidentification with the bodies of his mother and sister" (117). Telling the tale to his father figures is part of René's movement away from the feminine sphere toward a more acceptable masculinity. Père Souël's final words to René are harsh, but the narrator tells us that he harbors "un cœur compatissant" 'a sympathetic heart' (170 [Reboul]; my trans.). Students usually note that René grew up estranged from his father (145), and they hear Père Souël's admonishments as a message to "toughen up" or "be a man." The framing structure of the narrative, then, enacts a kind of paternal embrace of René and his story, bringing him into the fold of men. Ourika too grew up far from her biological parents, but the white, male, European doctor can neither provide surrogate parental support nor mediate inclusion into a gender-appropriate role for the black, female, African nun. Since he writes at the end that his medical treatment was useless (DeJean 45; Fowles 47), the doctor serves only to transmit to us her exotic story. The framing device maintains Ourika as other.

Analyzing the function of the narrative structure prepares students to think critically about the gender coding of the characters in each text. I have found it useful to begin these discussions with René, because his feminization is so obvious to students. My students typically find René whiny, weak, and effeminate, whereas they find Ourika sad, courageous, and strong. When pressed to explain, they say that Ourika has a concrete and insoluble problem while René's melancholy is vaguer, his behavior more passive. To provide context for René's character, we discuss the *mal du siècle*, drawing on Waller's seminal work in *The Male Malady*, which uncovers the gender politics at play in the construction of the Romantic hero. After detailing the ways in which René's language, attitude, and behavior can be described as stereotypically feminine (such as his emphasis on emotion and passion, his passivity, his lyrical melancholia), we compare him with his sister, Amélie. The comparative analysis of René and Amélie helps students understand the ways in which gender pervades the construction of these characters.

According to René, sister and brother were two peas in a pod (145 [Reboul]). His identification with his sister reinforces his own femininization; Waller points out, however, that René manages to valorize these feminine characteristics as part of a masculine vocation, recasting them as integral to his poetic sensitivity (*Male Malady* 41). Of course, Amélie, who is just as melancholy, just as sensitive, just as attuned to nature and reverie—in sum, just as Romantic as René— exhibits no poetic aspirations, only religious ones.

Students readily note that Amélie's *mal du siècle* is more physical. Her health deteriorates as she cares for René: "Elle maigrissait; ses yeux se creusaient; sa démarche était languissante, et sa voix troublée" 'She lost weight, her eyes grew hollow; her gait was listless, and her voice troubled' (159 [Reboul]; my trans.). This decline is the effect of the terrible secret she harbors. Once Amélie's incestuous desire is revealed to her brother, and thus to the reader, we can appreciate the degree to which the secret has been displaced from brother to sister. As Waller notes, "The story that had started out as the divulging of René's secret shifts to focus interest in unveiling hers" (47). Moreover, as Amélie weakens, René grows stronger. The disclosure of her desire occurs at the very moment she takes her final religious vows, a ceremony repeatedly figured as a sacrifice and a death. Amélie's first figurative death brings about a transformation in René: he is still miserable but takes enormous pleasure in having something specific to be miserable about. Meanwhile, Amélie suffers from a raging fever. Finally, her literal death is what prompts René to tell the story and authorizes him to make it his story. Weil observes that René tells his tale "over the dead body of his sister" (113). I would add that he also tells it on the body of his sister; desire and disease are imprinted on the female body.

Ourika, of course, also plays on the idea of the female body as impressionable surface. Students easily identify the similarities between Ourika and Amélie: both are sickly and melancholic; both suffer a "criminal" passion they dare not name. Having analyzed Amélie's function as René's other helps prepare students to understand Ourika as an entire society's other. It is interesting to point out to students that during our discussions of René and Amélie we do not talk of their whiteness, whereas it is difficult not to discuss Ourika's blackness. Like Amélie, Ourika suffers from a *mal du siècle* whose root cause is specific and which manifests itself physically. But unlike Amélie, Ourika believes that the physical is her affliction.

I ask my students to highlight the instances in the text that emphasize Ourika's belief that her skin color is the problem: she avoids looking in mirrors (DeJean 15; Fowles 15), she veils herself in elaborate clothing (27; 28), and she even imagines the contemptuous face of the white European in place of her own (28; 29). It is important to help students see, however, that the societal prejudice Ourika suffers results from the intersection of her race and her gender. As many critics have pointed out, Ourika's exclusion from white European society turns on the issue of marriage and procreation (Chilcoat, "Civility" 127; Massardier-Kenney 191; Weil 120). Nathaniel Wing writes, "Ourika as a child can be accommodated within the family; Ourika as a potential lover, wife, and mother becomes a threat of contaminating sexuality and miscegenation" (88). Ourika's skin color may be the patent sign of her difference, but her gender— and the gender role she is expected to maintain—is the more subtle factor that produces her exile. It is subtle, because, while the text critiques racial politics, it never questions the gender divide. As the marquise pointedly states, Ourika has been raised like every other aristocratic French girl of the time—groomed for marriage and motherhood within a particular class of society that will have nothing of her (DeJean 13; Fowles 13). And this desire that has been inculcated in

Ourika remains uninterrogated. While Ourika fantasizes about an unprejudiced society where skin color no longer isolates her (18–19; 19), she cannot imagine wanting anything outside of marriage and family for herself (17; 17–18). Body and mind restricted by her society, Ourika is always doubly trapped by her race and her gender.

Ourika, like Amélie, must follow the unmarried woman's path: convent, illness, and death. After reading the two texts, students grasp that women in nineteenth-century Europe had few options open to them, a fact that shapes the plot of each narrative. Although alienated from his father and his country, René has many more choices than either Ourika or Amélie. The Natchez tribe requires him to marry, but he is free to ignore his wife and live alone (143 [Reboul]). Ourika, of course, wants to marry in her society but cannot. Moreover, René has much greater mobility than Ourika. René's narrative is structured around his travels to Italy, Greece, within France, and finally to America. While Ourika's tale begins with her voyage to France, it is a displacement inaccessible to her own memory and one that was imposed on her: "Je fus rapportée du Sénégal" 'I was brought here from Senegal' (DeJean 7; Fowles 7).

Imposition is a recurring theme in *Ourika*. Bought by the chevalier de B., brought to France as a young child, and raised, caressed, and dressed by her adoptive mother, Ourika lives a life determined by others. Even the two major scenes of discovery emphasize her lack of agency. On both occasions it is the marquise who reveals information to Ourika: in the first, her impossible position in French society (12–14; 12–14), and, in the second, her forbidden love for Charles (40–41; 42–43). The first scene functions as a turning point in the plot, for this is when Ourika realizes that she can never belong to her adopted society. The second scene precipitates her entrance into the convent and ultimately her death. In both instances, Ourika is on the receiving end of the plot twist.

The second scene of revelation makes an interesting point of comparison with Amélie's revelation in *René*. The secret that the narrative wants to reveal is transferred from René to Amélie: Amélie's incestuous desire is the cause of René's hidden sorrow. When the marquise presses Ourika to bare her soul, Ourika insists that she harbors no secret: "Je n'ai point de secret . . . ma position et ma couleur sont tout mon mal, vous le savez" 'I have no secret. . . . You know very well what my problems are. My social situation. And the color of my skin' (40; 42). This statement echoes her earlier claim to the doctor: "Je n'ai point de secret: mon malheur, c'est l'histoire de toute ma vie" 'I have no secrets. The story of my unhappiness is the same as the story of my life' (5; 5). Nevertheless, the narrative demands that she have a secret, and so the marquise provides one, the *passion criminelle*.

The comparison of secrets between *Ourika* and *René* not only demonstrates to students the gendering of plot but also highlights the extent to which race and gender are inextricably knotted in Ourika's identity and her fate. Amélie's passion is forbidden because of the societal taboo on incest. Although Charles functions as a brother for Ourika, her love is criminal not because it is quasi-incestuous but because it poses the threat of racial miscegenation, as Wing reminds us (99). And in her final confrontation with Ourika, the marquise suggests that it is not Ourika's race but her sexual desire that is the cause of her unhappiness. Caught in the European construct of the black woman, Ourika can no more deny her passion than she can change the color of her skin. The only possible avenue is the convent, where she can mask both. Although the convent is the conventional end for the unmarried woman (as in *René*), in *Ourika* it serves to remove the black woman from a society that does not want to see her and that desires her story only on her death.

Students find the juxtaposition of these texts enlightening. Reading *Ourika* helps them realize that, despite his melancholia, René occupies a privileged position by virtue of his gender and race; *René* elucidates the role of gender in Ourika's plight. This approach to teaching *Ourika* and *René*, as well as the entire "he said she said" matrix could be adapted easily to a comparative literature or world-literatures-in-translation course that focuses on the intersection of gender and race in narrative. As part of a gender studies curriculum, *Ourika* and *René* would be useful model texts for a course designed to introduce undergraduates or graduate students to literary theory, such as feminist, multicultural, psychoanalytic, and even biographical criticism.

I am always impressed by the intensity with which students approach these texts. My students enjoy debating the different variables and imagining the narrative results: Should the chevalier de B. have left Ourika in Senegal? What if Ourika had been male? Would she have sought solitude like René? The paired reading engages students in a kind of shared textual universe, and they find the questions posed by these nineteenth-century novels to be important and pertinent to their own lives. *Ourika* and *René* are a compelling duo not only for teaching gender analysis but also for illustrating the power of literature to connect to real life.

Ourika in the Humanities Survey

Jen Hill

Sixteen weeks. Europe and the world from the Renaissance to the present in an interdisciplinary context. A required course with a nonspecialist audience. At its best, the course swiftly and broadly outlines some of the compelling issues, ideas, and events of the past five hundred years as it struggles to convey the complex nature of modernity. At its worst, it conveys modern history in reductive comic-book form. If ever a text were a solution to this potential pedagogical nightmare, it is Claire de Duras's *Ourika*.

Taught at exactly the midpoint in a second-year humanities survey, *Ourika* illuminates and extends arguments about race and culture discussed earlier in the semester in texts including New World "discovery" accounts and Aphra Behn's *Oroonoko* while enabling us to historicize central questions in postcolonial, postmodern, late-twentieth-century texts we will read later in the semester. Duras's novel also raises questions about the limits of Enlightenment ideals and the French Revolution and introduces the linked aesthetic and political concerns of Romanticism that we will examine in works by Robert Southey, William Wordsworth, and William Blake. These contexts are what we might think of as the factual and thematic matter of the course; the way in which Duras's text raises these issues makes it valuable for advancing the analytic reading and writing skills that are the mandate of the humanities survey.

Students' affective engagement with *Ourika* is a good starting point for discussion. Their identification with the character of Ourika can be as specific as being female students of color on a mostly white campus or as general as being the same age as she is. Asked for moments in the text that provoke these feelings of identification, students choose any number of passages, but those passages all engage our sympathy: we feel for Ourika, students point out after they read the lines aloud. The discussion moves quickly from how we feel about the text to how the text is able to make us feel, a discussion that forces us to pay attention to how Duras's style is as much part of her larger argument as the plot of the narrative. This concept is not news to literary scholars, but to nonmajors unfamiliar with the study of literature, *Ourika* offers an opportunity to understand more fully how literary texts work. The brevity of Duras's text makes students accountable for the evidence they use to support their arguments about the relation of sympathy to the text's sometimes oblique assertions about race, gender, and class.

Discussion of how and to what end Duras uses sympathy leads students to return to an earlier literary text from the syllabus that also examines the political potential and limits of sympathy, *Oroonoko*. By identifying the different narrative strategies of sympathy in both texts, we can comment more widely on how economies of sentiment can be marshaled and structured to confer or endorse otherwise impossible subject positions—as well as the pitfalls of this strategy—while identifying thematic and stylistic continuities and discontinuities across the centuries.

Behn's text details the life of the African prince Oroonoko, his capture by slavers, and his life as the rebellious slave leader Caesar in British Surinam. In its almost anthropological attention to Oroonoko/Caesar's life, the novel invests the protagonist with a subjectivity that the institution of slavery and colonial relations would deny him. Readers are invited to sympathize with his position and, although shocked by it, understand his ritualized, passionate murder of his pregnant wife, Imoinda, and his stoical resistance to his white oppressors. The bill for our sympathy comes due at the novel's end, in the detailed, horrifying description of Oroonoko's torture and death. In addition to revealing the effectiveness of sympathy as a strategy for political argument, the excessiveness of Oroonoko's final torture signals the murdering colonials' inability to contain the threat posed by the "Royal Slave" and, by extension, slaves and oppressed populations in general.

Asked to identify similar moments of excess in *Ourika*, students hesitate, for Duras's narrative is intimate; Ourika's suffering is private and hidden, her tale narrated only to the doctor. Students conclude that Behn's account is theatrical: Oroonoko's suffering is presented as a spectacle, demanding a reaction from its audience that reinforces the difference it wants its audience to question. In contrast, Ourika's first-person account of the narrow confines of her existence invites readers to experience her life vicariously, and their identification with her plight puts into question assumptions about difference. Duras seems to endorse sympathy as a means to negotiate or minimize difference; at the same time, she asserts that difference is fundamental. Students identify this paradox as a central issue of the Enlightenment. As ideas of equality and rights spread in the eighteenth century, so too is there a proliferation of individuals and therefore of difference.

Behn's and Duras's differing narrative strategies lead students to examine further the use of trope and literary convention in both texts. Behn's use of the noble savage brings into the debate Michel Montaigne's "On the Cannibals" and selections from Jean-Jacques Rousseau's *Discourse on the Origin and Foundations of Inequality among Men*; students then can discuss whether that trope is at work in *Ourika*'s discussion of difference and, if so, how. Similarly, the narration of *Oroonoko*, in which a female British colonist recounts the slave leader's story, invites comparison with the doctor's presentation and contextualization of Ourika's tale. Like the white colonial narrator of Behn's tale, the doctor structures and controls the work, authoring and authorizing the narrative. His is a profession dedicated to scientific rationality; he is at the convent to assess the nun's health and treat her condition. The doctor's failure to cure Ourika reveals the possible limits of empiricism and rationalism—concepts students link not only to scientific figures including Francis Bacon and Isaac Newton but also to Enlightenment figures like Immanuel Kant—as well as the limits of sympathy.

Finally, while Behn employs the conventions of romance to make Oroonoko and his plight legible, Duras uses Ourika's impossible love for Charles to create a role that the protagonist can fulfill. The doctor—the reader—is invited to understand her plight in the following terms: although there are many problems that confront her, it is the isolation of unrequited love that is somehow the most problematic, the implication being that political and social disenfranchisement would be bearable if only they did not preclude friendship, love, and the possibility of family. Ourika herself muses that the life of a slave might be preferable (DeJean 38; Fowles 39). The convention of the romantic love plot enables Ourika to see herself in a role she understands, to process or explain the effects of her isolation to herself in a comprehensible way, while offering Duras a way out of a narrative that has no easy resolution. But seeing this plot as a convention makes it more difficult to accept Ourika as a tragic romantic heroine and dismisses the larger structural issues behind her alienation.

The text's complex representation of religion also provides students with an opportunity to further their critical reading skills. Although they have just read *Candide*'s satirical portrait of the church as a self-serving and hypocritical institution, students are inclined to take Ourika's retreat into the convent at face value. The course has nonetheless discussed the church from the start as an institution, looking at the social and political contexts of the Inquisition, the Reconquest, the Reformation, and the Counter-Reformation, using texts such as the *Malleus Maleficarum* (1487) and selections from Erasmus and Martin Luther. From reading the abbé Emmanuel-Joseph Sieyès's "What Is the Third Estate?" and analyzing the cultural contexts of the French Revolution, students also have some sense of the complicated position of the church in eighteenth-century France. How sincerely are we to take Ourika's embrace of religion and faith as a solution to her problems? True, her exclusion from the marriage market is rectified in some way when she becomes a bride of Christ. Some students conclude that the failure of the postrevolutionary order to extend its promise of opportunity to Ourika leads her to lose faith in the promise of the revolution and to turn to the church as a repudiation of rationality and empiricism as well as an avenue to a kind of freedom that society denies her. Recognizing that she cannot find happiness here on earth, she defers her happiness until her death, when, according to Christian doctrine, she will have eternal life in heaven.

Nevertheless, Ourika's entrance into the convent seems an admission of how profoundly society has failed her. Is Ourika's avid embrace of the convent at book's end, like *Oroonoko*'s ending, a moment of excess that asks us to doubt Ourika's conclusions about rejecting the social for the spiritual? Perhaps Ourika's musings on the "nouveau jour" 'new light' of her situation and the "calme" 'calm' it brings her (DeJean 45; Fowles 46) are Duras's solutions to the narrative problem of what to do with this multiply alienated character.

Attention to the text's narrative strategies leads to a larger discussion of difference and identity, a discussion that connects to Enlightenment rights discourses.

Students quickly pick up on what they see as a disjunction between Ourika's interior and her exterior—between her intelligence and her self-knowledge, on the one hand, and the limited forms of agency extended to her as a black woman alienated from the culture and class in which she was raised, on the other. After "quelques espérances" '[the] wisp of hope' the revolution holds out to her (18; 19), Ourika recognizes the failures of the revolution to deliver her from her isolation. She expresses her disappointment in overtly political figures, "ces personnages qui voulaient maîtriser les événements" 'men . . . trying to control the course of events' (19; 19–20), and students connect her critique to political writings they have encountered by Sieyès, Olympe de Gouges (arts. 7–10), Mary Wollstonecraft, and Toussaint Louverture. Despite her critique, as a ward of an aristocratic household, Ourika, who is privileged and well educated in comparison with others in society, will be judged with a class to which she cannot, as she has discovered, ever belong.

Ourika's hope of belonging is further dampened by her exclusion from the marriage market. Her impossible love for Charles makes apparent the intertwined nature of race and gender. Because of her race, Ourika is excluded from marriage, the only available option for someone of her upbringing, gender, and class position. Ourika has received "tout ce qui devait former une éducation parfaite" 'all that is considered essential for a girl's perfect education' (9; 9): lessons in singing and painting, as well as exposure to literature. This is precisely the education that Wollstonecraft critiques in *Vindication of the Rights of Woman* as "disorderly" (159). For Wollstonecraft, "[n]ovels, music, poetry, and gallantry, all tend to make women the creatures of sensation," which necessarily prevents them from practicing "understanding [which], as life advances, is the only method pointed out by nature to calm the passions" (163). Ourika's education fails to prepare her for anything other than marriage into Mme de B.'s class; it also fails to prepare her intellectually to handle her discovery of her true position in society.

Ourika's inability to identify with other blacks in French society is due to both the formal education that Wollstonecraft critiques and her informal conditioning by the culture in which she inhabits. Students point to Ourika's deep revulsion at her racial difference as evidence of her internalization of the values and tastes of the aristocratic class (15; 15–16). The moment of consciousness is for Ourika a moment of terrible isolation; in discussions about Frantz Fanon's work on colonial practices later in the semester, students return to Ourika's experience and how her recognition of her difference violently imparts recognition of her alienation, rather than a new sense of belonging (20; 20).

Further, Ourika cannot reconcile herself to "[l]es massacres de Saint-Domingue" '[t]he Santo Domingo massacres' (20; 21). To counter Ourika's conclusions about the Haitian Revolution, students cite Toussaint Louverture's "Letter to the Directory, 28 October 1797," in which Toussaint Louverture describes the violent excesses of the rebellion as being the logical outcome of conditions that alienate blacks from the state of nature and deny them an education, conditions that lead to their being "classed apart from the rest of mankind" (168). Students find in Toussaint Louverture's argument support for their sense that Ourika's understanding of her position is a result of both her singularity and her poor education. But Ourika is quite literally an ocean away from Toussaint Louverture and black Haitians and can only perceive her difference from them as being as profound as her difference from the white society surrounding her.

Students' understanding of how Ourika's alienation is the result not only of her personal situation but also of larger political and economic systems is aided by discussion of excerpts from *The Letters of the Late Ignatius Sancho, an African*, Ottobah Cugoano's *Thoughts and Sentiments on the Evil of Slavery and Commerce of the Human Species*, and Olaudah Equiano's *The Interesting Narrative of the Life of Olaudah Equiano, or Gustavus Vassa the African*. These authors assert possibilities of subjectivity and agency denied Ourika and help students situate the fictional Ourika's experience in the lived experience of black Euopeans. Cugoano's abolitionist account of the history of slavery, of its underpinning of the economy and its moral costs, addresses social and historical issues relevant to Ourika's position that Duras's novel sidesteps. A closer nonfiction analogue to Ourika's experience is Mary Prince's Romantic-era account of her life in slavery, *The History of Mary Prince, a West Indian Slave*. Prince's description of terrible suffering under slavery, her education, and her life as a free woman in England counters the bleak tragedy of Ourika's death. Ourika's experience and sad end are imagined and written by a white Frenchwoman; Prince's account, although edited and influenced by others, is written by an ex-slave and models a black British identity available to its author in the early nineteenth century.

As Margaret Waller argues in her introduction to the MLA editions, *Ourika* both employs and departs from Romantic traditions. On the one hand, its emphasis on feeling, its embrace of sympathy, and its skepticism of rationality make it an excellent introduction to Romanticism for a nonspecialist audience. On the other hand, its serious engagement with politics, gender, and race complicates oversimplified, traditional representations of a masculine Romanticism that turns away from society toward nature. *Ourika* also becomes a general point of reflection and departure for students who are uneasy reading and discussing poetry. More comfortable with literature after having read Duras, they now turn to English poetry, reversing the course's chronology a bit by starting with an accessible, sentimental ballad by Southey, "The Sailor, Who Had Served in the Slave Trade." Using some of the reading strategies developed in our discussions of *Ourika*, students argue that the abolitionist ballad's tight rhyme scheme reinforces the wretchedness of the sailor who was forced to beat a slave to death on a slave ship and point out how Southey recruits sympathy to political ends: when the minister joins the guilty sailor in prayer at the poem's end, those who read the poem are asked to aid slaves everywhere in their prayers. Yet here, as in *Oroonoko*, sentiment stops short of empathy and reinforces the alterity of the black slave.

As we move on to poetry by Blake and Wordsworth, students extend their arguments about how sympathy and emotion work in texts while contextualizing *Ourika* broadly in relation to Romanticism. Like Southey's piece, selected poems from Blake's *Songs of Innocence* (1789) and *Songs of Experience* (1794) are accessible, yet have complex political motivations. The contradictions and challenges in Blake's poem "The Little Black Boy" strangely anticipate Ourika's position and her deferment of happiness to heavenly reward. In *Slavery and the Romantic Imagination*, Debbie Lee reads the poem as enabling "an altering vision where both self and other are preserved" (118), offering a counterbalance to Ourika's destruction—her withdrawal from society as well as her withering to nothingness and eventual death—and a possible antidote to Duras's depressing vision of isolation and difference. The "little black thing" in Blake's "The Chimney Sweeper" is a white child, blackened by his slave labor as a sweep. When he condemns not only his parents, who have sold him into slavery, but also "God & his Priest & King / Who make up a heaven of our misery," he states outright the structural complicities that remain buried in Duras's text. Yet Duras's novel is in the end an example of the accessible literature that Wordsworth champions in his "Preface to the *Lyrical Ballads*"; having read *Ourika*, students understand more fully the claims Wordsworth makes for the political potency of passion and pleasure in literature.

Teachings of *Ourika*

Barbara Woshinsky

This essay's title is a variation on the academic commonplace "readings of . . ." Like the term *readings*, *teachings* has a double implication: how *Ourika* can be taught to students and the insights it can bring to teachers and readers. One sign of a masterpiece is that it can be read on many levels. Claire de Duras's *Ourika* certainly meets this criterion.

I first taught the novel in 1996, in a combined graduate-undergraduate literature course on French women writers, and again in the following year, when the focus was on francophone literature. In those early classes, we read Claudine Herrmann's 1979 edition of *Ourika* in the Des Femmes collection. The publication of the excellent MLA critical editions has made this classic novel not only more available but also more accessible and rewarding to contemporary readers. Hence my colleagues and I have found ourselves using the novel in progressively less-advanced classes, from 300-level topics courses to introduction to literary analysis to a bridge course aiming to take students from their language studies to the level of literature. My colleague David R. Ellison's essay for this volume describes the teaching of *Ourika* in our bridge course. Here I share what I have learned from teaching the novel in introduction to literature and advanced literature courses. In reflecting on my many and varied teachings of *Ourika*, I find that all of them have in some way gravitated around the concatenation of race and gender that occurs within a sensitive female consciousness.

Teaching the Marriage Plot

My own first reading of *Ourika* was a revelation comparable only to my discovery of Mme de Lafayette's *La Princesse de Clèves* many years earlier. In both cases, my immediate responses were, "How could *this* novel have existed at *that* time?" and "Why didn't I know about it before?" These reactions are often echoed by my students. There is little need to pitch Lafayette or Duras to a class: though historical contexualization is necessary to fully understand and appreciate the works, students find both Mme de Clèves's and Ourika's stories compelling in themselves. Thus I first taught *Ourika* together with *La Princesse de Clèves* in a French women writers course that was cross-listed with women's studies. That context helped bring out continuities and contrasts with other works exploring and exploding the "marriage plot." While other women authors—including Lafayette—describe their heroine's rejection of marriage, Duras represents the tragedy of the impossibility of marriage for her eponymous character. I presented the novel as a tragedy of marriage denied. For a course on francophone women's writing the following year, the focus was still on marriage, but in a larger social context: I taught *Ourika* as a drama testing the limits of assimilation according to the French model, as its heroine runs up against the dual constraints of race and gender.

Would I offer these courses again today? On the one hand, I think rubrics like French Women Writers or Francophone Women's Writing belong to an earlier, necessary stage of women's studies, which required separating out the female voice in order to hear it, for the first time, in all its distinctness. On the other hand, the questioning of assimilation seems even more pertinent in the current social environment than it did ten years ago.

Today I might envision a course with a broader perspective—The Colonial Anatomy of Marriage—that would bridge gender, postcolonial, and cultural studies. Joan DeJean's introduction to the MLA *Ourika* edition gives an excellent summary of its historical and social context. Yet even more can be done to tie *Ourika* to the complex racial context of restoration France. I might begin by assigning two short background readings on marriage policy in the Old Regime: the Code Noir of 1685 (Sala-Molins 90–203) and Samuel Chatman's article "There Are No Slaves in France" (both texts are available online).

In the late seventeenth century, the focus of miscegenation legislation was less on race than on religion. After the annexation of Strasbourg in 1681, Louis XIV prohibited marriages between Catholics and Protestants. Forced conversions of Protestants begin in 1685, the same year as the promulgation of the Code Noir governing the treatment of African slaves in the colonies. In contrast to the treatment of non-Catholics, Louis XIV's and Jean-Baptiste Colbert's policy regarding miscegenation between blacks and whites in the colonies was relatively mild. Black concubines and their children were to be taken from their master, who was required to pay a fine. Unmarried white slaveholders were ordered to wed their slave mistresses in a Catholic ceremony; their children would be freed and legitimized (Sala-Molins, art. 8–9).

Yet what was tolerated in the colonies and what was acceptable in metropolitan France were two radically different matters. In principle, or at least in national myth, there were no slaves in France. In reality, a few slave owners brought their black maids and servants with them on their visits to the home country; the number of slaves present in France in the eighteenth century never exceeded five thousand, or .025 percent of the population (Chatman 144). Despite this low proportion, a growing perception developed in the mother country that blacks were arriving in ever-greater numbers and becoming a source of disorder. In response to these fears and prejudices, the monarchy issued a series of restrictive revisions to the Code Noir, culminating in a royal edict of 1778 that forbade blacks in France from marrying at all, for fear of racial mixing. Blacks were also prohibited from entering the country. Ourika may refer to these prohibitions in calling hers a "race proscrite" (DeJean 20; Fowles's translation, "race of outcasts" [21], does not quite convey this idea). But wealthy or aristocratic persons evidently found ways around this proscription (Woshinsky 168–69).

The Code Noir, suspended during the revolution, was reimposed in 1802 (DeJean, Introduction x). Ourika's experience implies that even if an interracial marriage could have been arranged at that time, it was, at the least, highly "frowned upon" (Chatman 149). Thus, in an elliptical and telescoped fashion, Duras's *tour d'horizon* of France from liberal Enlightenment through revolution to restoration traces the changes for the worse as "scientific racism" develops during that period (Chilcoat, "Civility" 132).

Teaching Racial Tensions

The fears and reactions provoked in the eighteenth and nineteenth centuries by the return of the repressed to the colonizer country prefigure the debates and violence around immigration in France today—not to mention the United States. As Alice L. Conklin states, current racial problems, troubling as they are, can at least make the teaching of French history and culture more accessible:

> A country that seemed eternally associated in the minds of students with berets, cheese and baguettes can now be presented to them as a sister republic founded on the same central contradiction as our own: an inspiring celebration of human rights and freedom in tandem with a troubled legacy of discrimination on the basis of race (not to mention gender).   (215)

Parallels between colonial and postcolonial tensions can be brought out through a series of class or online discussion questions: Is there a contradiction between "There are no slaves in France" and the reality of life in France in the eighteenth and nineteenth centuries? At the present time, what are the beliefs in France and the United States concerning minorities (assimilation, melting pot, etc.)? How do these beliefs (or myths) square with social reality? Papers could also be assigned on a topic such as "Hidden Racism in *Ourika*." One broad educational benefit of this approach is that students (like many other people) sometimes try to deny unpleasant social realities by placing them long ago and in another country. I occasionally receive comments on papers or exams such as "nineteenth-century French people were very racist."

Class time could be spent bringing out the connections between historical and ideological themes and the literary representation of racism as "lived" by the heroine in the text. As Michael Lucey puts it, Ourika "has to learn the implications of a racial and gendered identity of which she was initially unaware" (176). Close textual analysis helps students discover how Duras's up close and personal narrative makes readers undergo Ourika's painful apprenticeship alongside the heroine. I might also assign Jean Racine's *Phèdre* along with *Ourika*, to have students explore the themes of guilt and exclusion of the other common to the two works.

Teaching Narrative Strategies

In addition to working well in advanced courses, *Ourika* serves in an introductory literature class to develop an understanding of narrative. Two passages have proved particularly useful in this light: the introduction to the novel, where we see first see Ourika framed through the young doctor's eyes, and the famous "screen scene," where she overhears the fateful conversation between the marquise and Mme de B. Preparatory reading questions ask the students to examine closely the language of this passage, identifying different past tenses and explaining how they function in the narrative. In class, I often ask students to compare the screen episode with a five-act play: a prologue—"Il y avait dans le salon de Mme de B. un grand paravent de laque" 'There was, in Mme de B.'s drawing room, a large lacquer screen' (DeJean 11; Fowles 11)—and four sections alternating dialogue with subjective reaction. Students give technical answers to questions about verb usage but also comment on the repetition of the past definite, "je vis tout, je me vis négresse" (12). Fowles's translation eliminates the important shift in the French original from "je vis" (seeing how she is seen) to "je me vis" (seeing herself); instead, we have the abstract expression "I comprehended all. I was black" (12). It would be worthwhile to point out this difference when teaching the text in English.

After a preliminary class discussion of this passage, I sometimes distribute copies of an illustration of the scene from the 1826 edition (Little, "Table" xii, "Cahier" xx). This picture is rich in mixed cultural messages. On the one hand, Ourika's tapestry work, a favored occupation among leisured young ladies, and her fashionable dress, ironically "à l'orientale" 'oriental costume' (DeJean 8; Fowles 8), proclaim her high status. On the other hand, her bare black arms contrast with the puffy sleeves, long gloves, and pale skin of the white woman half-hidden in the left corner; Ourika's bulging eyes and open mouth, communicating her astonishment, turn her into a stereotype of an African girl. It is interesting to ask the students to compare the degree of racism in the illustration with that in Duras's text and to draw social conclusions. The visual representation of this scene also helps the students see the screen as a symbolic separation from white society. Opaque but permeable, it renders Ourika invisible while allowing the poisonous opinions of that society to penetrate. As my classes have progressed into the heart of the novel, probably the most compelling aspect for the students (mainly young women) has been the development of Ourika's love for her cousin Charles. Unrequited love is a universal experience that transcends the specificities of race and time and that makes Ourika's situation particularly poignant. One reading assignment that worked well was to have students follow the development of the relationship between Charles and Ourika and to find words in the text that signify its evolution from friendship to familial or maternal affection and finally to love. I gave variations on this assignment at four different points in our reading so that students would have a small number of pages to examine at a given time. Students noted that Ourika speaks of Charles first as her "conseil et . . . soutien" 'adviser . . . and defender' (9; 9); then as "un frère" for whom she is 'exactly as a sister' (17; 18); then she discovers "[l]a tendresse . . . d'une mère" 'my feelings for him had grown maternal' (28; 29); and, finally, "un amour coupable" 'a forbidden love' (41; 43). Most of the class concluded that Ourika was, indeed, in love with Charles and that her love, while forbidden, was not guilty. One student became so interested in this question that she wrote her final paper on the varieties of love in *Ourika*, arguing convincingly that love transcends categories.

Such final papers allow students to reflect globally on the narrative. Topics that I have found to work successfully include "Ourika entre race et genre" 'Ourika between Race and Gender'; "Paravent, voile et miroir" 'Screen, Veil, and Mirror'; "Le mal d'Ourika" 'Ourika's Sickness'; and "*Ourika*: 'Masque blanc, visage noir,'" '*Ourika*: "White Mask, Black Face,"' assigned in conjunction with David O'Connell's article based on the theories of Frantz Fanon. Recently a male student seemed to have difficulty identifying with the female heroine or finding a topic that interested him; I suggested he write on the topic "Si Ourika était un homme?" 'What If Ourika Were a Man?'

Teaching the Teacher

This rather technical, how-to description of my course experiences tends to obscure the most important component of teaching *Ourika*, which might be called meaningfulness. Students of color often respond strongly to the injustices of slavery shown in the novel; they are justifiably indignant at Ourika's astonishing statement, the more appalling for its very matter-of-factness, "M. de B. m'acheta" 'He took pity and bought me' (7; 7). Haitian American students in our classes help enlighten their classmates (and teachers) about their proud and tragic heritage. Understanding otherness requires little effort of the imagination in Miami, where nearly everyone—or her or his parents—is an exile from somewhere else—Cuba, the Caribbean, or the American North.

A final teaching I have drawn from my classroom experience with *Ourika* is the importance of religion in some students' lives and their ability to understand the ending of the novel in a way that I, like the modern, secularized doctor-narrator, would not have appreciated a few years ago. Some students, graduates of Catholic schools, have expressed satisfaction at the fact that Ourika finds refuge in the convent. Others, like me, view this refuge with some scepticism; after all, Ourika's last words are "Laissez-moi aller, Charles, dans le seul lieu où il me soit permis de penser sans cesse à vous…" 'Let me go, Charles, to the one place where I may still think of you day and night …' (45; 46). In many ways, the religious dimension of the novel is closer to Duras's sensibility than is twenty-first-century skepticism.

Whether in terms of family and love relationships, ethnicity, the role of women in society, racism, or general feelings of otherness—physical and spiritual exile—what *Ourika* teaches is the power of literature to engage us in very personal ways.

NOTES ON CONTRIBUTORS

Chantal Bertrand-Jennings is professor emerita at the University of Toronto. Her recent books include *Un autre Mal du siècle: Le Romantisme des romancières, 1800–1846* (2005) and *D'un siècle l'autre: Romans de Claire de Duras* (2001). She is the editor of *Masculin/Féminin: Le dix-neuvième siècle à l'épreuve du genre* (1999) and has published many articles on women writers. She is working on Simone de Beauvoir's fiction.

Mary Ellen Birkett is professor of French studies at Smith College. Her publications touch on Desbordes-Valmore, Fontenelle, Hugo, Lamartine, Nodier, Rousseau, Sainte-Beuve, Sand, Senancour, Stendhal, and Vigny. She is coeditor of *Religious Tolerance and Intolerance in Ancient and Modern Worlds* (2007) and author of *Lamartine and the Poetics of Landscape* (1982). She is studying the formation of French colonial policy in the Pacific in the first half of the nineteenth century.

Mary Jane Cowles is professor of French at Kenyon College. The author of articles on Rousseau, Mme de Staël, Balzac, Nodier, Nerval, Anatole France, and Dumas and film, she is working on a book tentatively titled "The Economy of Loss: The Absent Mother in French Literature, 1770–1850." Her teaching interests include psychoanalytic approaches to reading, representations of the French Revolution, and maternal themes in French literature.

Thérèse De Raedt is assistant professor of French at the University of Utah. She is writing a book manuscript tentatively entitled: "Visuality and Race: Figuring the African in France at the Turn of the Nineteenth Century." Her research interests also include minority discourse and comparative cultural approaches to foreigners in French-speaking cultures. She has studied Club Med and its intersections with postcolonial and post-Holocaust France.

Christine De Vinne is professor of English at Ursuline College. Her work on biography, autobiography, and confession has appeared in *Prose Studies*, *English Studies*, and *Doris Lessing Studies*. She is a contributor to *Onoma* and book review editor of *Names*. Her research and teaching interests include life writing, cultural theory, and names studies. She is working on a book-length study of confession in American autobiography.

Damon DiMauro is professor of French at Gordon College. He has published articles on French literature, particularly on writings from the Renaissance (Louis Des Masures, Antoine de Chandieu, André de Rivaudeau, Robert Garnier). He is working on a book on Garnier's *Les Juifves*.

David R. Ellison is Distinguished Professor in the Humanities at the University of Miami. He is the author of *Ethics and Aesthetics in European Modernist Literature: From the Sublime to the Uncanny* (2001), *Of Words and the World: Referential Anxiety in Contemporary French Fiction* (1993), *Understanding Albert Camus* (1990), and *The Reading of Proust* (1984). He is completing a book, "A Reader's Guide to *In Search of Lost Time*."

Carolyn Fay is an independent scholar in the San Francisco Bay area. She has published articles on *Les contes amoureux par Madame Jeanne Flore*, on Charles Perrault's "La Belle au bois dormant," and on the epistolary friendship of Claire de Duras and Rosalie de Constant. She is working on a book on sleep and dream in nineteenth-century France and is the creator of ImaginingSleep.com, an interdisciplinary online course on sleep and dream.

Dawn Fulton is associate professor in the Department of French Studies at Smith College. She is the author of articles on French Caribbean literature in *Romanic Review*, *Callaloo*, and *Studies in Twentieth and Twenty-First Century Literature* and of *Signs of Dissent: Maryse Condé and Postcolonial Criticism* (2008). She is at work on a project on francophone literature of urban migration.

Kathryn M. Grossman is professor of French at Penn State University, University Park. She is the author of Les Misérables: *Conversion, Revolution, Redemption* (1996), *Figuring Transcendence in* Les Misérables: *Hugo's Romantic Sublime* (1994), and *The Early Novels of Victor Hugo: Towards a Poetics of Harmony* (1986), and she coedited *Confrontations: Politics and Aesthetics in Nineteenth-Century France* (2001). Her current work focuses both on Hugo's later novels and on the pedagogy of literature.

Jen Hill is associate professor of English at the University of Nevada, Reno. She is the author of *White Horizon: The Arctic in the Nineteenth-Century British Imagination* (2007) and *An Exhilaration of Wings: The Literature of Birdwatching* (1999). She is preparing a book-length manuscript on natural history and landscape in nineteenth-century Britain.

Deborah Jenson teaches in the Department of Romance Studies at Duke University. She was previously director of the Center for the Humanities and professor of French at the University of Wisconsin, Madison. The author of *Trauma and Its Representations: The Social Life of Mimesis in Post-revolutionary France* (2001) and of *Beyond the Slave Narrative: Sex, Politics, and Manuscripts in the Haitian Revolution* (under contract), she is also the editor of an issue of *Yale French Studies* on Haiti (2005) and, with Doris Y. Kadish, of the MLA Text and Translation of *Sarah*.

Doris Y. Kadish is Distinguished Research Professor of Romance Languages and Women's Studies at the University of Georgia. She has published on Balzac, Condé, Flaubert, Gide, Sand, Simon, and Staël. Her books include *Translating Slavery* (1994), *Politicizing Gender* (1991), *The Literature of Images* (1987), and editions of the works of the French abolitionists Sophie Doin and Charlotte Dard. With Deborah Jenson, she is the editor of the MLA Text and Translation of *Sarah*. Her current interests focus on race, class, and gender in France and the French colonial societies.

Dorothy Kelly is professor of French at Boston University. She is the author of *Reconstructing Woman: From Fiction to Reality in the Nineteenth-Century French Novel* (2007), *Telling Glances: Voyeurism in the French Novel* (1992), and *Fictional Genders: Role and Representation in Nineteenth-Century French Narrative* (1989). She is working on a book on memory in nineteenth-century French literature.

Christopher L. Miller is Frederick Clifford Ford Professor of African-American Studies and French at Yale University. He is the author of *The French Atlantic Triangle: Literature and Culture of the Slave Trade* (2008), *Nationalists and Nomads: Essays on Francophone African Literature and Culture* (1998), and *Blank Darkness: Africanist Discourse in French* (1985).

Marshall C. Olds is Willa Cather Professor and Professor of Modern Languages at the University of Nebraska, Lincoln. He is the author of books and articles on nineteenth-century French poetry and narrative and has edited Gabrielle de Paban's *Le Nègre et la Créole, ou Mémoires d'Eulalie D°°°*, a novel written in response to *Ourika*. He is editor of the journal *Nineteenth-Century French Studies*.

Adrianna M. Paliyenko is professor of French at Colby College. She is the editor of *Engendering Race: Romantic-Era Women and French Colonial Memory* (2007), an issue of *L'Esprit Créateur*, and of *Récits des Antilles: Le Bois de la Soufrière*, by Anaïs Ségalas (2004), and the author of *Misreading the Creative Impulse: The Poetic Subject in Rimbaud and Claudel, Restaged* (1997). She is currently completing a book, "Genius Envy: Women Shaping French Poetic History, 1801–1900."

Sue Peabody is professor of history at Washington State University, Vancouver. She is the author of *"There Are No Slaves in France": The Political Culture of Race and Slavery in the Ancien Régime* (1996) and coeditor of two volumes, *Slavery, Freedom, and the Law in the Atlantic World* (with Keila Grinberg, 2006) and *The Color of Liberty: Histories of Race in France* (with Tyler Stovall, 2003). She is working on a monograph on the origins and effects of the concept of "Free Soil" in the legal courts of the Atlantic world.

Scott M. Powers is assistant professor of French at the University of Mary Washington. He has published articles on Céline and Frédéric Beigbeder. He is working on representations of the French Republic in contemporary French film and on a book-length study of the secularization of evil in modern French literature.

Christopher Rivers is professor of French at Mount Holyoke College. He is the editor and translator of *My Life and Battles* (2007), a memoir by Jack Johnson, and *Mademoiselle Giraud, ma femme* (2002) and the author of *Face Value: Physiognomical Thought and the Legible Body in Marivaux, Lavater, Balzac, Gautier, and Zola* (1994). He is at work on "The Idol of France," a book about the celebrated French boxer Georges Carpentier.

Mireille Rosello is director of the Amsterdam School of Cultural Analysis at the University of Amsterdam. Her publications include *France and the Maghreb: Performative Encounters* (2005) and *Postcolonial Hospitality: The Immigrant as Guest* (2001). She is completing a book entitled "The Reparative in Narratives: Works of Mourning in Progress."

Jocelyn Van Tuyl is professor of French at New College of Florida. She is the author of *André Gide and the Second World War: A Novelist's Occupation* (2006). She has written articles on Gide, Proust, Saint-Exupéry, the French Revolution, French literary approaches to 9/11, and historical epidemiology in French and English literature of the colonial era.

Kari Weil is visiting professor in the College of Letters at Wesleyan University. She is the author of *Androgyny and the Denial of Difference* (1992) and articles focusing on questions of gender in nineteenth-century French literature and culture and feminist theory. She is working on two book projects: the first entitled "Thinking Animals: An Introduction to Animal Studies" and the second on the representation of human-horse relations in nineteenth-century France.

Barbara Woshinsky is professor of French at the University of Miami. She has published articles on Claire de Duras and Racine and on Catherine de Villedieu's *Mémoires de la vie de Henriette-Sylvie de Molière*. She coedited (with Ralph Heyndels) *L'autre au XVII*e *siècle: Actes du colloque du Centre International de Rencontres sur le XVII*e *siècle* (1999). Her latest book, "Imagining Women's Conventual Spaces in Early Modern France, 1600–1800," is forthcoming from Ashgate Press.

SURVEY PARTICIPANTS

Chantal Bertrand-Jennings, *University of Toronto*
Ross Chambers, *University of Michigan, Ann Arbor*
Mary Jane Cowles, *Kenyon College*
Thérèse De Raedt, *University of Utah*
Christine De Vinne, *Ursuline College*
Carolyn Fay, *Penn State University, Altoona*
Kathryn M. Grossman, *Penn State University, University Park*
Jen Hill, *University of Nevada, Reno*
Deborah Jenson, *University of Wisconsin, Madison*
Dorothy Kelly, *Boston University*
David Mickelsen, *University of Utah*
Marshall C. Olds, *University of Nebraska. Lincoln*
Mireille Rosello, *Northwestern University*
Linda Rouillard, *University of Toledo*
Jocelyn Van Tuyl, *New College of Florida*
Margaret Waller, *Pomona College*

WORKS CITED

Acampo, Elinor Ann. "Integrating Women and Gender into the Teaching of French History, 1789 to the Present." *French Historical Studies* 27 (2004): 267–92. Print.

Achour, Christiane Chaulet, ed. *Ourika*. By Claire de Duras. Saint-Pourçain-sur-Sioule: Bleu Autour, 2006. Print.

Adanggaman. Dir. Roger Gnoan M'Bala. Abyssa, 2000. Film.

Albistur, Maïté, and Daniel Armogathe. *Histoire du féminisme français du Moyen-age à nos jours*. 2 vols. Paris: Des Femmes, 1977. Print.

"Alesso." *Dictionnaire de biographie française*. Vol. 1. Paris: Letouzey, 1933. 1443–46. Print.

Amazing Grace. Dir. Michael Apted. Four Boys, 2006. Film.

L'Anglaise et le duc [*The Lady and the Duke*]. Dir. Eric Rohmer. Rohmer, 2002. Film.

Aravamudan, Srinivas. *Tropicopolitans: Colonialism and Agency, 1688–1804*. Durham: Duke UP, 1998. Print.

Aron, Marguerite. *Les Ursulines*. Paris: Grasset, 1937. Print.

Augustine. *Confessions*. Trans. Henry Chadwick. New York: Oxford UP, 1991. Print.

Austin, J. L. *How to Do Things with Words*. Cambridge: Harvard UP, 1962. Print.

"Avis de parens de la mineure Ourika, 25 Frimaire III." Dl.U/1/21. 1794. Archives Départementales, Paris. Print.

Baculard d'Arnaud, François de. *Liebman*. 1775. Coulet, *Pygmalions* 111–71.

Banbuck, Cabuzel Andréa. *Histoire politique, économique et sociale de la Martinique sous l'Ancien Régime (1635–1789)*. Fort-de-France: Société de Distribution et de Culture, 1972. Print.

Bardoux, Agénor. *Études sociales et politiques: La duchesse de Duras*. Paris: Calmann-Levy, 1898. Print.

Barila, Beth, et al. "His Story / Her Story: A Dialogue about Including Men and Masculinities in the Women's Studies Curriculum." *Feminist Teacher* 16.1 (2005): 34–52. Print.

Baudelaire, Charles. "À une dame créole." *Œuvres complètes*. Paris: Gallimard, 1975. 62–63. Print.

Bearne, Catherine Mary Charlton. *Four Fascinating French Women: Adélaïde Filleul, comtesse de Flahaut, marquise de Souza; Claire de Kersaint, duchesse de Duras; Marie Caroline de Bourbon, duchesse de Berry; Princesse Mathilde Bonaparte, countess Demidoff*. London: Unwin, 1910. Print.

Beauvau, Marie-Anne Charlotte de Rohan-Chabot, maréchale princesse de. *Souvenirs de la maréchale de Beauvau (née Rohan-Chabot) suivis des mémoires du Maréchal Prince de Beauvau (recueillis et mis en ordre par Madame Standish, née Noailles, son arrière-petite-fille)*. Paris: Techener, 1872. Print.

Behn, Aphra. *Oroonoko*. 1688. Oroonoko, The Rover, *and Other Works*. Ed. Janet Todd. New York: Penguin, 2003. 75–154. Print.

Bellegarde-Smith, Patrick. *Haiti: The Breached Citadel*. Boulder: Westview, 1990. Print.

Bénichou, Paul. *Le sacre de l'écrivain*. Paris: Corti, 1973. Print.

Bénot, Yves. *La Révolution française et la fin des colonies*. Paris: Découverte, 1989. Print.

Bernardin de Saint-Pierre, Jacques-Henri. *Paul et Virgine*. Ed. Jean-Philippe Marty. Paris: Flammarion, 2002. Print.

Bertout, Anne. *Les Ursulines de Paris sous l'Ancien Régime*. Paris: Didot, 1935. Print.

Bertrand-Jennings, Chantal. *Un autre Mal du siècle: Le romantisme des romancières, 1800–1846*. Toulouse: PU du Mirail, 2005. Print.

———. "Condition féminine et impuissance sociale: Les romans de la duchesse de Duras." *Romantisme* 63.1 (1989): 39–50. Print.

———. *D'un siècle l'autre: Romans de Claire de Duras*. Jaignes: Chasse au Snark, 2001. Print.

———. "Problématique d'un sujet féminin en régime patriarcal: *Ourika* de Mme de Duras." *Nineteenth-Century French Studies* 23.1-2 (1994-1995): 42–58. Print.

Bessire, François. Préface. Boufflers 11–13.

Bissière, Michèle. "Union et désunion avec le père dans *Ourika* et *Edouard* de Claire de Duras." *Nineteenth-Century French Studies* 23.3-4 (1995): 316–23. Print.

Biver, Paul, and Marie-Louise Biver. *Abbayes, monastères, couvents de femmes à Paris des origines à la fin du XVIIIᵉ siècle*. Paris: PUF, 1975. Print.

Black Dawn. Dir. Robin Lloyd and Doreen Kraft. Green Valley Media, 1978. Film.

Blake, William. "The Chimney Sweeper." 1794. Mellor and Matlak 300.

———. "The Little Black Boy." 1789. Mellor and Matlak 278–79.

Bongie, Chris. Introduction. Hugo, *Bug-Jargal* [2004] 9–47.

Booth, Wayne C. *The Rhetoric of Fiction*. 2nd ed. Chicago: U of Chicago P, 1983. Print.

Boufflers, Stanislas, chevalier de. *Lettres d'Afrique à Madame de Sabran*. Ed. François Bessire. Paris: Actes Sud, 1998. Print.

Boulle, Pierre H. "Les gens de couleur à la veille de la Révolution." *L'image de la Révolution française*. Ed. Michelle Vovelle. Vol. 1. Paris: Pergamon, 1989. 159–68. Print.

Bourdieu, Pierre. *Masculine Domination*. Trans. Richard Nice. Stanford: Stanford UP, 2001. Print.

Bouteiller, Paul. *Le chevalier de Boufflers et le Sénégal de son temps (1785–1788)*. Paris: Lettres du Monde, 1995. Print.

Boutin, Aimée. *Maternal Echoes: The Poetry of Marceline Desbordes-Valmore and Alphonse de Lamartine*. Newark: U of Delaware P, 2001. Print.

Bulle et bref des Ursulines de la Congrégation de Paris, texte et histoire. Ed. H. M. Colombier. Paris: Berger-Levrault, 1877. Print.

Burton, Stacy, and Dennis Dworkin, eds. *Trials of Modernity: Europe and the World*. 3rd ed. Boston: Pearson, 2001. Print.

Butler, Judith. *Bodies That Matter*. New York: Routledge, 1993. Print.

Byron, George Gordon, Lord. *Childe Harold's Pilgrimage*. 1812. Byron, *Complete Poetical Works* 1: 44–76.

———. *The Complete Poetical Works*. Ed. Jerome J. McGann. 7 vols. Oxford: Clarendon; New York: Oxford UP, 1980–93. Print.

Capretz, Pierre J., et al. *French in Action*. 2nd ed. New Haven: Yale UP, 1994. Print.

Les caprices d'un fleuve. Dir. Bernard Giraudeau. Canal, 1995. Film.

Cardwell, Richard. Introduction. *The Reception of Byron in Europe: Southern Europe, France, and Romania*. Ed. Cardwell. Vol. 1. London: Thoemmes, 2004. 1–10. Print.

Césaire, Aimé. *Discourse on Colonialism*. New York: Monthly Review, 2000. Print.

———. *Discours sur le colonialisme*. Paris: Présence Africaine, 1955. Print.

Chalaye, Sylvie. *Du noir au nègre: L'image du noir au théâtre (1550–1960)*. Paris: Harmattan, 1998. Print.

———. *Les Ourika du boulevard*. Paris: Harmattan, 2003. Print.

Chapman, Herick, and Laura L. Frader, eds. *Race in France: Interdisciplinary Perspectives on the Politics of Difference*. New York: Bergahn, 2004. Print.

Chateaubriand, François-René de. *René*. *Atala*, *René*. Ed. Pierre Reboul. Paris: Flammarion, 1964. 141–72. Print.

———. *René*. *Œuvres romanesques et voyages*. Ed. Maurice Regard. 2 vols. Paris: Gallimard, 1969. 1: 100–46. Print.

Chatman, Samuel. "'There Are No Slaves in France': A Re-examination of Slave Laws in Eighteenth Century France." *Journal of Negro History* 85.3 (2000): 144–53. Print.

Chilcoat, Michelle. "Civility, Marriage, and the Impossible French Citizen: From *Ourika* to *Zouzou* and *Princesse Tam Tam*." *Colby Quarterly* 37.3 (2001): 125–44. Print.

———. "Confinement, the Family Institution, and the Case of Claire de Duras's *Ourika*." *Esprit Créateur* 38.3 (1998): 6–16. Print.

Choudhury, Mita. *Convents and Nuns in Eighteenth-Century French Politics and Culture*. Ithaca: Cornell UP, 2004. Print.

Cixous, Hélène. "Le sexe ou la tête?" *Les cahiers du GRIF* 13 (1976): 5–15. Print.

Cohen, William. *The French Encounter with Africans: White Response to Blacks, 1530–1880*. Bloomington: Indiana UP, 1980. Print.

Colette, Sidonie-Gabrielle. *La vagabonde*. Genève: Crémille, 1969. Print.

Côme, Jérémy, and Marie-Laure de Clermont-Tonnerre. "Casimir de Blacas: Bienvenue chez la Belle au bois dormant." *Gala* 1 June 2005: 54–57. Print.

Condillac, Étienne Bonnot de. *Traité des sensations*. 1754. Paris: Fayard, 1984. Print.

Condorcet, Marie-Jean-Antoine-Nicolas de Caritat, marquis de. *Réflexions sur l'esclavage des nègres*. N.p., 1781. Print.

Conklin, Alice L. "Boundaries Unbound: Teaching French History as Colonial History and Colonial History as French History." *French Historical Studies* 23.2 (2000): 215–38. Print.

Constant, Benjamin. *Adolphe*. Paris: Livre de Poche, 1972. Print.

Cooper, Barbara T. "Staging *Ourika* and the Spectacle of Difference." *Ethnography in French Literature*. Ed. Buford Norman. Amsterdam: Rodopi, 1996. 97–114. Print. French Literary Series 23.

Cottin, Sophie. *Amélie Mansfield*. Paris: Giguet, 1803. Print.

Coulet, Henri. "Présentation: Pygmalions des lumières." Coulet, *Pygmalions* 7–29.

———, ed. *Pygmalions des lumières*. Paris: Desjonquères, 1998. Print.

Coypel, Antoine. *Jeune noir tenant une corbeille de fruits et jeune fille caressant un chien*. Musée du Louvre, Paris. *Joconde*. Web. 20 Feb. 2008.

Crichfield, Grant. *Three Novels of Madame de Duras:* Ourika, Edouard, Olivier. The Hague: Mouton, 1975. Print.

Crofts, Marylee S. "Duras's *Ourika*: Race and Gender in Text and Context." Diss. U of Wisconsin, 1992. Print.

Cugoano, Ottobah. *Thoughts and Sentiments on the Evil of Slavery and Commerce of the Human Species*. 1787. Mellor and Matlak 58–61.

Dangerous Liaisons. Dir. Stephen Frears. Lorimar, 1988. Film.

Danton. Dir. Andrzej Wajda. Gaumont, 1983. Film.

Datlof, Natalie, Jean Fuchs, and David Powell, eds. *The World of George Sand*. New York: Greenwood, 1991. Print.

Davis, David Brion. *The Problem of Slavery in the Age of Revolution, 1770–1823*. Ithaca: Cornell UP, 1975. Print.

DeJean, Joan. Introduction. DeJean, *Ourika* vii–xiii.

———, ed. *Ourika*. By Claire de Duras. Introd. DeJean and Margaret Waller. New York: MLA, 1994. Print.

Delvaux, Martine. "Le tiers espace de la folie dans *Ourika, Juletane* et *L'amant*." *Mots pluriels* 7 (1998): n. pag. Web. 3 Sept. 2008.

Denby, David J. *Sentimental Narrative and the Social Order in France, 1760–1820*. Cambridge: Cambridge UP, 1994. Print.

De Raedt, Thérèse. "Ourika en noir et blanc: Une femme africaine en France." Diss. U of California, Davis, 2000. Print.

———. "*Ourika* in Black and White: Textual and Visual Interplay." *Women in French Studies* 12 (2004): 45–69. Print.

———. "Ourika: L'inspiration de Mme de Duras." *Dalhousie French Studies* 73 (2005): 19–34. Print.

Desbordes-Valmore, Marceline. *Huit femmes*. Paris: Chlendowski, 1845. Print.

———. "Le retour en Europe." Desbordes-Valmore, *Huit femmes* 1–9.

———. *Sarah*. Desbordes-Valmore, *Huit femmes* 25–211.

Deslandes, André-François. *Pygmalion, ou la statue animée*. 1741. Coulet, *Pygmalions* 47–70.

Diderot, Denis. *Entretien entre D'Alembert et Diderot*. 1769. *Œuvres philosophiques*. Ed. Paul Vernière. Paris: Garnier, 1964. Print.

———. *La religieuse*. Paris: Livre de Poche, 1966. Print.

———. *Salons*. Ed. Jean Seznec and Jean Adhémar. Vol. 1. Oxford: Clarendon, 1957. Print.

Diethelm, Marie-Bénédicte, ed. *Ourika*. By Claire de Duras. *Madame de Duras: Ourika, Edouard, and Olivier*. Paris: Gallimard, 2007. 61–96. Print.

DiMauro, Damon. "*Ourika*; or, Galatea Reverts to Stone." *Nineteenth-Century French Studies* 28.3-4 (2000): 187–211. Print.

Doin, Sophie. *La famille noire, ou La traite et l'esclavage, suivie de trois nouvelles blanches et noires*. 1825–26. Ed. Doris Y. Kadish. Paris: Harmattan, 2002. Print.

Doyle, William. *The French Revolution: A Very Short Introduction*. Oxford: Oxford UP, 2001. Print.

Dubois, Laurent. *Avengers of the New World: The Story of the Haitian Revolution*. Cambridge: Harvard UP, 2004. Print.

Duras, Claire de. *Olivier ou le secret*. Ed. Denise Virieux. Paris: Corti, 1971. Print.

———. *Ourika*. Paris: Ladvocat, 1824. Print.

———. *Ourika: A Tale from the French*. Boston: Carter, 1829. Print.

"Elegant Apartments in Central Paris." *Voyage Europe*. Voyage Europe, n.d. Web. 13 Feb. 2008.

Equiano, Olaudah. *The Interesting Narrative of the Life of Olaudah Equiano, or Gustavus Vassa the African*. 1789. Burton and Dworkin 90–96.

"État des Pièces Remises au Directeur des Domaines nationaux . . . provenant de la Sucession en Desherence de Charlotte Catherine Benezet." DQ/10/461, pièce 106. 1795–99. Archives Départementales, Paris. Print.

Fanon, Frantz. *Black Skin, White Masks*. Trans. Charles Lam Markmann. New York: Grove, 1967. Print.

———. *Peau noire, masques blancs*. Paris: Seuil, 1952. Print.

Finch, Alison. *Women's Writing in Nineteenth-Century France*. Cambridge: Cambridge UP, 2000. Print.

Fowles, John. Foreword. Fowles, *Ourika* xxvii–xxxi.

———. *The French Lieutenant's Woman*. 1969. Boston: Little, 1998. Print.

———, trans. *Ourika*. By Claire de Duras. Austin: Taylor, 1977. Rev. ed. Introd. Joan DeJean and Margaret Waller. New York: MLA, 1994. Print.

The French Revolution. Dir. Doug Shultz. Partisan, 2005. Film.

Freud, Sigmund. "Mourning and Melancholia." 1917. *The Standard Edition of the Complete Psychological Works of Sigmund Freud*. Trans. and ed. James Strachey. Vol. 14. London: Hogarth, 1961. 239–60. Print.

Gates, Henry Louis. "Critical Fanonism." *Critical Inquiry* 17.3 (1991): 457–70. Print.

———. *Figures in Black: Words, Signs, and the "Racial" Self*. New York: Oxford UP, 1987. Print.

Gautier, Arlette. *Les soeurs de solitude: La condition féminine dans d'esclavage aux Antilles du XVIIᵉ au XIXᵉ siècle*. Paris: Caribéennes, 1985. Print.

Gautier, Théophile. *Histoire du romantisme*. Paris: Charpentier, 1927. Print.

Gautier-Dagoty, Jean-Baptiste André. *Jeanne Bécu, Comtesse du Barry. Joconde*. Joconde, n.d. Web. 20 Feb. 2008.

Gay, Sophie. *Anatole*. 1815. *Œuvres complètes de Sophie Gay*. Ed. Michel Lévy. 2 vols. Paris: Nouvelle, 1872. 2: 3–264. Print.

Genlis, Stéphanie Félicité de. *Mademoiselle de Clermont*. 1802. Paris: Deforges, 1977. Print.

———. *Mémoires inédits de Madame la comtesses de Genlis, sur le dix-huitième siècle et la Révolution française depuis 1756 jusqu'à nos jours*. Vol. 7. Paris: Ladvocat, 1825. 292–94. Print.

———. *Pygmalion et Galatée, ou la statue animée depuis vingt-quatre heures*. [c. 1790]. *Nouveaux contes moraux et nouvelles historiques*. Vol. 6. Paris: Lecointe, 1825. 233–309. Print.

Gide, André. *L'immoraliste*. Paris: Gallimard, 1973. Print.

Gouges, Olympe de. *Declaration of the Rights of Woman*. Burton and Dworkin 148–52.

———. *L'esclavage des nègres ou l'heureux naufrage*. 1789. Ed. Sylvie Chalaye and Jacqueline Razgonnikoff. Paris: Harmattan, 2006. Print.

Graffigny, Françoise de. *Lettres d'une Péruvienne*. 1774. Introd. Joan DeJean and Nancy K. Miller. New York: MLA, 1993. Print.

Grégoire, Henri. *De la noblesse de la peau, ou du préjugé des blancs contre la couleur des Africains et celle de leurs descendans, noirs et sang-mèlés*. Paris: Baudouin, 1826. Print.

Grossman, Kathryn M. *The Early Novels of Victor Hugo: Towards a Poetics of Harmony*. Genève: Droz, 1986. Print.

Gueudré, Marie de Chantal. *Histoire de l'Ordre des Ursulines en France*. 3 vols. Paris: Saint-Paul, 1963. Print.

Haudrère, Philippe, and Françoise Vergès. *De l'esclave au citoyen*. Paris: Gallimard, 1998. Print.

Herrmann, Claudine. Introduction. Herrmann, *Ourika* 7–22.

———, ed. *Ourika*. By Claire de Duras. Paris: Femmes, 1979. Print.

Hoffmann, Léon-François. *Le nègre romantique: Personnage littéraire et obsession collective*. Paris: Payot, 1973. Print.

Hugo, Victor. *Bug-Jargal* [première version]. *Œuvres complètes*. Ed. Jean Massin. Vol. 2. Paris: Club Français du Livre, 1967–70. 351–79. Print.

———. *Bug-Jargal*. Trans. and ed. Chris Bongie. Peterborough: Broadview, 2004. Print.

———. *Han d'Islande*. 1823. Lausanne: Recontre, 1967. Print.

———. *Les Misérables*. 1856. Ed. Maurice Alem. Paris: Gallimard, 1986. Print.

Hunt, Lynn. *The Family Romance of the French Revolution*. Berkeley: U of California P, 1992. Print.

———, ed. *The French Revolution and Human Rights: A Brief Documentary History*. Boston: Bedford, 1996. Print.

Hutcheon, Linda. *A Poetics of Postmodernism: History, Theory, Fiction*. New York: Routledge, 1988. Print.

Ingersoll, Earl G. "The Appropriation of Black Experience in the *Ourika* of Claire de Duras." *CEA Critic* 60.3 (1998): 1–14. Print.

James, C. L. R. *The Black Jacobins: Toussaint L'Ouverture and the San Domingo Revolution*. New York: Vintage, 1989. Print.

Jégou, Marie-Andrée. *Les Ursulines du Faubourg St-Jacques à Paris (1607–1662): Origine d'un monastère apostolique*. Paris: PUF, 1981. Print.

Jenson, Deborah. *Trauma and Its Representations: The Social Life of Mimesis in Post-revolutionary France*. Baltimore: Johns Hopkins UP, 2001. Print.

Kadish, Doris Y. "Cultural Diversity and Nineteenth-Century French Studies." *Modern French Literary Studies in the Classroom: Pedagogical Strategies*. Ed. Charles J. Stivale. New York: MLA, 2004. 154–63. Print.

———. *Francophone Slavery*. *University of Georgia*. U of Georgia, n.d. Web. 3 June 2008.

———. Introduction. Kadish and Massardier-Kenney 1–7.

———. "*Ourika*'s Three Versions: A Comparison." Kadish and Massardier-Kenney 217–28.

———. "Rewriting Women's Stories: *Ourika* and *The French Lieutenant's Woman*." *South Atlantic Review* 62.2 (1997): 74–87. Print.

Kadish, Doris Y., and Françoise Massardier-Kenney, eds. *Translating Slavery: Gender and Race in French Women's Writing, 1783–1823*. Kent: Kent State UP, 1994. Print.

Krüdener, Julie de. *Valérie*. 1804. Ed. Michel Mercier. Paris: Klincksieck, 1974. Print.

Lafayette, Madame de. *La princesse de Clèves*. 1678. Ed. Antoine Adam. Paris: Garnier-Flammarion, 1972. Print.

Laguarigue, Jean-Luc de. *Les habitations: Livre cartes postales, Martinique maisons créoles*. Le Pallet: Traces, 2003. Print.

La Tour du Pin, Henriette Lucy de, marquise de. *Mémoires de la marquise de La Tour du Pin: Journal d'une femme de cinquante ans, 1778–1815*. Paris: Mercure de France, 1989. Print.

———. *Memoirs of Madame de La Tour du Pin*. Trans. Felice Harcourt. London: Century, 1985. Print.

Lee, Debbie. *Slavery and the Romantic Imagination*. Philadelphia: U of Pennsylvania P, 2002. Print.

Lescure, M. de. Notice. *Ourika*. By Claire de Duras. Ed. Lescure. Paris: Lib. des Bibliophiles, 1878. i–xxiii. Print.

Liebersohn, Harry. "Discovering Indigenous Nobility: Tocqueville, Chamisso, and Romantic Travel Writing." *American Historical Review* 99.3 (1994): 746–66. Print.

Lierheimer, Linda. *Female Eloquence and Maternal Ministry: The Apostolate of Ursuline Nuns in Seventeenth-Century France*. Ann Arbor: UMI, 1994. Print.

Little, Roger. "Bibliographie selective." Little, *Ourika* 125–26.

———. "Cahier iconographique." Little, *Ourika* xiii–xx.

———. "Madame de Duras et Ourika." Little, *Ourika* 33–106.

———. "Le nom et les origines d'Ourika." *Revue d'histoire littéraire de France* (1998): 633–37. Print.

———, ed. *Ourika*. By Claire de Duras. Exeter: U of Exeter P, 1998. Print.

———. "Peau noire, masque blanc." Little, *Ourika* vii–ix.

———. "Table d'illustrations." Little, *Ourika* xii.

Loriot-Raymer, Gisèle, Michèle E. Valet, and Judith A. Muyskens. *À vous d'écrire: Atelier de français*. McGraw, 1996. Print.

Lovell, Terry. "Bourdieu, Social Suffering, and Working-Class Life." *Reading Bourdieu on Society and Culture*. Ed. Bridget Fowler. Malden: Blackwell; Sociological Review, 2000. 27–48. Print.

Lucey, Michael. Rev. of *Between Genders: Narrating Difference in Early French Modernism*, by Nathaniel Wing. *Nineteenth-Century French Studies* 34.1-2 (2005): 174–76. Print.

Lux-Sterritt, Laurence. *Redefining Female Religious Life: French Ursulines and English Ladies in Seventeenth-Century Catholicism*. Aldershot: Ashgate, 2005. Print.

Magdelaine-Andrianjafitrimo, Valérie. "La Galatée noire ou la force d'un mot: *Ourika* de Claire de Duras, 1823." *Orages. Littérature et culture, 1760–1830* 2 (2003): n. pag. Web. 3 Sept. 2008.

Mannière, Fabienne. *Les prémices de la Révolution, 1774–1788. Herodote.net*. Herodote.net, 2008. Web. 26 Aug. 2008.

Mansel, Philip. *Paris between Empires, 1814–1852*. London: Murray, 2001. Print.

Massardier-Kenney, Françoise. "Duras, Racism, and Class." Kadish and Massardier-Kenney 185–93.

Massardier-Kenney, Françoise, and Claire Salardenne, trans. *Ourika*. By Claire de Duras. Kadish and Massardier-Kenney 194–216.

Maugras, Gaston de, and Comte P. De Croze-Lemercier. *Delphine de Sabran, Marquise de Custine*. Paris: Plon Mourrit, 1912.

———, trans. *Memoirs of Delphine de Sabran, Marquise de Custine*. London: Heinemann; New York: Doran, 1912. Print.

McIntosh, Peggy. "White Privilege: Unpacking the Invisible Knapsack." *Peace and Freedom* July-Aug. 1989: 10. Print.

Mellor, Anne K., and Richard E. Matlak, eds. *British Literature, 1780–1830*. New York: Harcourt, 1996. Print.

Mercier, Louis-Sébastien. "Petits Nègres." *Le tableau de Paris: Nouvelle édition*. Amsterdam: n.p., 1783. 253–54. Print.

Merici, Angela. "Counsels of Angela Merici." *Angela Merici and the Company of St. Ursula*. Ed. Teresa Ledóchowska. Trans. Mary Teresa Neylan. Vol. 1. Rome: Pontifical Gregorian U, 1968. Print.

Mérimée, Prosper. "Tamango." 1829. *Nouvelles complètes*. Ed. Pierre Josserand. 2 vols. Paris: Gallimard, 1973–74. 1: 53–75. Print.

Miller, Christopher L. *Blank Darkness: Africanist Discourse in French*. Chicago: U of Chicago P, 1985. Print.

———. "Forget Haiti: Baron Roger and the New Africa." *The Haiti Issue*. Ed. Deborah Jenson. Spec. issue of *Yale French Studies* 107 (2005): 39–69. Print.

———. *The French Atlantic Triangle: Literature and Culture of the Slave Trade*. Durham: Duke UP, 2008. Print.

Moitt, Bernard. *Women and Slavery in the French Antilles, 1635–1848*. Bloomington: Indiana UP, 2001. Print.

Montaigne, Michel. "On the Cannibals." 1572. Burton and Dworkin 54–62.

Morgan, Jennifer L. *Laboring Women: Reproduction and Gender in New World Slavery*. Philadelphia: U of Pennsylvania P, 2004. Print.

Musset, Alfred de. *La confession d'un enfant du siècle. Œuvres complètes en prose*. Ed. Maurice Allem and Paul-Courant. Paris: Gallimard, 1960. 65–288. Print.

Nora, Pierre, ed. *Les lieux de mémoire*. 7 vols. Paris: Gallimard, 1984. Print.

La nuit de Varennes. Dir. Ettore Scola. France 3, 1983. Film.

O'Connell, David. "The Black Hero in French Romantic Fiction." *Studies in Romanticism* 12 (1973): 516–29. Print.

———."*Ourika*: Black Face, White Mask." *French Review* 47.6 (1974): 47–56. Print.

Ovid. "Pygmalion." *Metamorphoses*. 2 vols. Cambridge: Harvard UP, 1958. 2: 80–85. Print.

Paban, Gabrille de. *Le Nègre et la Créole, ou Mémoires d'Eulalie D****. 1825. Ed. Marshall C. Olds. Paris: Harmattan, 2008. Print.

Pageux, Daniel-Henri. "Ourika ou la religieuse sénégalaise." *Cahiers du CRA* 5 (1987): 215–26. Print.

Pailhès, Gabriel. *La duchesse de Duras et Chateaubriand d'après des documents inédits*. Paris: Perrin, 1910. Print.

Paliyenko, Adrianna M. *FR 356: Cultural Legacies of Nineteenth-Century France. Colby College*. Dept. of French and Italian, Colby Coll., n.d. Web. 20 Feb. 2008.

Paraillous, Alain. "Chateaubriand et la duchesse de Duras." *Le revue de l'Agenais* 3 (1995): 271–86. Print.

Passage du milieu. Dir. Guy Deslauriers. Dorlis, 1999. Film.

Peabody, Sue. *"There Are No Slaves in France": The Political Culture of Race and Slavery in the Ancien Régime*. New York: Oxford UP, 1996. Print.

Peabody, Sue, and Tyler Stovall, eds. *The Color of Liberty: Histories of Race in France*. Durham: Duke UP, 2003. Print.

Pétré-Grenouilleau, Olivier. *La traite des noirs*. 2nd ed. Paris: PUF, 1997. Print.

Pineau, Gisèle. *Exile according to Julia*. Trans. Betty Wilson. Charlottesville: U of Virginia P, 2003. Print.

———. *L'exil selon Julia*. Paris: Stock, 1996. Print.

Prabhu, Anjali. "Deux nègres à Paris: La voix de l'autre." *Romance Languages Annual* 7 (1995): 133–37. Print.

Prévost, Antoine-François. *Manon Lescaut*. Paris: Fayard, 1947. Print.

Prince, Mary. *The History of Mary Prince, a West Indian Slave*. 1831. Mellor and Matlak 868–80.

Proust, Marcel. "A propos du 'style' de Flaubert." *Contre Sainte-Beuve, précédé de Pastiches et Mélanges et suivi de Essais et Articles*. Ed. Pierre Clarac and Yves Sandre. Paris: Gallimard-Pléiade, 1971. 586–600. Print.

Rameau, Jean-Philippe. *Pygmalion. Œuvres complètes*. Ed. Maurice Emmanuel and Martial Ténéo. Vol. 17, pt. 1. Paris: Durand, 1913. 1–107. Print.

Rancière, Jacques. *Le maître ignorant*. Paris: Fayard, 1987. Print.

Ransom, Amy. "Mademoiselle Aïssé: Inspiration for Claire de Duras's *Ourika*?" *Romance Quarterly* 46.2 (1999): 84–98. Print.

Rapley, Elizabeth. *The Dévotes: Women and Church in Seventeenth-Century France*. Montreal: McGill-Queen's UP, 1990. Print.

———. *A Social History of the Cloister: Daily Life in the Teaching Monasteries of the Old Regime*. Montreal: McGill-Queen's UP, 2001. Print.

Règlemens des religieuses Ursulines de la Congrégation de Paris. Vol. 3. Paris: Josse, 1741. Print. 3 vols.

Reinhold, Meyer. "The Naming of Pygmalion's Animated Statue." *Classical Journal* 66.4 (1971): 316–19. Print.

Rétif de la Bretonne, Nicolas-Edme. *Le nouveau Pygmalion*. 1780. Coulet, *Pygmalions* 173–207.

La Revolution française: La revolution et la royauté. Dir. Robert Enrico. Ariane, 1989. Film.

Ridicule. Dir. Patrice Leconte. Canal, 1996. Film.

Rigaud, Hyacinthe. *Jeune nègre tenant un arc*. Musée de Beaux-Arts, Dunkerque. *Musenor*. Web. 20 Feb. 2008.

Rogers, Nancy. "The Wasting Away of Romantic Heroines." *Nineteenth-Century French Studies* 11. 3-4 (1983): 246–55. Print.

Rousseau, Jean-Jacques. *Discourse on the Origin and Foundations of Inequality among Men*. 1755. Burton and Dworkin 118–30.

———. *Pygmalion*. 1762. Coulet, *Pygmalions* 99–110.

Sainte-Beuve, Charles-Augustin. "Madame de Duras." *Œuvres*. Vol. 2. Paris: Gallimard, 1951. 1042–58. Print. 2 vols.

Sala-Molins, Louis. *Le Code noir, ou, Le calvaire de Canaan*. Paris: PUF, 1987. Print.

Sancho, Ignatius. *The Letters of the Late Ignatius Sancho, an African*. 1782. Burton and Dworkin 135–38.

Savage, John. Letter to Sue Peabody. 17 June 2005. MS.

Schama, Simon. *Citizens: A Chronicle of the French Revolution*. New York: Knopf, 1989. Print.

Scheler, Lucien. "Un best-seller sous Louis XVIII: *Ourika* par Mme de Duras." *Bulletin du bibliophile* 1 (1998): 11–28. Print.

Schwarz-Bart, André, and Simone Schwarz-Bart. *La mulâtresse Solitude*. Paris: Seuil, 1972. Print.

Scott, Joan Wallach. *Gender and the Politics of History*. New York: Columbia UP, 1999. Print.

Seltzer, Mark. *Bodies and Machines*. New York: Routledge, 1992. Print.

Sepinwall, Alyssa. Message to Sue Peabody. 16 June 2005. E-mail.

Shelley, Mary Wollstonecraft. *Frankenstein; or, The Modern Prometheus: The 1818 Text*. Ed. James Rieger. Chicago: U of Chicago P, 1982. Print.

Sherman, Carol L. "Race, Melancholy, and Therapeutic Narrative in *Ourika*." *Journal of Early Modern Cultural Studies* 1.1 (2001): 88–116. Print.

Sieyès, Emmanuel-Joseph. "What Is the Third Estate?" Burton and Dworkin 139–43.

Singley, Carol. "Alternative Syllabi: 'Engaging Pairs.'" *Heath Anthology of American Literature Newsletter* 2 (1989): 10–11. Print.

Sister Act. Dir. Emile Ardolino. Touchstone Pictures, 1992. Film.

Somdah, Marie-Ange. "Ourika ou l'univers antithétique d'une héroïne." *LittéRéalité* 8.2 (1996): 53–63. Print.

Southey, Robert. "The Sailor, Who Had Served in the Slave Trade." 1798. Mellor and Matlak 68–70.

Staël, Germaine de. *Corinne ou l'Italie.* 1807. Ed. Simone Balayé. Paris: Gallimard, 1985. Print.

———. *De la littérature.* 1800. 2 vols. Genève: Droz, 1959. Print.

———. *De l'Allemagne.* 1810. 2 vols. Paris: Garnier, 1968. Print.

———. *Delphine.* 1802. Ed. Claudine Herrmann. Paris: Des Femmes, 1981. Print.

———. *Mirza.* Kadish and Massardier-Kenney 271–81.

———. *Mirza.* Trans. Françoise Massardier-Kenney. Kadish and Massardier-Kenney 146–57.

Steele, Ross, et al. *La civilisation française en évolution I: Institutions et culture avant la Ve République.* New York: Heinle, 1996. Print.

Stein, Robert Louis. *The French Slave Trade in the Eighteenth Century: An Old Regime Business.* Madison: U of Wisconsin P, 1979. Print.

Stendhal [Marie-Henri Beyle]. "*Ourika, ou la négresse,* par Mme la duchesse de ———." *1823–1824.* Vol. 2 of *Chroniques pour l'Angleterre: Contributions à la presse britannique.* Ed. Keith G. McWatters. Trans. Renée Dénier. Grenoble: U de Grenoble, 1982. Print. 8 vols. 1980–95.

Swenson, J. "A Small Change in Terminology or a Great Leap Forward? Culture and Civilization in Revolution." *MLN* 112.3 (1997): 322–48. Print.

Switzer, Richard. "Mme de Staël, Mme de Duras, and the Question of Race." *Kentucky Romance Quarterly* 20 (1973): 303–16. Print.

Tamango. Dir. John Berry. Cyclope, 1957. Film.

Tezenas du Montcel, R. "Madame de Duras, cette inconnue." *La revue des deux mondes* (1968): 364–84. Print.

Todorov, Tzvetan. *Nous et les autres: La réflexion française sur la diversité humaine.* Paris: Seuil, 1989. Print.

Toews, John E. "Intellectual History after the Linguistic Turn: The Autonomy of Meaning and the Irreducibility of Experience." *American Historical Review* 92.4 (1987): 879–907. Print.

Tourasse, L[éonel] de la. *Le château du Val dans la Forêt de Saint-Germain.* St. Germain-en-Laye, 1924. Print.

Toussaint Louverture. "Letter to the Directory, 28 October 1797." Burton and Dworkin 167–68.

Tropiques Amers. Dir. Jean-Claude Barny. Lizland, 2007. Film.

Trousson, Raymond. Introduction. Trousson, *Romans* 965–84.

———, ed. *Ourika.* By Claire de Duras. Trousson, *Romans* 985–1007.

———, ed. *Romans de femmes du XVIIIe siècle*. Paris: Laffont, 1996. Print.

Vaget-Grangeat, Nicole. *Le Chevalier de Boufflers et son temps: Etude d'un échec*. Paris: Nizet, 1976. Print.

Van Tuyl, Jocelyn, and Miriam L. Wallace. "The French Revolution in the Cultural Imagination: Eighteenth-Century France and Britain." *Teaching the Eighteenth Century: Three Courses* 6 (1998): 1–18. Print.

Waller, Margaret. Introduction. DeJean, *Ourika* xiii–xxi.

———. *The Male Malady: Fictions of Impotence in the French Romantic Novel*. New Brunswick: Rutgers UP, 1993. Print.

Warburton, Eileen. "Ashes, Ashes, We All Fall Down: *Ourika*, *Cinderella*, and *The French Lieutenant's Woman*." *Twentieth Century Literature* 42.1 (1996): 165–86. Print.

Weil, Kari. "Romantic Exile and the Melancholia of Identification." *Differences* 7.2 (1995): 111–26. Print.

Whiting, T. Denean Sharpley. *Black Venus: Sexualized Slaves, Primal Fears, and Primitive Narratives in French*. Durham: Duke UP, 1999. Print.

Wing, Nathaniel. *Between Genders: Narrating Difference in Early French Modernism*. Newark: U of Delaware P, 2004. Print.

Wollstonecraft, Mary. *Vindication of the Rights of Women*. 1792. Burton and Dworkin 157–65.

Wordsworth, William. "Preface to the *Lyrical Ballads*." 1800. Mellor and Matlak 184–88.

Woshinsky, Barbara. "Tombeau de *Phèdre*: Repression, Confession and Métissage in Racine and Claire de Duras." *Les epreuves du labyrinthe: Essais de poétique et d'herméneutique raciniennes*. Spec. issue of *Dalhousie French Studies* 49 (1999): 167–81. Print.

INDEX

Modern Language Association of America

Approaches to Teaching World Literature

Joseph Gibaldi, series editor

Achebe's Things Fall Apart. Ed. Bernth Lindfors. 1991.
Arthurian Tradition. Ed. Maureen Fries and Jeanie Watson. 1992.
Atwood's The Handmaid's Tale *and Other Works*. Ed. Sharon R. Wilson,
     Thomas B. Friedman, and Shannon Hengen. 1996.
Austen's Emma. Ed. Marcia McClintock Folsom. 2004.
Austen's Pride and Prejudice. Ed. Marcia McClintock Folsom. 1993.
Balzac's Old Goriot. Ed. Michal Peled Ginsburg. 2000.
Baudelaire's Flowers of Evil. Ed. Laurence M. Porter. 2000.
Beckett's Waiting for Godot. Ed. June Schlueter and Enoch Brater. 1991.
Beowulf. Ed. Jess B. Bessinger, Jr., and Robert F. Yeager. 1984.
Blake's Songs of Innocence and of Experience. Ed. Robert F. Gleckner and
     Mark L. Greenberg. 1989.
Boccaccio's Decameron. Ed. James H. McGregor. 2000.
British Women Poets of the Romantic Period. Ed. Stephen C. Behrendt and
     Harriet Kramer Linkin. 1997.
Charlotte Brontë's Jane Eyre. Ed. Diane Long Hoeveler and Beth Lau. 1993.
Emily Brontë's Wuthering Heights. Ed. Sue Lonoff and Terri A. Hasseler. 2006.
Byron's Poetry. Ed. Frederick W. Shilstone. 1991.
Camus's The Plague. Ed. Steven G. Kellman. 1985.
Writings of Bartolomé de Las Casas. Ed. Santa Arias and Eyda M. Merediz. 2008.
Cather's My Ántonia. Ed. Susan J. Rosowski. 1989.
Cervantes' Don Quixote. Ed. Richard Bjornson. 1984.
Chaucer's Canterbury Tales. Ed. Joseph Gibaldi. 1980.
Chaucer's Troilus and Criseyde *and the Shorter Poems*. Ed. Tison Pugh and
     Angela Jane Weisl. 2006.
Chopin's The Awakening. Ed. Bernard Koloski. 1988.
Coleridge's Poetry and Prose. Ed. Richard E. Matlak. 1991.
Collodi's Pinocchio *and Its Adaptations*. Ed. Michael Sherberg. 2006.
Conrad's "Heart of Darkness" and "The Secret Sharer." Ed. Hunt Hawkins and
     Brian W. Shaffer. 2002.
Dante's Divine Comedy. Ed. Carole Slade. 1982.
Defoe's Robinson Crusoe. Ed. Maximillian E. Novak and Carl Fisher. 2005.
DeLillo's White Noise. Ed. Tim Engles and John N. Duvall. 2006.
Dickens's Bleak House. Ed. John O. Jordan and Gordon Bigelow. 2009.
Dickens's David Copperfield. Ed. Richard J. Dunn. 1984.
Dickinson's Poetry. Ed. Robin Riley Fast and Christine Mack Gordon. 1989.
Narrative of the Life of Frederick Douglass. Ed. James C. Hall. 1999.
Duras's Ourika. Ed. Mary Ellen Birkett and Christopher Rivers. 2009.

Early Modern Spanish Drama. Ed. Laura R. Bass and Margaret R. Greer. 2006

Eliot's Middlemarch. Ed. Kathleen Blake. 1990.

Eliot's Poetry and Plays. Ed. Jewel Spears Brooker. 1988.

Shorter Elizabethan Poetry. Ed. Patrick Cheney and Anne Lake Prescott. 2000.

Ellison's Invisible Man. Ed. Susan Resneck Parr and Pancho Savery. 1989.

English Renaissance Drama. Ed. Karen Bamford and Alexander Leggatt. 2002.

Works of Louise Erdrich. Ed. Gregg Sarris, Connie A. Jacobs, and
    James R. Giles. 2004.

Dramas of Euripides. Ed. Robin Mitchell-Boyask. 2002.

Faulkner's The Sound and the Fury. Ed. Stephen Hahn and Arthur F. Kinney. 1996.

Fitzgerald's The Great Gatsby. Ed. Jackson R. Bryer and Nancy P. VanArsdale. 2009.

Flaubert's Madame Bovary. Ed. Laurence M. Porter and Eugene F. Gray. 1995.

García Márquez's One Hundred Years of Solitude. Ed. María Elena de Valdés and
    Mario J. Valdés. 1990.

Gilman's "The Yellow Wall-Paper" and Herland. Ed. Denise D. Knight and
    Cynthia J. Davis. 2003.

Goethe's Faust. Ed. Douglas J. McMillan. 1987.

Gothic Fiction: The British and American Traditions. Ed. Diane Long Hoeveler
    and Tamar Heller. 2003.

Grass's The Tin Drum. Ed. Monika Shafi. 2008.

Hebrew Bible as Literature in Translation. Ed. Barry N. Olshen and
    Yael S. Feldman. 1989.

Homer's Iliad *and* Odyssey. Ed. Kostas Myrsiades. 1987.

Ibsen's A Doll House. Ed. Yvonne Shafer. 1985.

Henry James's Daisy Miller *and* The Turn of the Screw. Ed. Kimberly C. Reed and
    Peter G. Beidler. 2005.

Works of Samuel Johnson. Ed. David R. Anderson and Gwin J. Kolb. 1993.

Joyce's Ulysses. Ed. Kathleen McCormick and Erwin R. Steinberg. 1993.

Works of Sor Juana Inés de la Cruz. Ed. Emilie L. Bergmann and Stacey Schlau. 2007.

Kafka's Short Fiction. Ed. Richard T. Gray. 1995.

Keats's Poetry. Ed. Walter H. Evert and Jack W. Rhodes. 1991.

Kingston's The Woman Warrior. Ed. Shirley Geok-lin Lim. 1991.

Lafayette's The Princess of Clèves. Ed. Faith E. Beasley and
    Katharine Ann Jensen. 1998.

Works of D. H. Lawrence. Ed. M. Elizabeth Sargent and Garry Watson. 2001.

Lazarillo de Tormes *and the Picaresque Tradition*. Ed. Anne J. Cruz. 2009.

Lessing's The Golden Notebook. Ed. Carey Kaplan and Ellen Cronan Rose. 1989.

Mann's Death in Venice *and Other Short Fiction*. Ed. Jeffrey B. Berlin. 1992.

Marguerite de Navarre's Heptameron. Ed. Colette H. Winn. 2007.

Medieval English Drama. Ed. Richard K. Emmerson. 1990.

Melville's Moby-Dick. Ed. Martin Bickman. 1985.

Metaphysical Poets. Ed. Sidney Gottlieb. 1990.

Miller's Death of a Salesman. Ed. Matthew C. Roudané. 1995.

Milton's Paradise Lost. Ed. Galbraith M. Crump. 1986.

Milton's Shorter Poetry and Prose. Ed. Peter C. Herman. 2007.

Molière's Tartuffe *and Other Plays.* Ed. James F. Gaines and
Michael S. Koppisch. 1995.

Momaday's The Way to Rainy Mountain. Ed. Kenneth M. Roemer. 1988.

Montaigne's Essays. Ed. Patrick Henry. 1994.

Novels of Toni Morrison. Ed. Nellie Y. McKay and Kathryn Earle. 1997.

Murasaki Shikibu's The Tale of Genji. Ed. Edward Kamens. 1993.

Nabokov's Lolita. Ed. Zoran Kuzmanovich and Galya Diment. 2008.

Poe's Prose and Poetry. Ed. Jeffrey Andrew Weinstock and Tony Magistrale. 2008.

Pope's Poetry. Ed. Wallace Jackson and R. Paul Yoder. 1993.

Proust's Fiction and Criticism. Ed. Elyane Dezon-Jones and
Inge Crosman Wimmers. 2003.

Puig's Kiss of the Spider Woman. Ed. Daniel Balderston and Francine Masiello. 2007.

Pynchon's The Crying of Lot 49 *and Other Works.* Ed. Thomas H. Schaub. 2008.

Novels of Samuel Richardson. Ed. Lisa Zunshine and Jocelyn Harris. 2006.

Rousseau's Confessions *and* Reveries of the Solitary Walker. Ed. John C. O'Neal
and Ourida Mostefai. 2003.

Shakespeare's Hamlet. Ed. Bernice W. Kliman. 2001.

Shakespeare's King Lear. Ed. Robert H. Ray. 1986.

Shakespeare's Othello. Ed. Peter Erickson and Maurice Hunt. 2005.

Shakespeare's Romeo and Juliet. Ed. Maurice Hunt. 2000.

Shakespeare's The Tempest *and Other Late Romances.* Ed. Maurice Hunt. 1992.

Shelley's Frankenstein. Ed. Stephen C. Behrendt. 1990.

Shelley's Poetry. Ed. Spencer Hall. 1990.

Sir Gawain and the Green Knight. Ed. Miriam Youngerman Miller and
Jane Chance. 1986.

Song of Roland. Ed. William W. Kibler and Leslie Zarker Morgan. 2006.

Spenser's Faerie Queene. Ed. David Lee Miller and Alexander Dunlop. 1994.

Stendhal's The Red and the Black. Ed. Dean de la Motte and Stirling Haig. 1999.

Sterne's Tristram Shandy. Ed. Melvyn New. 1989.

Stowe's Uncle Tom's Cabin. Ed. Elizabeth Ammons and Susan Belasco. 2000.

Swift's Gulliver's Travels. Ed. Edward J. Rielly. 1988.

Teresa of Ávila and the Spanish Mystics. Ed. Alison Weber. 2009.

Thoreau's Walden *and Other Works.* Ed. Richard J. Schneider. 1996.

Tolstoy's Anna Karenina. Ed. Liza Knapp and Amy Mandelker. 2003.

Vergil's Aeneid. Ed. William S. Anderson and Lorina N. Quartarone. 2002.

Voltaire's Candide. Ed. Renée Waldinger. 1987.

Whitman's Leaves of Grass. Ed. Donald D. Kummings. 1990.

Wiesel's Night. Ed. Alan Rosen. 2007.

Works of Oscar Wilde. Ed. Philip E. Smith II. 2008.

Woolf's To the Lighthouse. Ed. Beth Rigel Daugherty and Mary Beth Pringle. 2001.

Wordsworth's Poetry. Ed. Spencer Hall, with Jonathan Ramsey. 1986.

Wright's Native Son. Ed. James A. Miller. 1997.